# THE WOMEN WHO KNEW TOO MUCH

# THE WOMEN WHO KNEW TOO MUCH

## SECOND EDITION

Hitchcock and Feminist Theory

Tania Modleski

Routledge
Taylor & Francis Group
New York   London

Published in 2005 by
Routledge
Taylor & Francis Group
270 Madison Avenue
New York, NY 10016

Published in Great Britain by
Routledge
Taylor & Francis Group
2 Park Square
Milton Park, Abingdon
Oxon OX14 4RN

© 2005 by Taylor & Francis Group, LLC
Routledge is an imprint of Taylor & Francis Group

Printed in the United States of America on acid-free paper
10 9 8 7 6 5 4 3 2 1

International Standard Book Number-10: 0-415-97362-7 (Softcover)
International Standard Book Number-13: 978-0-415-97362-5 (Softcover)

**Library of Congress Cataloging-in-Publication Data**

Catalog record is available from the Library of Congress

Taylor & Francis Group
is the Academic Division of T&F Informa plc.

Visit the Taylor & Francis Web site at
http://www.taylorandfrancis.com

and the Routledge Web site at
http://www.routledge-ny.com

# Dedication

for Clare and Frank Modleski

# Contents

# Acknowledgments

I want to thank Patrice Petro for her encouragement when it was most needed, for her invaluable help on this project, and for her friendship. Without her this book would not have been written. I also want to thank Jane Nardin, who not only read and commented on the manuscript, but watched some of the films with me and on more than one occasion provided crucial insights that became central to my analyses. She sustained me in important ways throughout the writing of this book. Dana Polan read and reread chapters of the manuscript and, as he always does, made scholarly collaboration both richly rewarding and lots of fun. I am deeply grateful to my friends who read and critiqued all or part of the manuscript: Devon Hodges, Nadia Medina, and Abigail Solomon-Godeau.

A slightly altered version of Chapter 1 was first published as "Rape versus Mans/laughter: Hitchcock's *Blackmail* and Feminist Interpretation," *PMLA* 102, no. 3 (May 1987): 304–15. A slightly altered version of Chapter 3 was first published as "Never to Be Thirty-Six Years Old: *Rebecca* as Female Oedipal Drama," *Wide Angle* 5, no.1 (1982): 34–41.

# Introduction

## Hitchcock, Feminism, and the Patriarchal Unconscious

*Hitchcock and Feminist Film Theory*

In providing for a number of his films to be withheld from circulation for re-release many years later, Alfred Hitchcock ensured that his popularity with a fickle film-going public would remain as strong as ever. With this ploy, by which he managed to continue wielding an unprecedented power over a mass audience, Hitchcock betrays a resemblance to one of his favorite character types—the person who exerts an influence from beyond the grave. That this person is often a woman—Rebecca in the film of the same name, Carlotta and Madeleine in *Vertigo*, Mrs. Bates in *Psycho*—is not without interest or relevance to the thesis of this book: Hitchcock's great need (exhibited throughout his life as well as in his death) to insist on and exert authorial control can be related to the fact that his films are always in danger of being subverted by females whose power is both fascinating and seemingly limitless.

Such ghostly manipulations on Hitchcock's part would be ineffective, however, were it not for the fact that the films themselves possess an extraordinary hold on the public's imagination. Of course, some critics have been inclined to dismiss the films' appeal by attributing it simply to the mass audience's desire for sensational violence—usually directed against women—and "cheap, erotic" thrills, to quote "Mrs. Bates." While these critics find themselves increasingly in the minority, it is nevertheless somewhat surprising to reflect on the extent to which *feminists* have found themselves compelled, intrigued, infuriated, and inspired by Hitchcock's works.

In fact, the films of Hitchcock have been central to the formulation of feminist film theory and to the practice of feminist film criticism. Laura Mulvey's essay, "Visual Pleasure and Narrative Cinema," which may be considered the founding document of psychoanalytic feminist film theory, focuses on Hitchcock's films to show how women in classic Hollywood cinema are inevitably made into passive objects of male voyeuristic and sadistic impulses; how they exist simply to fulfill the desires and express the anxieties of the men in the audience; and how, by implication, women filmgoers can only have a masochistic relation to this cinema.[1] Since the publication of Mulvey's essay in 1975, a number of feminist articles on Hitchcock films have tended to corroborate her insights.

1

Believing that the representation of women in film is more complicated than Mulvey's article allows, I published an article in 1982 on Hitchcock's first American film, *Rebecca,* which was based on the bestselling "female Gothic" novel by Daphne du Maurier (this essay is included, in modified form, in the present volume).[2] There I argued that some films do allow for the (limited) expression of a specifically female desire and that such films, instead of following the male oedipal journey, which film theorists like Raymond Bellour see as the trajectory of *all* Hollywood narrative, trace a female oedipal trajectory, and in the process reveal some of the difficulties for women in becoming socialized in patriarchy.[3] Subsequently, Teresa de Lauretis in *Alice Doesn't* referred to that essay and to Hitchcock's films *Rebecca and Vertigo* to develop a theory of the female spectator. According to de Lauretis, identification on the part of women at the cinema is much more complicated than feminist theory has understood: far from being simply masochistic, the female spectator is always caught up in a double desire, identifying at one and the same time not only with the passive (female) object, but with the active (usually male) subject.[4]

Mulvey herself has had occasion to rethink some of her essay's main points and has done so in part through a reading of Hitchcock's *Notorious* that qualifies the condemnation of narrative found in "Visual Pleasure."[5] Other feminists have returned, almost obsessively, to Hitchcock to take up other issues, fight other battles. In an extremely interesting essay on *The Birds,* for example, Susan Lurie analyzes a segment that has also been analyzed by Raymond Bellour: the ride out and back across Bodega Bay. Lurie is concerned to dispute the Lacanian theory relied on so heavily by Bellour and Mulvey—particularly in the latter's argument that woman's body signifies lack and hence connotes castration for the male. In Lurie's view, women like Melanie Daniels in *The Birds* are threatening not because they automatically connote castration, but because they *don't,* and so the project of narrative cinema is precisely to "castrate" the woman whose strength and perceived wholeness arouse dread in the male.[6] Thus, if de Lauretis is primarily interested in complicating Mulvey's implied notion of femininity, Lurie is chiefly concerned with questioning certain aspects of Mulvey's theory of masculinity and masculine development. And both develop their arguments through important readings of Hitchcock's films.

Recently, Robin Wood, a male critic who has been a proponent of Hitchcock's films for many years, has become interested in these issues.[7] In the 1960s, Wood's book—the first in English on Hitchcock—set out to address the question, "Why should we take Hitchcock seriously?" In the 1980s, Wood declares, the question must be, "Can Hitchcock be saved for feminism?"—though his very language, implying the necessity of rescuing a favorite *auteur* from feminist obloquy, suggests that the question is fundamentally a rhetorical one. And indeed, although Wood claims in his essay not to be interested in locating "an uncontaminated feminist discourse in the films," he proceeds to minimize the misogyny in them and to analyze both *Rear Window* and *Vertigo* as exposés of the twisted logic of patriarchy, relatively untroubled by ambivalence or contradiction.

It may be symptomatic that in contrast to the female critics I have mentioned, the stated goal of the one male critic concerned with feminism is to reestablish the authority of the artist—to "save" Hitchcock. For Wood, political "progressiveness" has come to replace moral complexity as the criterion by which to judge Hitchcock's art, but the point remains the same—to justify the ways of the auteur to the filmgoing public. The feminist critics I have mentioned, by contrast, use Hitchcock's works as a means to elucidate issues and problems relevant to women in patriarchy. In so doing, these critics implicitly challenge and decenter directorial authority by considering Hitchcock's work as the expression of cultural attitudes and practices existing to some extent outside the artist's control. My own work is in the irreverent spirit of this kind of feminist criticism and is, if anything, more explicitly "deconstructionist" than this criticism has generally tended to be. Thus, one of my book's main theses is that time and again in Hitchcock films the strong fascination and identification with femininity revealed in them subverts the claims to mastery and authority not only of the male characters but of the director himself.

This is not to say that I am entirely unsympathetic to Wood's position. Indeed, this critic's work seems to me an important corrective to studies that see in Hitchcock only the darkest misogynistic vision. But what I want to argue is *neither* that Hitchcock is utterly misogynistic *nor* that he is largely sympathetic to women and their plight in patriarchy, but that his work is characterized by a thoroughgoing ambivalence about femininity—which explains why it has been possible for critics to argue with some plausibility on either side of the issue. It also, of course, explains why the issue can never be resolved and why, when one is reading criticism defending or attacking Hitchcock's treatment of women, one continually experiences a feeling of "yes, but ..." This book aims to account, often through psychoanalytic explanations, for the ambivalence in the work of Hitchcock. In the process, it continually demonstrates that despite the often considerable violence with which women are treated in Hitchcock's films, they remain resistant to patriarchal assimilation.

To explain the ambivalence in these films, I will be especially concerned with showing the ways in which masculine identity is bound up with feminine identity—both at the level of society as well as on the individual, psychological level. In this respect, the book will confirm that what Fredric Jameson says about ruling class literature is also true of patriarchal cultural production. According to Jameson in *The Political Unconscious,* consciousness on the part of the oppressed classes, expressed, "initially, in the unarticulated form of rage, helplessness, victimization, oppression by a common enemy," generates a "mirror image of class solidarity among the ruling groups. ... This suggests ... that the *truth* of ruling-class consciousness … is to be found in working-class consciousness."[8] Similarly, in Hitchcock, the "truth" of patriarchal consciousness lies in feminist consciousness and depends precisely on the depiction of victimized women found so often in his films. The paradox is such, then, that male solidarity (between characters, director, spectators, as the case may be) entails giving expression to women's feelings of "rage, helplessness, victimization, oppression." This point is of the greatest consequence for a theory of the female spectator. As I argue in the chapters on *Blackmail* and *Notorious*, insofar as Hitchcock films repeatedly reveal the way women are oppressed in patriarchy, they allow the female spectator to feel an anger that is very different from the masochistic response imputed to her by some feminist critics.

Not only is it possible to argue that feminist consciousness is the mirror of patriarchal consciousness, but one might argue as well that the patriarchal *unconscious* lies in femininity (which is not, however, to equate femininity with the unconscious). Psychoanalysis has shown that the process by which the male child comes to set the mother at a distance is of very uncertain outcome, which helps to explain why it is continually necessary for man to face the threat woman poses and to work to subdue that threat both in life and in art. The dynamics of identification and identity, I will argue, are fraught with difficulties and paradoxes that are continually reflected and explored in Hitchcock films.[9] To take an example suggestive of Jameson's mirror metaphor, when Scottie Ferguson in *Vertigo* begins investigating the mysterious Madeleine Elster, the first point-of-view shot shows him as a mirror image of the woman, and the rest of the film traces the vicissitudes of Scottie's attempts to reassert a masculinity lost when he failed in his performance of the law.

By focusing on the problematics of identity and identification, then, this study aims to insert itself in the debates circulating around Hitchcock's films and to examine some of the key theoretical issues developed in the various critiques. On the one hand, the book seeks to engage the problem of the female spectator, especially in the analysis of those films told from the woman's point of view (i.e., *Blackmail*, *Rebecca*, and *Notorious*). But even some of those films that seem to adopt the male point of view exclusively, like *Murder!*, *Rear Window*, or *Vertigo*, may be said either to have woman as the ultimate point of identification or to place the spectator—regardless of gender—in a classically "feminine" position. On the other hand, then, my intent is to problematize *male* spectatorship and masculine identity in general. The analysis will reveal that the question that continually—if sometimes implicitly—rages around Hitchcock's work as to whether he is sympathetic toward women or misogynistic is fundamentally unanswerable because he is both.[10] Indeed, as we shall see, the misogyny and the sympathy actually entail one another—just as Norman Bates' close relationship with his mother provokes his lethal aggression toward other women.

## The Female Spectator

As the figure of Norman Bates suggests, what both male and female spectators are likely to see in the mirror of Hitchcock's films are images of ambiguous sexuality that threaten to destabilize the gender identity of protagonists and viewers alike. Although in *Psycho* the mother/son relationship is paramount, I will argue that in films from *Rebecca* on it is more often the mother/daughter relationship that evokes this threat to identity and constitutes the main "problem" of the films. In *Vertigo*, for example, Madeleine is the (great grand) daughter of Carlotta Valdez, who seems to possess the heroine so thoroughly that the latter loses her individuality. *Rebecca's* heroine experiences a similar difficulty in relation to the powerful Rebecca, first wife of the heroine's husband. *Marnie's* main "problem"—as far as patriarchy is concerned—is an excessive attachment to her mother that prevents her from achieving a "normal," properly "feminine," sexual relationship with a man. In other films, the mother figure is actually a mother-in-law, but one who so closely resembles the heroine that it is impossible to escape the suspicion that the mother/daughter relationship is actually what is being evoked. In *Notorious*, both Alicia and her mother-in-law have blonde hair and foreign accents; and in *The Birds*, there is an uncanny resemblance between Melanie Daniels and Mitch's mother, Lydia. In all these films, moreover, Hitchcock manipulates point of view in such a way that the spectator him/herself is made to share the strong sense of identification with the (m)other.

As feminists have recently stressed, the mother/daughter relationship is one of the chief factors contributing to the bisexuality of women—a notion that several critics have argued is crucial to any theory of the female spectator seeking to rescue women from "silence, marginality, and absence." Very soon after the publication of Mulvey's essay, feminist critics began to approach this idea of female bisexuality to begin to explain women's experience of film. A consideration of this experience, they felt, was lacking in Mulvey's work, which thereby seemed to collaborate unwittingly in patriarchy's plot to render women invisible. In a much quoted discussion among film critics and filmmakers Michelle Citron, Julia Lesage, Judith Mayne, B. Ruby Rich, and Anna Marie Taylor that appeared in *New German Critique* in 1978, one of the major topics was the bisexuality of the female spectator. In the course of the discussion, the participants, attempting to counter what might be called the "compulsory heterosexuality" of mainstream film, concluded that more attention needs to be paid to women's erotic attraction to other women—to, for example, Marlene Dietrich not only as a fetishized object of male desire, which is how Mulvey had seen her, but as a female star with an "underground reputation" among lesbians as "a kind of subcultural icon."[11] Several of the participants stressed that female eroticism is obviously going to differ from male eroticism; the experience of the female spectator is bound to be more complex than a simple passive identification with the female object of desire or a straightforward role reversal—a facile assumption of the transvestite's garb. Julia Lesage insisted, "Although women's sexuality has been shaped under a dominant patriarchal culture, clearly women do not respond to women in film and the erotic element in quite the same way that men do, given that patriarchal film has the structure of a male fantasy" (p. 89). In other words, there must be other options for the female spectator than the two pithily described by B. Ruby Rich: "to identify either with Marilyn Monroe or with the man behind me hitting the back of my seat with his knees" (p. 87).

Several of the women in this discussion were strenuously anti-Freudian, claiming that Freud's framework cannot account for the position of female spectators. Recent Freudian and neo-Freudian accounts of women's psychic development in patriarchy and applications of these accounts to issues in feminist film theory have, however, suggested otherwise. Thus Gertrud Koch, addressing the question of "why women go to men's movies," refers to Freud's theory of female bisexuality, which is rooted in woman's pre-oedipal attachment to her mother. This attachment, it will be remembered, came as a momentous discovery to Freud and resulted in his having to revise significantly his theories of childhood sexuality and to recognize the fundamental asymmetry in male and female development.[12] The female's attachment to the mother, Freud came to understand, often goes "unresolved" throughout woman's life and coexists with her later heterosexual relationships. Hence, Teresa de Lauretis's notion of a "double desire" on the part of the female spectator—a desire that is *both* passive and active, homosexual and heterosexual. Koch speculates that men's need to prohibit and punish female voyeurism is attributable to their concern about women's pleasure in looking at other women: "Man's fear of permitting female voyeurism stems not only from fear of women looking at other men and drawing (to him perhaps unfavorable) comparisons but is also connected to a fear that women's bisexuality could make them competitors for the male preserve."[13]

In her book *Women and Film: Both Sides of the Camera*, feminist film critic E. Ann Kaplan draws on the neo-Freudian work of Julia Kristeva to make a similar point about men's repression of the "nonsymbolic" (pre-oedipal) aspects of motherhood. According to Kristeva/Kaplan, patriarchy must repress these nonsymbolic aspects of motherhood because of the "homosexual components" involved in the mother/daughter relationship.[14] Elsewhere, Kaplan analyzes *Stella Dallas*, a film about an intense mother/daughter relationship, in order to argue that the process of repression is enacted in classical cinema and that the female spectator herself comes to desire this repression and to endorse the heterosexual contract that seals the film at its end.[15] Another analysis of *Stella Dallas* by Linda Williams argues against this view and persuasively postulates a contradictory "double desire" on the part of the female spectator; on the one hand, we identify with the working class Stella and share her joy at having successfully sacrificed herself in giving away her daughter to the upper-class father and boyfriend and, on the other hand, because of the way point of view has been handled in the film, we are made to experience the full poignancy and *undesirability* of the loss of the close affective relationship with the daughter.[16] In other words, we could say that the spectator simultaneously experiences the symbolic *and* the nonsymbolic aspects of motherhood, despite patriarchy's attempts to repress and deny the latter.

In stressing the contradictory nature of female spectatorship, Williams' essay can be seen as a critique not only of the position that, given the structure of classic narrative film as male fantasy, the female spectator is forced to adopt the heterosexual view, but also of the opposite position, most forcefully articulated by Mary Ann Doane, which sees the pre-oedipal relationship with the mother as the source of insurmountable difficulties for the female spectator. To disqualify female voyeurism, Doane draws on the work of Christian Metz and his theories of spectatorship based on male fetishism and disavowal. According to Doane, whose essay "Film and the Masquerade: Theorising the Female Spectator," I will consider at greater length in the next chapter, woman's putative inability to achieve a distance from the *textual* body as related to her inability to separate decisively from the *maternal* body. Because women lack a penis, they lack the possibility of losing the "first stake of representation," the mother, and thus of symbolizing their difference from her (a "problem" that we shall see is at the heart of *Rebecca*): "this closeness to the body, this excess, prevents the woman from assuming a position similar to the man's in relation to signifying systems. For she is haunted by the loss of a loss, the lack of that lack so essential for the realization of the ideals of semiotic systems."[17] There are, I believe, several ways for feminists to challenge such a nihilistic position. One might, for example, point out the tortuous logic of these claims, as Hélène Cixous has done ("She lacks lack? Curious to put it in so contradictory, so extremely paradoxical a manner: she lacks lack. To say she lacks lack is also, after all, to say she doesn't miss lack … since she doesn't miss the lack of lack.")[18] Or, one might say with Linda Williams and B. Ruby Rich that the female spectator does indeed experience a "distance" from the image as an inevitable result of her being an exile "living the tension of two different cultures."[19] Or, one might, as I shall do in the chapters that follow, question the very "ideals" of the "semiotic systems" invoked by Doane—and, in particular, the ideal of "distance," or what in Brechtian theory is called "distanciation."

According to Doane, woman's closeness to the (maternal) body means that she "overidentifies with the image": "The association of tears and 'wet wasted afternoons' (in Molly Haskell's words) with genres specified as feminine (the soap opera, the 'woman's picture') points very precisely to this type of overidentification, this abolition of a distance, in short this inability to fetishize."[20] Now, as I have mentioned, many of Hitchcock's films actually thematize the "problem" of "overidentification"—the daughter's "overidentification" with the mother and, in at least one film *(Rear Window)*, the woman's "overidentification" with the "textual body." Given Hitchcock's preoccupation with female bisexuality and given his famed ability to draw us into close identifications with his characters—so many of them women—his work would seem to provide the perfect testing ground for theories of female spectatorship.

But the question immediately arises as to why a male director—and one so frequently accused of unmitigated misogyny—would be attracted to such subjects. I want to suggest that woman's bisexual nature, rooted in pre-oedipality, and her consequent alleged tendency to overidentify with other women and with texts, is less a problem for *women*, as Doane would have it, than it is for patriarchy. And this is so not only for the reason suggested by Gertrud Koch (that female bisexuality would make women into competitors for "the male preserve"), but far more fundamentally because it reminds man of his *own* bisexuality (and thus his resemblance to Norman Bates), a bisexuality that threatens to subvert his "proper" identity, which depends upon his ability to distance woman and make her his property. In my readings of Hitchcock, I will demonstrate how men's fascination and identification with the feminine continually undermine their efforts to achieve masculine strength and autonomy and is a primary cause of the violence toward women that abounds in Hitchcock's films. These readings are meant to implicate certain Marxist/psychoanalytical film theories as well, since by uncritically endorsing "distanciation" and detachment (however "passionate" this detachment is said to be) as the "proper"—i.e., politically correct—mode of spectatorship, they to some extent participate in the repression of the feminine typical of the "semiotic system" known as classic narrative cinema.[21]

## Men at the Movies

The psychiatrist, the voice of institutional authority who "explains" Norman Bates to us at the end of *Psycho*, pronounces matricide to be an unbearable crime—"most unbearable to the son who commits it." In my opinion, though, the crime is "most unbearable" to the victim who suffers it, and despite the fact that a major emphasis of my book is on masculine subjectivity in crisis, its ultimate goals are a deeper understanding of women's victimization—of the sources of matrophobia and misogyny—and the development of female subjectivity, which is continually denied women by male critics, theorists, and artists (as well as by their female sympathizers). Some feminists, however, have recently argued that we should altogether dispense with analysis of masculinity and of patriarchal systems of thought in order to devote full time to exploring female subjectivity. Teresa de Lauretis, for example, has declared that the "project of women's cinema [by which she means also feminist film theory] is no longer that of destroying or disrupting man-centered vision by representing its blind spots, its gaps or its repressed"; rather, she argues, we should be attending to the creation of another—feminine or feminist—vision.[22] Although I fully share de Lauretis's primary concern, I do not agree that we should forgo attempting to locate the gaps and blind spots in "man-centered vision." One of the problems with Mulvey's theory was that her picture of male cinema was so monolithic that she made it seem invincible, and so, from a political point of view, feminists were stymied. An analysis of patriarchy's weak points enables us to avoid the paralyzing nihilism of a position that accords such unassailable strength to an oppressive system and helps us more accurately to assess our *own* strengths relative to it. Moreover, I believe we *do* need to destroy "man-centered vision" by beginning to see with our own eyes—because for so long we have been not only fixed in its sights, but also forced to view the world through its lens.

While, as we have seen, some feminists have criticized Mulvey's "inadequate theorization of the female spectator," others have objected to her restriction of the *male* spectator to a single dominant position, arguing that men at the movies—at least at *some* movies—may also be feminine, passive, and masochistic. Studies like D.N. Rodowick's "The Difficulty of Difference," Janet Bergstrom's "Sexuality at a Loss," and Gaylyn Studlar's "Masochism and the Perverse Pleasure of the Cinema" take issue with the view of sexual difference as organized according to strict binary oppositions (masculinity = activity; femininity = passivity, etc.) and emphasize the bisexuality of *all* human beings and "the mobility of multiple, fluid identifications" open to every spectator, including men.[23] These critics point to certain Freudian pronouncements to the effect that each individual "displays a mixture of the character traits belonging to his own and to the opposite sex."[24] In "Sexuality at a Loss: The Films of F.W. Murnau," for example, Janet Bergstrom refers to this aspect of Freudian theory in arguing that Murnau's films displace sexuality from the female body to the male body and thus carry "a shifting, unstable homoerotic charge" enabling viewers to "relax rigid demarcations of gender identification and sexual orientation."[25] Bergstrom concludes from this analysis that the issue of gender is not pertinent to a psychoanalytically oriented criticism, which ought to stress the bisexuality of all individuals, and should concern only those critics interested in "historical and sociological perspectives"—as if it were possible to divide up the human subject in this way.[26]

A passage from Bergstrom's earlier essay "Enunciation and Sexual Difference" helps to illuminate the problem involved in considering the male spectator to be similar to the female spectator in his bisexual response. In that essay, Bergstrom had called for attention to be paid to "the movement of identifications, whether according to theories of bisexuality, power relations ... or some other terms."[27] The weakness of this formulation, however, lies in its assumption that notions of bisexuality can be considered *apart* from power relations. On the contrary, in patriarchy the feminine position alone is devalued and despised, and those who occupy it are powerless and oppressed. The same

Freud who spoke of bisexuality also, after all, spoke of the normal masculine "contempt" for femininity.[28] Freud showed very precisely how men tend to repress their bisexuality to avoid being subjected to this contempt and to accede to their "proper" place in the symbolic order. A discussion of bisexuality as it relates to spectatorship ought, then, to be informed by a knowledge of the way male and female responses are rendered asymmetrical by a patriarchal power structure. As Hitchcock films repeatedly demonstrate, the male subject is greatly threatened by bisexuality, though he is at the same time fascinated by it; and it is the woman who pays for this ambivalence—often with her life itself.

An interesting challenge to Mulvey's theorization of male spectatorship has been mounted by critics who have questioned its exclusive emphasis on the male spectator's sadism, man's need to gain mastery over the woman in the course of the narrative. A pioneering essay by Kaja Silverman entitled "Masochism and Subjectivity" and a later study by Gaylyn Studlar on the films of Josef Von Sternberg stress the male spectator's masochistic pleasures at the movies. In placing emphasis on this aspect of male subjectivity, both critics point to the importance of the pre-oedipal phase in masculine development. Hitherto, as I have said, many film theorists have insisted on the fact that narrative cinema closely follows the male oedipal trajectory outlined by Freud, and in doing so cements the male spectator into the male symbolic order. In the Freudian scenario, the child renounces pre-oedipal bisexuality and the mother as "love object" for "the requirements of the Oedipus Complex," and in the process assumes his castration.[29] Arguing against this view, Gaylyn Studlar generalizes from an analysis of the films Josef Von Sternberg made with Marlene Dietrich to argue that at the cinema we all regress to the infantile pre-oedipal phase, submitting ourselves to and identifying (fusing) with the overwhelming presence of the screen and the woman on it. "Castration fear and the perception of sexual difference," Studlar says, "have no importance" in her aesthetic, which aims to "replace" Mulvey's theory with a more benign version of spectatorship. Studlar's model "rejects" a position that emphasizes "the phallic phase and the pleasure of control or mastery" and thus, she maintains, can help deliver feminist psychoanalytic theory from the "dead end" in which it supposedly finds itself.[30]

While I believe that male masochism is indeed an important area for feminists to explore—is, in fact, one of the blind spots or "repressed" aspects of male-centered vision—the point surely is that this masochism, and the pre-oedipal relationship with the mother in which it is rooted, *are* in fact repressed by the male in adult life, as Studlar at one point acknowledges. For me the crucial question facing feminist theory is, "What are the sources and the consequences *for women* of this repression?" For that matter, what are the sources and consequences of the "dread of woman," of "ambivalence" toward the mother, of the equation of women with death, all of which are mentioned by

Studlar as crucial components of the masochistic aesthetic? How do the answers to these questions illuminate the undeniable fact that Mulvey had sought to understand and that Studlar disregards: i.e., that women are objectified and brought under male domination in the vast majority of patriarchal films?

The fact that men are driven to repress their pre-oedipal attachment to their mothers in acceding to a patriarchal order would seem to invalidate any attempt simply to "replace" a political critique that focuses on the phallic, sadistic, oedipal nature of narrative cinema with an aesthetic that privileges its oral, masochistic, and pre-oedipal components. As Christian Metz noted some time ago, although cinema is situated in the realm of the Imaginary—of the pre-oedipal—the male spectator himself has already passed through the Symbolic,[31] has, then, internalized the "normal contempt" for femininity, repressed it in himself, and met—more or less—the "requirements of the Oedipus complex." Hence, the necessity of discussing the way sadistic and masochistic, oedipal and pre-oedipal, symbolic and nonsymbolic aspects of male spectatorship interrelate. In this complex undertaking Kaja Silverman's work on masochism seems to me to be of utmost importance.

In "Masochism and Subjectivity," Silverman examines Lacan's theory of the mirror stage and Freud's discussion of his grandson's "fort/da" game, on which Lacan's theory is based, and concludes that in decisive moments in the history of the subject, the individual learns to take pleasure in pain and loss. Cinematic activity, like many other forms of cultural activity, replays these moments of loss, which are as pleasurable for the male spectator as for the female spectator. Referring to theories of cinematic suture, for example, Silverman explains that, in relating to films, we experience "a constant fluctuation between the imaginary plenitude of the shot, and the loss of that plenitude through the agency of the cut."[32] Yet, she admits, there is a significant contradiction here, since in films themselves it is most often women who are "placed in positions of passivity, and more generally men than women who occupy positions of aggressivity. On the other hand, the subject—whether male or female—is passively positioned and is taught to take pleasure in his/her pain" (p. 5). Silverman "resolves" this contradiction by referring to Freud's theory of dreams, in which the dreamer, though perhaps absent *"in propria persona"* from the dream, may be represented by a variety of people, onto whom the dreamer displaces his/her own fears and desires. In films where the female character occupies a passive position, she enacts *on behalf of the male viewer* "the compulsory narrative of loss and recovery" (p. 5). Unfortunately, Silverman's essay, like Studlar's, ultimately refuses to cede any importance to sadism in the male viewer's response. Silverman writes, "Indeed, I would go so far as to say that the fascination of the sadistic point of view is *merely* that it provides the best vantage point from which to watch the masochistic story unfold" (p. 5, emphasis mine). Yet the reference to Freudian dream theory points to a way not of canceling or "resolving" the contradiction she describes, but of understanding how it works *as* a contradiction. Just as Freud showed that the meaning of the dream resides neither in its latent content nor in its manifest content, but in the complex interaction of the two—in the dreamwork itself—so the male viewer's response might best be understood in the Freudian sense of a sadomasochistic dialectic rather than of pure sadism (as in Mulvey) or "mere" masochism.[33]

Thus, whereas Studlar's article places sole emphasis on the female as a possible figure of male identification—and mentions only in passing the fact that this identification is the "'source of deepest dread,'"— Silverman's analysis helps to explain the workings of both the identification *and* the dread; the dream mechanism of displacement enables the male subject simultaneously to experience and deny an identification with passive, victimized female characters. By acknowledging the importance of denial in the male spectator's response, we can take into account a crucial fact ignored by the articles discussed in this section—the fact that the male finds it necessary to repress certain "feminine" aspects of himself, and to project these exclusively onto the woman, who does the suffering for both of them.

It is part of my project here to explore this dialectic of identification and dread in the male spectator's response to femininity—the movement between the two poles Alice Jardine has said characterize contemporary culture: "hysteria" (confusion of sexual boundaries) and "paranoia" (their reinforcement).[34] The paranoia may be seen as a consequence of the hysteria—the two interacting in a way to be described in my chapter on *Murder!*—but, as Jardine elsewhere observes, it is fundamentally a reaction against women who know not only too much, but anything at all. "Man's response in both private and public to a woman who *knows* (anything) has most consistently been one of paranoia."[35] "I know a secret about you, Uncle Charlie," says Charlie the niece to her uncle in *Shadow of a Doubt*, thereby arousing his murderous rage. Charlie is a typical Hitchcock female, both because her close relationship to her mother arouses in her a longing for a different kind of life from the one her father offers them and because she seems to possess special incriminating knowledge about men. Charlie's attitude is representative of the two types of resistance to patriarchy I have been discussing here—that which seeks to know men's "secrets" (patriarchy's "blind spots, gaps, and repressed areas") and that which knows the kinds of pleasure unique to women's relationship with other women. This book is devoted to understanding how female spectators may be drawn into this special relationship and how men may react to women who are suspected of possessing such valuable secret knowledge.

## A Frankly Inventive Approach

All of this is to suggest that Hitchcock films as I read them are anything but exemplary of Hollywood cinema. Rather, if the films do indeed invoke typical patterns of male and female socialization, as Raymond Bellour has repeatedly argued, they do so only to reveal the difficulties inherent in these processes—and to implicate the spectator in these difficulties as well. Interestingly, even Mulvey's essay, which uses Hitchcock films as the main evidence in her case against Hollywood cinema, actually ends up claiming that *Vertigo* is critical of the kinds of visual pleasure typically offered by mainstream cinema, a visual pleasure that is rooted in the scopic regime of the male psychic economy. In her reading of the film, Mulvey thus unwittingly undercuts her own indictment of narrative cinema as possessing no redeeming value for feminism.

Of course, Mulvey is not the first commentator to discover in Hitchcock films self-reflexive critiques of voyeurism and visual pleasure—a whole tradition of criticism celebrates the director's ability to manipulate spectators so as to make us uncomfortably aware of the perverse pleasures of cinema going. But for all the claims of traditional critics to have had their eyes opened to the moral ambiguities inherent in film viewing, most remain incredibly blind to the relation of voyeurism to questions of sexual difference. For example, male critics frequently point to *Psycho* as a film that punishes audiences for their illicit voyeuristic desires, but they ignore the fact that within the film not only are women objects of the male gaze, they are also recipients of most of the punishment. It is left to feminist criticism to point out that after Marion Crane is killed in the shower, the camera focuses on her sightless eye; that when Mother is finally revealed, it is Marion's sister who is forced to confront the horrible vision; that while she screams out in fright, the swinging lightbulb is reflected in the eye sockets of the female corpse; and that, finally, at the end of the film, "Mother" is agonizingly aware of being stared at and tries desperately to demonstrate her harmlessness to her unseen observers by refusing to swat a fly. In acknowledging such sexual asymmetry in desire and its punishment (where men possess the desire and women receive the punishment), we are forced to relinquish the more facile notions about Hitchcock's self-reflexivity and his critiques of voyeurism—at the very least we would need to invoke the notions discussed earlier of male masochism and its denial or displacement.

An analysis of voyeurism and sexual difference is only one of the ways in which a book taking a specifically feminist approach can provide a much needed perspective on Hitchcock's films. Indeed, there are many questions that I think begin to look very different when seen by a woman. What, for example, happens to the frequently noted theme of the "transference of guilt" when we insist against the grain of an entire history of Hitchcock criticism that a certain heroine is innocent because she was defending herself against rape? In patriarchy woman's sexual "guilt" is unique to her and is not "transferable" to men. Or, to take another example, how do the theatrical motifs so common in Hitchcock films change their meaning when considered in the light of Western culture's association of femininity with theater and spectacle? Or, again, how may we begin to rethink Hitchcock's "Catholicism" when we view it in the context of Julia Kristeva's work on religion and matrophobia—matrophobia being so strong an element in Hitchcock that it is acknowledged by even the most traditional of nonfeminist critics? While not the primary focus of this work, such concerns, which have been central to Hitchcock studies, will be given a new inflection in my readings. I am, however, by no means claiming to advance comprehensive, definitive interpretations of the films. Less ambitiously, I think of my book as a sustained meditation on a few of the issues that have been of paramount interest to feminist film theory.

In his recent work *The World, the Text, and the Critic,* Edward Said has beautifully described the critic as one who "is responsible to a degree for articulating those voices dominated, displaced, or silenced by the textuality of texts. Texts are a system of forces institutionalized by the reigning culture at some human cost to its various components. … The critic's attitude … should …be frankly inventive, in the traditional sense of *inventio* so fruitfully employed by Vico, which means finding and exposing things that otherwise may be hidden beneath piety, heedlessness, or routine."[36] Feminism, too, has by now its pieties and routines. Insofar as it all too readily accepts the ideals of male semiotic systems, feminism also needs to be challenged by a "frankly inventive" approach, an approach that, if it seems alien at first, is so only because it is situated in the realm of the uncanny—speaking with a voice that inhabits us all, but that for some of us has been made strange through fear and repression.

If it did not sound more frivolous than I intend to be, then, I would say that part of my intention in these pages is to defend that much maligned woman, Mrs. Bates, whose *male* child suffers such a severe case of "overidentification" with her that he is driven to matricide and to the rape/murder of various young women. At the end of the film, "Mrs. Bates" (who has the last word) speaks through her son's body to protest her innocence and place the blame for the crimes against women on her son. I think she speaks the truth. As I will argue, the sons are indeed the guilty ones, and, moreover, it is my belief that the crime of matricide is destined to occur over and over again (on the psychic plane) until woman's voice allows itself to be heard—in women and men alike.

# 1
# Rape vs. Mans/laughter
## *Blackmail*

The issue of sexual violence must be central to any feminist analysis of the films of Alfred Hitchcock. In film studies, Hitchcock is often viewed as the archetypal misogynist, who invites his audience to indulge their most sadistic fantasies against the female. Some critics have even argued that Hitchcock's work is prototypical of the extremely violent assaults on women that make up so much of our entertainment today. Thus, Linda Williams has claimed that *Psycho* is the forerunner of the slasher films of the 1970s and 1980s (films like *Halloween* and *Friday the Thirteenth* and their numerous sequels), however superior it may be in aesthetic value to these later films.[1] As might be expected, such films are usually thought to appeal largely to males; women, it is claimed, can enjoy such films only by assuming the position of "masochists."[2] Rape and violence, it would appear, effectively silence and subdue not only the woman *in* the films—the one who would threaten patriarchal law and order through the force of her anarchic desires—but also the women watching the films: female spectators and female critics.

Recent criticism has explored the relation between interpretation in the arts and interpretation in legal discourse. Not surprisingly, analyses like Ronald Dworkin's "Law as Interpretation," while insisting that interpretation is necessarily political, ignore the significance of gender and thereby perpetuate the myth that the legal system is, in Catharine MacKinnon's words, "point-of-viewless" and "universal," that it can incorporate and adjudicate women's experience as fully as it does men's.[3] Women like MacKinnon who wish to expose the partiality of the legal system have done so by focusing on the issue of rape in order to show how interpretation always locates the meaning of the act in the man's point of view. "Under conditions of sex inequality, with perspective bound up with situation, whether a contested interaction is rape comes down to whose meaning wins."[4] I suggest that the question of whose meaning wins is equally pertinent to interpretation in literary and film criticism and that to insist on the very different meaning a given text may have for women is in fact an act of survival of the kind Adrienne Rich believes is always at stake in feminist re-visions.[5]

*Blackmail* (1929) is the story of a shopkeeper's daughter, Alice White, one of the first in a long line of tormented blonde heroines that Hitchcock featured throughout his career. Our introduction to this character is postponed, however, until the end of the film's lengthy, entirely silent, opening sequence, which shows the capture, interrogation, and booking of a criminal. Following this sequence, shot in quasidocumentary style, the film's detective hero, Frank Webber (John Longden), meets his fiancée, Alice White (Anny Ondra), in the outer rooms of Scotland Yard. Alice is petulant because Frank has kept her waiting for half an hour, but she perks up when a heavy, mustachioed detective whispers something in her ear. She exits laughing, pointedly excluding Frank from the joke, although he valiantly tries to share in the mirth. At the café they go to for their date, Alice deliberately picks a quarrel with Frank so that she can keep an assignation she has made with another man, an artist named Crewe (Cyril Ritchard), who at the end of the evening persuades the hesitant Alice to come up to his studio. Their conversation outside the building is punctuated by closeups of a mysterious man listening intently to hear what they are saying. The man calls to the artist, who explains to Alice that the interloper is a "sponger." Once inside the building, Crewe stops in the foyer and—so much for passionate seduction scenes—checks his mail, queries his landlady about a disturbing note he has received, and finally ascends the staircase with Alice, the camera emphasizing this movement by recording it in a single impressive crane shot from the side of the stairwell. *Blackmail* is one of the first of many Hitchcock films associating a room at the top of the stairs with sexuality and with danger and violence to a woman. There ensues a very curious scene that ends with the artist assaulting Alice, dragging her screaming and struggling to his bed, where she finally stabs him to death—an event that occurs off screen, behind the bed curtains. We simply see her hand reach out and grab a knife conveniently placed near some bread on a night table; then there is an ominous silence, and the artist's lifeless arm falls outside the curtains. Alice sneaks home after an agonized night of wandering the streets and manages to get into bed just before her mother comes up to wake her.

Meanwhile, Scotland Yard enters the case, and Frank finds Alice's glove during a search of the studio. When he visits her father's shop, where the family also lives, and takes Alice into the phone booth to talk, the two are surprised by the stranger who was lurking about the studio the night before—a Mr. Tracy (Donald Calthrop). Tracy has found Alice's other glove, and he begins to blackmail the pair, installing himself comfortably at the breakfast table with her puzzled parents. But when Frank learns that Tracy was observed by the artist's landlady the night before and is now Scotland Yard's chief suspect, he gleefully begins to taunt and threaten Tracy despite Alice's protests. There ensues a frantic chase that eventually winds up on the domed roof of the British Museum, where Tracy plunges through a skylight while on the verge of identifying Alice as the killer. The chase is intercut with closeup shots of Alice paralyzed with guilt and fear, and it ends as Alice decides to write a note to Frank declaring her intention to confess, since she cannot bear the thought of an innocent man's suffering for something she has done. When she gets into the office of the Chief Inspector, however, she finds Frank there and before she can disclose the truth, the phone rings, and the inspector instructs Frank to handle the matter. Frank removes her from the office and acknowledges awareness of what she has done; on their way out they encounter the mustachioed detective who ushered Alice in and who laughingly asks Frank, "Well, did she tell you who did it? You want to look out or she'll be losing your job, my boy." The men laugh heartily at the thought of "lady detectives" on the police force, of women usurping male roles and possessing masculine knowledge, and the camera tracks in on Alice visually caught between them, trying to force herself to laugh along. Then, as she catches sight of something out of the frame, her expression sobers, and the final shot of the film shows us what she sees: a picture of a laughing, pointing jester painted by the murdered artist, which recedes from a closeup view as a detective carries it down the hall.[6]

Even so cursory a summary suggests the extent to which the film, through a classically Hitchcockian "parallel reversal," may be viewed as a "set-up" of the woman, who begins the film by flirtatiously laughing at another man's joke to provoke her lover and ends by standing between two detectives who share a joke at her expense. Here, the woman literally and figuratively occupies precisely that place that Freud assigned to women in the structure of the obscene joke: the place of the object between two male subjects.[7] It might be argued that one of the main projects of the film is to wrest power from the woman, in particular the power of laughter, and to give the men the last laugh, thereby defusing the threat of woman's infidelity, her refusal to treat with proper seriousness patriarchal law and authority. Alice's private joke with the second detective is, after all, occasioned by her expecting "the entire machinery of Scotland Yard to be held up to please" her, as Frank sarcastically observes. In other words, she unreasonably demands that the law conform to her, instead of accepting the reverse.

It is scarcely accidental that contemporary feminist theory has stressed the subversive potential of woman's laughter, as for example, Hélène Cixous does in "Castration or Decapitation?" where she recounts the parable of the warrior Sun Tse. Instructed by the king to train the king's wives in the arts of war, Sun Tse found that "instead of learning the code very quickly, the ladies started laughing and chattering and paying no attention to the lesson." So he threatened them with decapitation, whereupon they stopped laughing and learned their lessons very well. "Women," concludes Cixous, "have no choice other than to be decapitated, and in any case, the moral is that if they don't actually lose their heads by the sword, *they only keep them on condition that they lose them*—lose them, that is, to complete silence, turned into automatons."[8]

If castration is, as Laura Mulvey has persuasively argued, always at stake for the male in classical narrative cinema, then decapitation is at stake for the female—in the cinema as elsewhere. In the scene in the studio, Alice tries to paint a picture on the artist's canvas, and she draws the head of a woman. The artist takes her hand, guiding it to "complete the masterpiece," and draws a nude female body, which Alice then signs, authorizing, as it were, man's view of woman and thereby consenting to the silencing of her own possibly different ideas about herself. Maurice Yacowar writes of this episode, "That routine is a comic miniature of the scene in the studio, the girl having gone to his room for some playful headwork, conversation, but (artists being what they are) finding the body soon forced into play."[9] Thus does the critic, with his little oxymoronic witticism about rape, add his voice to the chorus of male laughter that ends the film.

The nude is only one of two important pictures in *Blackmail*. The second is the jester. In the artist's studio Alice at first laughs at the picture and even points back at it, but after she has stabbed Crewe it seems to accuse her, and she lashes out and tears it. Later, when Frank discovers Alice's glove in the studio, he immediately confronts the jester, who appears to be mocking Frank's cuckoldry. At the end, a realignment has clearly taken place, and the sound of male laughter, Frank's included, accompanies the image of the laughing jester pointing at an Alice who can no longer even smile. According to Yacowar, "the clown is the spirit of corrective comedy, recalling the shrewd, manic wisdom of the jester in *King Lear*. … The painting, like its dapper, elegant artist, works as a test of the people it meets. It is the very spirit of irony, seeming innocent but a tricky test of its viewer's moral alertness."[10] Every jester, I suppose, is bound to recall *King Lear*, but in any case, what the spirit of this jester comically "corrects" is a world in which the female is temporarily in control. If Yacowar is right to see a self-reflexive element in the painting, to see, that is, the artist in the film as a representative of Hitchcock the artist, then by extension, the filmmaker's work of art, *Blackmail*, would be like the painting in the final shot, a cruel but not unusual joke on woman, a joke which the critic retells in his own style.

Commentators have most often praised *Blackmail* for its innovative and creative use of sound. In particular, they have pointed to the breakfast table scene, in which Alice, having stabbed a man to death just hours before, listens to a chattering neighbor deplore the killer's choice of a knife for the murder weapon; the voice becomes a mumble, with only the often-repeated word "knife" clearly audible; then with the camera fixed on a closeup of Alice, her father's voice comes on the soundtrack asking her to "cut us a bit of bread." As the voluble neighbor drones on, another closeup shows Alice's hand reaching out hesitantly to pick up the utensil, which she sends flying when the word "knife" suddenly screams out at her. Generally, critics of the film content themselves with celebrating the cleverness of such manipulations of sound without discussing its narrative function; they simply admire the way Hitchcock "so masterfully controls [this element] by turning the cinematic screws."[11] And even when they do consider the matter further, they tend to discuss Hitchcock's concern with "the limits and the problems of human communication."[12] What is remarkable to me, however, is that this first British sound film specifically foregrounds the problems of *woman's* speaking.

To begin with, we can cite a historical accident, one that nevertheless profoundly affects the way we experience the film. Since Anny Ondra, the Czech actress who plays Alice, had much too pronounced an accent for the daughter of a British shopkeeper, Hitchcock had another woman, Joan Barry, stand near the camera and say the lines that Ondra mimed. In a way, the film is uncannily prophetic, anticipating all those sound films for decades to come in which women are more spoken than speaking, hysterics reduced to communicating in "body language," to use Yacowar's telling phrase.[13] As Ondra clearly hesitates before each line, listening for her cue, and then accompanies the lines with slightly exaggerated gestures, she does indeed resemble Cixous's "automatons"—a word, moreover, that captures the marionette-like nature of Alice's movements after the murder when she emerges from the bed dazed and "out of herself," holding the knife in what Deborah Linderman notes is a "phallic position."[14] She has, after all, usurped the male prerogative of aggression against the opposite sex.

Further, as we have seen, the film apparently works to reduce Alice to a silent object between two male subjects—and this objectification occurs not just at the end. The film repeatedly places Alice in a triangular relationship with two men: Frank and the artist; the artist and the film's spectator; Frank and the blackmailer; and Frank and the laughing detective. One of the most famous shots occurs in the artist's studio and involves a "split screen" effect: Alice changes clothes on one side of the artist's screen while on the other side Crewe sings and plays the piano with his back to Alice, whose undressing is thus presented pornographically for the sole delectation of the film spectator. As Deborah Linderman observes, woman is here positioned at the point of a triangle "completed by two male sightlines," which subsequently collapse into "a single point of identification" between the male viewer and Crewe. For Linderman, this scene provides evidence for Raymond Bellour's thesis that "in classical cinema the spectator is *always* male."[15]

Alice appears at the point of another triangle later when Frank is gloating over the turned tables in his dealing with the blackmailer. She is seated, quaking, in the foreground of the image, and the blackmailer and Frank stand talking on either side of her in the background. Frank maintains that though Tracy will try to blame the murder on Alice, "our word's as good as, or perhaps a bit better than, that of a jailbird." At one point during the scene the camera cuts to a medium closeup of the blackmailer, who says, "When the surprise comes, it won't be for me." There is a pan to Alice, and he continues,

"It's *my* word against hers." Unable to bear it any longer, Alice gets up and goes round to Frank's side, with the camera following, and says, "Frank, you … you can't do this"; he tells her to be quiet, and she walks around behind the two men, where she is again caught between them as the camera pans back and forth. When Tracy asks, "Why can't you let her speak?" Frank replies, "You mind your own business. And in any case she'll speak at the right moment." Tracy begins to plead and even tries to return the blackmail money, but Frank ignores it. As the camera follows the blackmailer's hand pulling the money back in front of Alice's body, the shot neatly captures her role as object of exchange between males. When Frank continues to disregard Tracy's pleas, Tracy falls back on his previous formula, "All right, then, it's still *my* word against hers."

But what might Alice say about her situation if she could speak about it? What language adequately describes the episode in the artist's studio? What, in short, *is* the woman's "word" against which the blackmailer pits his own? Lindsay Anderson describes the incident leading to the murder as a seduction;[16] Donald Spoto calls it an act of "violent love" on the part of the artist: "his passion overcomes him and he attempts to make violent love to her."[17] John Russell Taylor characterizes it as "a fairly violent pass."[18] Hitchcock himself uses the word "rape" on one occasion and "seduction" on another, suggesting that for him, as for many men, there's not much difference between the two.[19] Eric Rohmer and Claude Chabrol also speak of rape, but only to introduce a doubt. They write, "He apparently tries to rape her," and they go on to suggest that she gets what she deserves: "To defend her virtue, which one would have thought to be less precious to her, she stabs him with a bread-knife."[20] Raymond Durgnat actually subjects Alice to a mock trial; after appearing to consider both sides of the issue, he concludes, "Hitchcock would not have been allowed to show incontrovertible evidence of rape even if he had wanted to so there's room for doubt even on the issue of whether Alice is right in thinking she's being raped rather than merely forcibly embraced."[21] "Forcible embrace" or "violent love": the oxymorons seem to proliferate when rape is the issue. In the court over which he presides Durgnat effectively eradicates the very category of rape (at least as far as the film world is concerned) by ruling that a condition of its legal existence must be the kind of "incontrovertible evidence" that it is illegal to show. Another Alice finds herself in Wonderland. In any case, it is impossible to imagine what would constitute adequate proof for the male critic, since it is a question here of *attempted* rape. The film, after all, does have the artist begin to pull Alice across the room while she screams to be let go, then we see the shadows of their figures projected on the wall as he pushes her into his bed, where the struggle continues until shortly after Alice seizes the knife. Interestingly, since the episode is not presented directly to the spectator's view, it is a question here of accepting the veracity of the woman's words, her expression of protest and fear. As frequently occurs in real life, critics in the main refuse to accept the woman's negative, claiming that Alice unconsciously wishes to be ravished.[22]

Like Frank denying Alice the right to speak, then, the critics seem intent on silencing an interpretation of the film that would adopt the woman's point of view. For the film is indeed susceptible to this kind of interpretation, which, moreover, would not necessarily require reading entirely "against the grain." The very fact that critics resort to such tortuous language and logic to discredit a reading of the film that as yet nobody has proffered suggests that *they* may be the ones who are going against the grain in trying to acquit the artist and convict the woman. John Russell Taylor, who adopts the guise of prosecuting attorney, remarks, "After all, the victim had only taken her up to his apartment (willingly enough on her part) and made a fairly violent pass at her—it would be difficult even to maintain that she killed him while resisting rape. So she would seem to be guilty of at least an unpremeditated panic killing, worse than manslaughter."[23] Like prosecutors in real life, the critics consider the woman's willingness to go with the man sufficient justification for any liberty, however violent, he chooses to take. The question becomes: to what extent does the film share this point of view and make us condemn the woman for her sexual availability? Here it is important to stress that while Alice is nervously flirtatious, she is hardly the one-dimensional vamp of so many films of the period. As a matter of fact, the scene in the artist's studio strikes me as remarkable for its subtle nuances and complexities. First, as even Yacowar unwittingly concedes, Alice is clearly much more interested in "headwork," conversation, with that exotic species of being, the artist, who flatters the shopkeeper's daughter with his attentions. Second, she is persuaded to don the revealing costume by the lure of participating in the artistic process, since Crewe has promised to let her model for him. After she emerges from behind the screen in this outfit, she prances gaily around the room, more like a child playing dressup than a woman of doubtful virtue.

And if we turn to consider the artist's role, Cyril Ritchard's performance does little to suggest the passionate nature critics continually project onto his character: from the moment Crewe checks his mail in the foyer to the time he sings the jaunty tune, "Miss Up-to-Date," at the piano, while Alice strips behind a screen, his behavior is thoroughly nonchalant. His abrupt violence is all the more startling and disturbing for the contrast it makes to his earlier casual air. Critics have taken the lyrics of the song, which suggest that modern woman has abandoned old-fashioned morality, as further proof of Alice's guilt. But the artist's declaration, "That's a song about you, my dear," clearly points to an alternate reading of the scene. For the artist continually works to *construct* the woman as sexual and hence as responsible for her attack; in the song he sings, in the painting he "helps" her finish, in his gesture of pulling the straps of her costume down from her shoulder—in all these acts, the artist reveals that the sexual woman is a product of male desire and male artistic practice.[24]

The point is, then, that the same scene can elicit very different responses depending on its viewers' experience and values. It is possible for a male critic to celebrate the tendency of art to "force" woman's "body into play," while a feminist critic might see a self-reflexive element here and be led to deplore the way art so easily becomes the alibi for sexual violence against women. Since the scene is presented more or less "objectively"—or, if anything, slightly emphasizes Alice's reactions—a feminist interpretation is available to the female spectator without her necessarily having to adopt the position of "resisting viewer" (to paraphrase Judith Fetterley).[25]

In such an interpretation, moreover, the issue of guilt that critics continually invoke in discussions of Hitchcock films gets inflected very differently. Rohmer and Chabrol write, "*Blackmail* ... prefigures other aspects of films to come ... especially, the famous notion of the 'transfer' of guilt, which we see expressed here for the first time in the parallel editing showing on the one hand the blackmailer's desperate flight from the police and on the other, an admirable series of close-ups of the true murderess prostrate in remorse and prayer."[26] Now, of course, whether or not the "transfer" occurs depends on whether or not the woman is guilty in the first place; and the purpose of my analysis has been to challenge the assumption of her guilt by activating a word that is never uttered in the film—and that male critics continually strike from the record—in order to argue that Alice is the victim of an attempted rape (and thus acts in self-defense). Certainly, however, Alice experiences a great deal of guilt, which is acutely rendered not only in the sequences referred to by Rohmer and Chabrol but in the shots detailing her night of wandering the London streets following the murder. As she walks aimlessly about in a state of shock, shots of passersby are superimposed over her image, lending the objective world around her a ghostly air; the arm of a traffic cop metamorphoses into the arm of the murdered man; a neon sign depicting a gin bottle is transformed into a knife moving up and down. The sign reads "White for Purity" (White is, of course, Alice's surname), and many critics take it to be an ironic commentary on Alice's so-called "panic killing" of a man to defend a purity "which one would have thought to be less precious to her."[27] The scene ends as Alice suddenly comes upon a tramp sprawled in the street with his arm outstretched in the manner of the dead man. Her scream merges into the scream of the landlady who, in the next shot to which Hitchcock abruptly cuts, has just discovered the murdered man.[28] The entire sequence works to draw us deeply into Alice's subjectivity, to make us identify with her anguish and fear (and this empathy is encouraged through and beyond the famous breakfast table scene discussed earlier). An ironic—hence distanced—reading of the "White for Purity" sign thus goes against the grain of the sequence, which suggests rather the extent to which Alice feels sullied and dirtied by her experience. That the experience of sexual violence induces guilt in woman is understandable when we reflect on how patriarchy would convict her not only of murder, but, preeminently, of sexuality as well (we recall Taylor's condemnation of Alice simply for accompanying the artist). Given such attitudes on the part of men, women's guilt over the latter "crime" may easily be as great as over the former—a state of affairs that the film captures by the image of Alice sneaking up to bed in the morning just as she would have if she had been enjoying a love tryst rather than tormentedly walking the streets after having stabbed a man to death. Woman's sexual guilt, a major preoccupation in Hitchcock's films, is obviously not "transferable" to men, and until such sexual asymmetry is recognized, the real complexity of the theme of guilt in the films cannot be fully grasped.

The point I wish to stress here is that while on the surface *Blackmail* seems to offer an exemplary instance of Hitchcock's misogyny, his need to convict and punish women for their sexuality, the film, like so many of his other works, actually allows for a critique of the structure it exploits and for a sympathetic view of the heroine trapped within that structure. This means that the female spectator need not occupy either of the two viewing places typically assigned her in feminist film theory: the place of the female masochist, identifying with the passive female character, or the place of the "transvestite," identifying with the active male hero. In an important and influential essay, "Film and the Masquerade: Theorising the Female Spectator," Mary Ann Doane discusses these positions in the light of psychoanalytic theories of femininity. Interestingly for our purposes (since we have been considering *Blackmail* an elaborate joke on woman), Doane offers a visual "joke" as an analogy for the situation of the female spectator at the cinema. Her example is a 1948 photograph by Robert Doisneau, *"Un regard oblique,"* in which a man and a woman (the woman centered in the frame) stand before a picture of which we see only the back. The woman is looking intently at the picture, but the man to her left is glancing across to the other side of the frame, which reveals the picture of a female nude. Doane remarks, "[N]ot only is the object of [the woman's] look concealed from the spectator, her gaze is encased by the two poles defining the masculine axis of vision. ... On the other hand, the object of the male gaze is fully present, *there* for the spectator. The fetishistic representation of the nude female body, fully in view, insures a masculinisation of the spectatorial position. The woman's look is literally outside the triangle which traces a complicity between the man, the nude, and the spectator."[29]

Doane proceeds to analyze this photographic joke in the light of Freud's discussion of obscene jokes, which, in contrast to "smut," require the female as object of desire to be absent, while a third party, a man, comes to take the place of the woman and "becomes the person to whom the smut is addressed" (p. 30). Although in *Blackmail*, the question is not consistently one of "smut" or obscenity,[30] nevertheless, there are striking similarities to the situation described by Freud, as Alice, the original addressee of the joke, finds her place ultimately usurped by a man who laughs at a joke told at her expense. It might be tempting to see in *Blackmail* what Doane sees in the Doisneau photograph: a little parable of the female spectator, inevitably excluded from the terms of the film's address. Doane argues that because women cannot "fetishize" and therefore cannot adopt the "distance so necessary for an adequate reading of the image, ... Doisneau's photograph is not readable by the female spectator—it can give her pleasure only in masochism. In order to 'get' the joke, she must ... assume the position of transvestite" (p. 87). But are these indeed the only options available to the female spectator?

There seems to me in Doane's formulation a major confusion between the notion of "getting," or reading, a joke and the idea of receiving pleasure from it. While it may be true that in order to derive pleasure from the joke, a woman must be masochistic (we will return to this issue), surely a woman (*as* woman) may at least "get" the joke even if she doesn't appreciate it, just as, say, a Black may comprehend a racist joke without adopting the guise of a white person or assuming the position of masochist. It even seems reasonable to suppose that the oppressed person may see more deeply into the joke than the oppressor is often able or willing to do, as well as into many other situations in which he or she is ridiculed, attacked, or persecuted (we might speculate that Freud's Judaism contributed to his analysis of tendentious jokes). Surely Doane herself in her analysis, or "reading," of the joke is speaking neither as a masochist nor as a man (a transvestite) but as a woman who deeply understands the experience of women's oppression under patriarchy—and not only understands it, but quite rightly resents it. Thus there is at least one response to the joke other than the pleasure of the masochist or the immediate enjoyment of the male spectator, and that response seems to me crucial in theorizing the female spectator: I am referring to the anger that is provoked in the object of a hostile or obscene joke at the moment of "getting" it, even if that anger remains unconscious or is quickly suppressed. In my opinion, feminist film theory has yet to explore and work through this anger, which for women continues to be, as it has been historically, the most unacceptable of all emotions.

As for Doane's denial of pleasure to the female spectator, women are undoubtedly prevented from indulging in the same unreflecting laughter enjoyed by male spectators, but this deprivation is of course hardly a loss and, in any case, other pleasures remain possible. First of all, pleasure is involved in analysis itself, in understanding how the joke works even when it works against women. In the context of a study like Doane's, the joke may actually become a source of feminist humor or make a feminist point by itself. Shoshana Felman has shown how a change in modes of address may transform the objects of laughter into subjects. At a feminist conference Felman repeated Freud's witty exclusion of women from his examination of femininity, and in doing so she elicited laughter from her largely female audience, thereby demonstrating the power of recontextualization.[31] Similarly, I think of my study here as a contribution to the development of female subjectivity in that it analyzes in the context of a feminist inquiry the works of the filmmaker whom some would call the greatest practical joker as well as the greatest misogynist.

Secondly, one can find pleasure in acknowledging and working through one's anger, especially when that anger has long been denied or repressed. This is a pleasure Hitchcock's films repeatedly make available to women. It has long been noted that the director is obsessed with exploring the psyches of tormented and victimized women. While most critics attribute this interest to a sadistic delight in seeing his leading ladies suffer,[32] and while even I am willing to concede this point, I would nevertheless insist that the obsession often takes the form of a particularly lucid exposé of the predicaments and contradictions of women's existence under patriarchy. We have already touched upon the ways *Blackmail* may be read—"got" or interpreted—by women. It shows, for example, the dilemma of women continually charged with sexual guilt even when they are the victims of male violence. And it shows women reduced to objects in men's relations with each other.[33] A recurring, almost archetypal shot in Hitchcock's films focuses on the heroine trapped between a figure of the law and one of lawlessness—in *Blackmail*, between Frank, the lover/detective, and Tracy, the blackmailer. This placement and the woman's discomfort indicate that *both* men are threatening to her, that she is caught within a structure that needs her to ensure "human communication" (men's dealings with other men, as Lévi-Strauss has theorized them), but at the price of negating her own language and experience. Hitchcock's films have the merit of revealing woman's status as radically outside the law; on the one hand, she is not like the blackmailer, a criminal who can be readily named and identified as such, despite Rohmer and Chabrol's suggestion of the psychic interchangeability of the two. On the other hand, patriarchal law can hardly consider her innocent, nor can it possibly offer her real justice, since its categories precisely exclude her experience—an exclusion to which the critics we have quoted amply bear witness as they strain the limits of patriarchal discourse in order to subdue the truth of this experience.

It is a commonplace in discussions of Hitchcock's films that even though the director may be considered a stern moralist, he nevertheless continually exhibits a profound distrust and fear of the forces of the law. This attitude potentially places him in a sympathetic relation to his outlaw heroines. Obviously, it is not necessary to assume conscious intention on the director's part; as a matter of fact, there is virtually decisive evidence that Hitchcock was oblivious to the interest and sympathy he created for his heroine. In a discussion of the art of film direction, for instance, Hitchcock gave the following précis of *Blackmail*'s plot:

> Imagine an example of a standard plot—let us say a conflict between love and duty. This idea was the origin of my first talkie, *Blackmail*.

The hazy pattern one saw beforehand was duty–love—love vs. duty. ...
I had first to put on the screen an episode expressing duty. ... I showed
the arrest of a criminal by Scotland Yard detectives and tried to make it
as concrete and detailed as I could. You even saw the detectives take the
man to the lavatory to wash his hands—nothing exciting, just the routine of duty. Then the young detective says he's going out that evening
with his girl: They are middle-class people. The love theme doesn't run
smoothly; there is a quarrel and the girl goes off by herself, just because
the young man has kept her waiting a few minutes. So your story starts;
the girl falls in with the villain—he tries to seduce her and she kills him.
Now you've got your problem prepared. Next morning, as soon as the
detective is put onto the murder case, you have your conflict—love versus duty. The audience know that he will be trying to track down his
own girl, who has done the murder, so you sustain their interest: They
wonder what will happen next.[34]

Aside from the inaccuracies of plot, this description, repeated by some
critics, distorts the film's psychological and emotional interests, which are
centered in Alice, not the detective. In fact, the film is so strongly invested in
the heroine and *her* conflicts that Frank becomes almost a secondary character, or, perhaps more accurately, a symbolic embodiment *of* these conflicts. In
her room after the murder, Alice looks up at the wall and sees a photograph of
Frank in his policeman's uniform staring down at her; the shot vividly and
poignantly conveys the conflict between love and pride, on the one hand, and
shame, guilt, and especially fear, on the other. The conflict continues to be the
focus of the film's interest—for example, at the breakfast table, shortly after
the knife episode, when the camera lingers on a closeup of Alice and, in the
words of John Longden, "the ring of the shop-door bell [is] lengthened and
magnified like a note of doom."[35] Interestingly, Longden incorrectly remem-
bers this as the moment when the blackmailer enters the shop, but the fact
that it is Frank who slowly and inexorably enters the frame while Alice stands
behind the counter waiting for her fate to be sealed, that it is Frank who, as her
future husband and the representative of law and justice, signals the heroine's
doom, makes the scene much more ironic.

Indeed, throughout the film, Hitchcock continually points an accusatory
finger at the law in general and Frank in particular, indicating both their lack
of human compassion and their complicity in the criminality to which they
are theoretically opposed. The dissolve in the opening sequence from the
criminal's face in closeup to a gigantic fingerprint is one such instance of
Hitchcock's sarcastic treatment of the police, as is the later cut from the chief
inspector wringing his hands to the blackmailer performing the same gesture
at the White's breakfast table. In the context of such round condemnations of
the penal system, Hitchcock's decision to cut away from Alice during the rape

scene to a high-angle shot of the policeman below, walking his beat in total oblivion (a shot that repeats an earlier one taken from Alice's point of view), suggests a sympathy for and possible identification with the imperiled woman. Finally, Frank himself becomes strongly implicated in the film's critique of the law. Immediately upon discovering that Scotland Yard is after Tracy for the murder of the artist, Frank begins to taunt, threaten, and abuse the suspect, knowing full well, as he later admits, that Alice, not Tracy, has killed Crewe. Frank, then, is morally responsible for the death of a man innocent of the crime for which he is unofficially executed.

The ironies in *Blackmail* are, finally, much more subtle and prolific than those Hitchcock originally intended. He wanted to end the film with Alice being apprehended, and Frank, in the washroom as he was in the beginning, being asked by a fellow detective, "Are you going out with your girl tonight?" to which he would respond, "No, not tonight." Again, the actual film displaces Frank as the center of interest to focus on Alice and her predicament—a predicament that renders ironic both the film's title and its "happy" ending, and does so, moreover, from the woman's point of view. It hints, as *Marnie* will do years later and much more strongly, that the bond linking the man and the woman is his knowledge of her guilty secret (guilty, that is, in patriarchal terms), that the union is founded on the man's ability to blackmail the woman sexually.[36]

As for the last shot, which seems to point the finger directly at Alice, as the jester is carried down the hall (the nude portrait on the reverse side), thus suggesting the collusion of the director and audience with the male characters, my interpretation of the film has been meant to elicit other possible readings of this ending. In particular, we note that the film withholds the reverse shot, which would confirm the sense that it is Alice at whom the joke is aimed. Without the reverse shot, it is as if the spectator himself becomes the final butt of the film's humor—perhaps that very male spectator to whom all classical cinema is supposedly addressed, he who thinks himself secure in his masculine identity, at one with the other male figures in the film. My concern has been, in part, to show the extent to which the film undermines patriarchal law and creates sympathy for and an identification with the female outlaw. It is precisely the possibility of such an identification that is the source of so much desire and so much dread in so many Hitchcock films to come.

# 2
# Male Hysteria and the "Order of Things"
## *Murder!*

*Blackmail,* as we saw, is about the problem of women and the law. On the one hand, the film's project is to punish the woman for subordinating the law to her own desire and for flaunting the bond that ties her to it (her engagement to a member of the police force). On the other hand, in the process, we are shown the complicated relations between women and the law and the impossibility of the legal system's accommodating women's experience in patriarchal society. At first glance, Hitchcock's 1930 film, *Murder!* would seem to be a very different sort of story. For one thing, the point of view is strictly male—i.e., the story is told predominantly from the vantage of the man playing the detective, the actor/ aristocrat Sir John Menier (Herbert Marshall). Unlike in *Blackmail,* where the woman's consciousness is central, in *Murder!* the heroine is seldom even on stage—that is, until the end of the film when she is literally "on stage," acting in a play that Sir John has presumably written and produced. The question of the woman's guilt, moreover, is not really the focus of the film's interest, since the hero is so strongly convinced of her innocence. In contrast to *Blackmail,* then, we seem to have here a relatively straightforward case of miscarriage of justice, which eventually gets corrected by the hero. Despite its differences from the earlier film, however, *Murder!* is very much concerned with the complicated configurations of femininity and the law, as are so many of the Hitchcock films that feature male protagonists. More precisely, the film suggests that the law performs the crucial function for men of keeping femininity at a psychic distance.

That the law "performs" such a function may literally be the case in this detective story set in the world of the theater. *Murder!* opens at night with a clock striking, a woman's screaming, the shadow of a cat scurrying down an empty street. Characteristically, Hitchcock stresses at the outset the theme of voyeurism and introduces the metaphor of theatricality: the camera tracks across a building past various windows out of which people poke their heads to see what the commotion is all about, and stops at the window of stage manager Edward Markham (Edward Chapman) and his wife Doucie (Phyllis Konstam).

As the two strain out their window, which keeps falling on their necks like a guillotine, Doucie spots a policeman, who inexplicably disappears before her husband looks, and then just as inexplicably reappears a few seconds later. It turns out that a woman named Edna Druce has been murdered at the apartment of Diana Baring (Norah Baring), who is immediately arrested for murder. At her trial, Diana testifies that she and Edna had been in the midst of a quarrel about a man, whose identity she refuses to divulge, when everything went blank; as a result she has no recollection of what occurred during the murder.

There follows an elaborate scene of the jury deliberations. A few jurors, among them Sir John, to whom we are introduced for the first time, hold out for a verdict of innocent, but are gradually persuaded to change their minds. After the trial, Sir John determines to do some detective work on his own, applying, as he continually says, "the technique of his art to the problems of life." Soliciting the help of Markham and his wife, he discovers that the real murderer is an actor named Handel Fane (Esme Percy), a female impersonator in love with Diana. Fane had killed Edna when she was on the verge of disclosing the secret that Fane is a "half-caste." Tirelessly applying the technique of his art, Sir John writes a play based on the Baring murder trial and gets Fane to audition for it, hoping to trap him into a confession. The ploy does not work immediately, but that night Sir John goes to the circus, where Fane is performing as a trapeze artist in drag, and looks on as Fane hangs himself during the act. Diana is released from prison and the final shot of the film shows her coming into a drawing room to embrace Sir John; as the camera pulls back, however, it reveals that the two are actually on stage acting in a play. The film ends as the curtain descends.

"The law has no sense of drama," declares Sir John to Fane during the fake audition. But the film shows this to be far from the case. Rather, at the very heart of the film, is the fear that theater may so infuse and confuse reality that proper distinctions and the boundaries by which we make sense of life no longer hold true. Emblematic of this fear is the scene in which the police go to the theater to question Diana Baring's fellow actors in the play in which she and Edna Druce were performing. The police stand in the wings while the play is going on and question Markham about the various players making their entrances and exits. One of the actors is Fane, dressed up as a woman—"one hundred per cent he-woman," says Markham—and another is dressed up as a policeman. While the two performers are being questioned by the detectives, they execute a change of clothing, so that by the end of the discussion, the policeman has become a woman, while Fane has been transformed into a policeman. Fane then makes his entrance onto the stage, and the man dressed in woman's clothing is tied up and sent out after him, whereupon Doucie enters dressed in *masculine* fashion, wearing riding clothes and brandishing a riding crop. In this scene we witness a carnivalesque defiance of certain social and "biological" categories, as the woman (who is not really a woman at all) is transformed into a representative of patriarchal law. It turns out that this man/woman's ability to masquerade as the law is what enables him temporarily to get away with murder since we discover that Fane was the policeman Doucie thought she saw on the night of the crime.

The sexual and social confusion of the farce seems to bleed over into the film's next scene, into the serious business of the courtroom. The trial is introduced in a highly theatrical manner, with scroll and musical fanfare, and the defense attorney is revealed to be a female in powdered wig—a female "impersonating" a male—who resoundingly proclaims the innocence of her client. This image is even more unsettling than a simple reversal of sex roles would typically be, since the wig seems especially superfluous on the head of a woman and hence serves as a reminder of a time when masculinity was more "feminine"—that is, more exhibitionist and more theatrical—than it has come to be in our time.[1] Hitchcock further stresses the theatricality of the trial by focusing on the jurors' voyeuristic interest in the proceedings, as they swivel their heads to and fro while the lawyers parade before them. This is only one of many episodes which merge theatrical motifs with legal ones, especially ones signifying punishment and death. For example, an earlier shot cuts from a curtain rising on a stage to a shutter being raised on Diana in her prison cell. The culmination of this blending of motifs occurs in the circus sequence when Fane commits his own execution by hanging himself with the trapeze rope, thereby saving Diana from being hanged on the gallows that had earlier been shown shadowed on the prison wall.

Fane's condition, like that of Roland Barthes's castrato in *SZ*, is contagious, threatening to infect everything around him and to disrupt not only the integrity of the most basic patriarchal institutions, like the law, but the psychological unity of the other characters as well.[2] Thus, the policeman whom Doucie thought she saw and who disappeared and then reappeared a few seconds later, turns out to be, as Sir John says, "two people." As a result, Diana is taken to be a murderess rather than the sweet innocent girl that she appears to be and that one of the jurors keeps insisting she therefore *must* be. During the jury deliberations, one of the women argues for a verdict of innocent because Diana's crime was supposedly committed in a state of "disassociation." Another female juror concludes that this is precisely the reason Diana must be imprisoned: "If we set this bad personality free, we must be prepared to shoulder the responsibility." The theme of the dual personality is present as well in the film's motif of the understudy, an individual who replaces another individual who in turn is pretending to be—acting as—somebody else (both Diana and Sir John have their roles taken over by understudies in the course of the film).

As in so many Hitchcock films, then, images of split or multiple personalities, of psychic disintegration, abound. At one point, Sir John attempts to prove to Diana's landlady, Mrs. Mitcham, that she may have been mistaken in assuming that no man had entered the room while the women were quarrel-ing. "You can't mistake a woman's voice," insists the landlady, whereupon Sir John goes into the next room and mimics Alice the maid calling for the land-lady. The gullible woman falls for the trick and tries to run to see what is the matter. "No, no, it was I," says Sir John, forestalling her movement. "Or is it me? Do you know, Markham? I can never remember." The linguistic confu-sion is symptomatic.

In *Murder!*, the theater is the signifier of disunity, standing for the realm of appearances rather than essences, and Fane's ability to transform himself into a woman is the quintessential theatrical gesture, transgressing as it does the most basic, because "biological," boundary.[3] Fane represents theater at its most "debased": farces and circuses, the world of spectacle rather than of serious drama—a world evoked in the climactic scene in which he enters the circus arena garbed in women's clothing and elaborate feathered headdress, throws off his cape, and ascends the rope ladder to drum rolls while the breathless crowd looks on and the camera fetishistically follows from under-neath. In contrast to Fane, Sir John represents the theater as "art." He continu-ally speaks of his "art" and its techniques, and he plays in "high brow shockers" and Shakespearean drama; his superiority in this respect is stressed during a conversation in which he visibly suppresses a smile when Markham tells of how he once threatened Doucie that if she didn't get hold of herself in a certain farce she was acting in, they might have to stoop to playing Shakespeare.

The associations of the drama with masculinity and of the theater with femininity are old ones in Western culture. Woman and the theater are felt to be on the side of the inauthentic and the spectacular (the visible), whereas the drama is linked to authenticity, Truth, and the Word. Like Lacan's "feminin-ity," the theater involves masquerade, excess, histrionics; it is more than a mere linguistic coincidence, for example, that the term "histrionic" has replaced "hysteric" in some mental health manuals. As Georges Didi-Huberman argues at some length in his recent book *Invention de l'hystérie*, hysteria in the nine-teenth century was a "theatrical" as well as primarily a feminine disease, involving the patients in very complicated kinds of role playing and constantly threatening to draw the doctors into a world of appearances, illusion, and duplicity[4]—precisely the world in which so many Hitchcock heroes find them-selves. But although it is a critical commonplace that the world of false appear-ances is a menacing one in Hitchcock's films, it has not yet been sufficiently recognized that this world is so dreadful to men *precisely because it is a femi-nine and feminizing space.*

In the crucial scene in which Sir John determines to solve the crime, he confronts his image in the mirror, a prop that is frequently reserved for women in the cinema. As he muses on the deceptive nature of appearances (on how the other jurors could have seen Diana so differently from the way he did) and goes over in his mind the events of the crime and the trial, the radio

plays the overture from Wagner's *Tristan und Isolde*. Sir John's voiceover histri-
onically accompanies the overture, so that whenever the music crescendos, his
ruminations become more intense and melodramatic, and when the music
subsides he becomes calmer and more reflective. The choice of music could
not be more appropriate, given that Wagner has been characterized—notably
by Nietzsche—as at once theatrical (signifying "the emergence of the actor in
music") *and* feminine: "No one," wrote Nietzsche, "brings along the finest
senses of his art to the theater, least of all the artist who works for the theater—solitude is lacking; whatever is perfect suffers no witnesses. In the theater one becomes people, herd, female, pharisee, voting cattle, patron,
idiot—Wagnerian." For Nietzsche, the most dangerous aspect of Wagnerian
opera is its appeal to the individual to yield himself to the power and beauty of
the music; thus it entails a loss of mastery and control and involves its auditor
in a submissive, "feminine" attitude: "One walks into the sea, gradually loses
one's secure footing, and finally surrenders oneself to the elements without
reservation."[5] What seems to be at stake for Sir John—loner, aristocrat, dra-
matist, male—is the temptation and the fear of being immersed in the seductive and feminine world of appearances, in what Luce Irigaray, speaking of
Plato's cave, calls the *hystera*—the womb, the cave, the realm of illusion—the
"*circle* or circus ring, the *theatrical arena* of [the cave's] representation."[6] Thus
it is at this point that Sir John determines to take charge of events and to
become the stage director of a plot over which he has hitherto had little
control. And it is significant that the decision he makes in his solitude, as the
"hysterical" music shapes and guides his thoughts, leads directly to the
punishment of a man who embraces and exploits his femininity.

It is also significant that Sir John makes his decision to search out truth and
eradicate error as he stands in front of a mirror. The "I" and the "me" here
confront one another, and he faces the possibility of his *own* doubleness. In
Lacanian theory, of course, the mirror is the place where the subject is first
confronted with the irreducible fact of his split nature: the fact that he *is* in
some sense a "dual" personality. As Kaja Silverman has pointed out, the male
subject has great difficulty reconciling himself to his lack of wholeness and so
he projects it onto the female when he becomes aware of her anatomical difference: he needs to see woman as castrated so that he can assure himself of his
essential unity and wholeness. Yet, Silverman writes, "It is hardly surprising ...
that at the heart of woman's otherness there remains something strangely
familiar, something which impinges dangerously upon male subjectivity.
From the very outset the little boy is haunted by this similitude—by the fear
of becoming like his sexual other."[7] It is precisely this "similitude" that more
or less literally "haunts" the male characters in some of Hitchcock's most
memorable films.

Aside from *Psycho, Murder!* is probably the Hitchcock film in which the
stakes for the male are made the clearest, since rather than projecting guilt

onto a female character, the film locates it in a man who freely avows his similitude to his sexual other and makes it the source of his power. The full complexity of Fane's characterization is seldom acknowledged in Hitchcock criticism. Many critics claim, for example, that Fane is a homosexual, disregarding the fact that the most disturbing thing about this character is his defiance of any simple categorization.[8] Fane not only impersonates women but also takes them as objects of his desire; thus he is Sir John's rival in a romantic triangle with Diana (during the jury deliberations, the camera shows a closeup of Sir John's startled face as he receives the unwelcome knowledge that Fane was in love with her). Rather than being the simple embodiment of falsehood and duplicity that feminine figures so frequently are in Western culture, Fane instead, and much more radically, challenges the categories, boundaries, and dichotomous structures that sustain patriarchal culture. He is a white man with black blood, a man who can both *be* woman and love woman, who can masquerade as the law in order to perpetrate a crime, and who, as we have seen, spreads this sexual and social confusion like a contagious disease. Given the threat Fane poses to Truth itself, it is no wonder that the project of the film is to restore order through Sir John's detective work, and to reinstate important social boundaries, particularly the boundary between masculinity and femininity, affirmed at last in the apparent triumph of clear-cut heterosexual love.

This triumph is the culmination of a whole series of triumphs for Sir John, who, because he is so threatened by the loss of mastery and control, must be shown to be superior in a number of different respects. For example, as many critics have observed, the film works overtime to establish Sir John's admirable aristocratic manners and nature by contrasting him with the ignorant and opportunistic, though amusing, lower-class characters.[9] Even those critics who try to argue against this view of Sir John's character only end up confirming it: thus, for example, Maurice Yacowar states that "the film has nothing to do with the class system. Hitchcock neither sneers at nor admires any class here.... As a gentleman, as a celebrity, and as an artist, Hitchcock's Sir John charmingly descends to deal generously with someone else's problem on a lower stratum" (p. 134).[10] These words, of course, exactly duplicate the *film's* patronizing attitude towards the "lower stratum." I have already mentioned one instance of this attitude—in Sir John's amused reaction to Markham's story about threatening his wife with playing Shakespeare. Later on in this same scene, in which Sir John calls in Markham and his wife to aid him in his detective work, the film engages in an extended play around cocktails, the whole point of which seems to be to mock Doucie's discomfort because Sir John has placed his olive on the servant's tray and she is left holding hers in the air all the while he questions her and Markham about the events on the night of the murder. In this interchange, during which Doucie's predicament and her appalled expression become the focus of our interest, the ostensible subject of the film—the issue of "who done it"—threatens to fade entirely into the background, and the film comes close to exposing the fact that it has *everything* to do with the class system and with the need to assert its hero's superiority to those around him. And in fact the scene actually continues along these lines, as the three sit down to lunch, all the while discussing the murder, and Doucie chooses the wrong spoon; Sir John notices her error and picks up the corresponding utensil, whereupon the camera tracks in on him heroically attempting to finish his soup using the tiny spoon.

In a later sequence, Sir John spends the night at the policeman's house in order to pick up some clues about the murder. The next morning, the wife comes in carrying a crying baby and bringing in tow several noisy children and a kitten. The bemused Sir John lies in bed in the midst of this domestic disaster area while the baby squalls and the wife shrilly rattles on, eventually letting drop an important clue to the murder. Here lower-class domestic space threatens to engulf poor Sir John, who the night before had almost changed his mind and gone to his club instead. The film audience shares in Sir John's confusion, since it is virtually impossible for us to follow the conversation with all the distractions and with the crying baby dominating the soundtrack. "Solitude," to recall Nietzsche's words, is definitely "lacking" here. It is all the more remarkable, then, that Sir John is able to find in all this chaos the one element that will restore law and order and bring us to narrative closure.

As if it were a gloss on the Nietzschean text I quoted earlier, *Murder!* not only relentlessly insists on the hero's aristocratic nature but stresses his status as a solitary loner who fights for justice against the lawlessness of the mob—feared precisely because it seems to pose a feminine threat of loss of identity (as in Nietzsche's series, "people, herd, female"). Thus, the moment of untruth occurs when the crowd of jurors, presented like a chorus in a play, close in on Sir John and force him to acquiesce in a verdict of guilty against his better judgment. Only by putting on his own play, one that he both writes and directs, can Sir John counter this mere "show" of justice.

It is here, however, that the film begins to deconstruct the oppositions on which it appears to depend. To be sure, the film seems rigorously to uphold the hierarchical polarities of art and spectacle, truth and falsehood, masculinity and femininity, polarities which critics like Yacowar are also at pains to uphold: "Of course, Sir John can also assume roles, false identities, such as Mrs. Mitcham's maid or Fane's ostensible employer. But the actor plays with roles to arrive at the truth, not to deceive. The chaos of life can be brought to order by an artist's clear, humble and balanced vision" (p. 131). As a case in point he refers to the two cut-in "food shots," one of which contradicts Doucie's reference to her "little tid-bit" of lunch by showing a bottle of Guinness and a large chunk of cheese. The other is a shot of the "sumptuous feast" Sir John fantasizes when he is tempted to go to his club instead of spending the night at the policeman's. The latter shot presumably "tells the truth for the artist," while the former "exposes the imposter . ... The difference is that the artist controls his fancy towards the projection of the truth. The imposter—Doucie here on a small scale; the female-impersonator working under an assumed name later ...—uses image for disguise" (p. 131). Yet surely, what is interesting about the two subjective shots is the way they suggest a link between the woman and the man—a link that is emphatically established a little earlier when both Sir John and Doucie prepare to halt the investigation in order to have dinner (they are, however, shamed into continuing by Markham). Had the film been concerned to make the strongest case possible for Sir John and his identification with Truth, it would certainly have eliminated a shot that indicates his readiness to abandon his quest for truth to obtain a moment of sensory gratification. This sensuousness feminizes Sir John, as does a certain quality in Herbert Marshall's portrayal of the aristocrat, whose very status makes him an ambiguous, androgynous sort of figure. For, in the twentieth century, both the aristocrat and the artist have occupied a more feminine position than the one Nietzsche in the nineteenth century had claimed for each.

Just as the two subjective cut-in shots, although perhaps intended to reinforce the difference between the man and the woman, actually reveal a certain similarity in their natures, so too does the entire film suggest that sexual difference is ultimately a matter not simply of denying the male's "similitude" to the female but of his *risking feminization and hystericization* in order to achieve mastery and control. Thus, at one point in the film, Sir John himself becomes a female impersonator—when he mimics Alice the maid to persuade Mrs. Mitcham of her error in maintaining that "you can't mistake a woman's voice." Even more important is the fact that he must identify with the film's heroine, Diana, must put himself in her position (like the actor he is) in order to think through the crime. Finally, in the scene before the mirror as he surrenders himself to the power of the histrionic Wagnerian music and lets it direct his thoughts and emotions, Sir John immerses himself in the "feminine" element and allows it to control him so that he can achieve the appropriate mastery over appearances.

It seems possible to speculate that critics of the film insist so strenuously on Sir John's "art" because it provides the rationalization for a feminine wish lying at the heart of the narrative. Here we might invoke Freud's Dr. Schreber, the paranoid man who fantasized being a woman. According to Freud, Schreber's illness began with a conscious wish to be a woman submitting to sexual intercourse with a man, but such a thought was so abhorrent that it underwent repression, and various paranoid fantasies arose in its place. However, the wish was allowed to become conscious again when Schreber was able to reconcile it with what he continually called "the order of things": he began to believe that God had destined him to undergo the transformation into a woman so that a new race of men would be born from him.[11] Religion thus provided the necessary rationalization for Schreber's fantasied femininity just as Truth, Law and, especially, Art provide this rationalization in *Murder!*—as well as *for Murder!*. Sir John's actions, we are led to perceive, are consonant with the narrative "order of things," whereas Fane's feminine masquerade is a disturbance to this order.

This is not to argue, however, that we are dealing with a latently aberrant protagonist. On the contrary, Freud often noted that part of the *typical* masculine trajectory involves a "feminine" phase—an insight that has not received much attention in film theory. (Interestingly, however, Laura Mulvey in her "Afterthoughts on 'Visual Pleasure and Narrative Cinema'" has stressed the importance of the "masculine" phase in the female.[12]) Whereas a theorist like Raymond Bellour assumes an unproblematic heterosexual orientation from the outset and sees the oedipal trajectory of the male as involving simply "the symbolization of the death of the father" and "the displacement from the attachment to the mother to the attachment to another woman,"[13] Freud himself increasingly stressed, in the words of Richard Klein, "a homoerotic identification with [the boy's] father, a position of effeminized subordination to the father, as a condition of finding a model for his own heterosexual role." Klein writes:

> Conversely, in this theory, the development of the male homosexual requires the postulation of the father's absence or distance and an abnormally strong identification by the child with the mother, in which the child takes the place of the father. There results from this scheme a surprising neutralization of polarities: heterosexuality in the male ... presupposes a homosexual phase as the condition of its normal possibility: homosexuality, obversely, requires that the child experience a powerful heterosexual identification.[14]

Glossing this quotation, Eve Kosofsky Sedgwick notes the paradoxically "feminizing potential of desire for a woman" (as well as the "masculinizing potential of subordination to a man").[15] Perhaps it is this feminizing potential that Fane, who is passionately in love with Diana, embodies, and that Sir John, upon falling in love with her himself, must risk and ultimately vanquish. In any case, for Hitchcock heroes, the lure and the threat of feminization is ever present as the heroes painfully grope their way towards their "proper" heterosexual role, which is rarely achieved with total success.

In order to reinstate the sexual polarities that Fane threatens to "neutralize," Sir John must, as I have said, put on a show to counter the "show" of justice, the travesty of patriarchal law that has been dramatized and made visible throughout the film. But for all that the film tries to make a sharp distinction between art and spectacle, truth and illusion, the distinctions break down precisely because Sir John has to resort to the imposter's tactics (role playing, female impersonating, etc.) in order to triumph over him. In this he resembles the doctors in Charcot's clinic, who, according to Didi-Huberman, would often be obliged to elicit and repeat the hysterics' symptoms in their attempts to exorcise those symptoms. Paradoxically, they "invented a theater against hysterical 'theatricality' in order to denounce the latter as simulation, excess and sin of mimesis."[16] (Charcot in particular was fond of speaking of his "art," fond of applying the techniques of his art to problems of life.) Similarly, Fane indulges in an "excess of mimesis" that confounds the "truth/fantasy" pair sustaining patriarchal thought; and he is destroyed by Sir John's theatrical ploys—driven, in a kind of paroxysm of poetic and patriarchal justice, to hang himself with his theatrical props.

Didi-Huberman goes on to argue that the *mise-en-scène* of the clinic and the spectacle of female hysteria displayed at Charcot's Tuesday sessions were designed to put hysteria at a safe distance. The very fact, however, that the doctors were irresistibly drawn into the hysterical condition—driven, for example, to counter spectacle with spectacle—not only precluded the possibility of a "cure," but actually resulted in an exacerbation of the hysteria, a redoubling of the disease and of efforts to eradicate it—what he calls a *"surenchère expérimentale."*[17] This "upping of the stakes" is analogous to the contagion I have noted in *Murder!*, at the narrative level as well as the formal level. Of course, it is possible to argue that narrative closure puts an end to this play which has all along implicated the male artist in the process of feminization, possible to argue that masculinity, heterosexuality, truth, and justice ultimately prevail over that which has blocked and opposed them. Yet even here, at the end of the film, the truth does not unequivocally win out. For although the final scene begins with a clichéd view of Diana entering a room to be embraced by Sir John, the camera tracks back to reveal that the two are acting on stage and are not "really" kissing. The film leaves us in a state of uncertainty about the formation of the couple and the extent to which the play mirrors or reflects their "real" situation. It might even be argued that in making this reference to theater, the film engages in a certain avant-gardism; as Stephen Heath has argued, because theorists have so often compared cinema to the theater in order to demonstrate cinema's superior ability to mirror reality, "the exact reference to the theater" in a film may be a way of calling into question the quest for the real.[18] In any case, the concluding scene *of Murder!* suggests that as spectators we may still be caught up in theatrical illusion rather than being recipients of the film's superior—"masculine"—truth.

Narrative film, philosophy, art, medicine, even psychoanalysis all conspire to put femininity at a distance. In the process, however, they very often compromise themselves, showing the impossibility of definitively rejecting the feminine, of placing it, like the Sphinx in the myth of Oedipus, forever outside the gates of the city. At this point I want to put in play one further suggestion: that is, that film theory too, even when it appears to speak for women and for feminism, is often engaged in an attempt to keep femininity at a safe distance.

Indeed, I would venture to assert that this is frequently the purport of the critical emphasis on "distanciation" and anti-illusionism in so much contemporary theoretical discourse. Paul Willemen's "Distanciation and Douglas Sirk," a typical *Screen* article dealing with the theory of Brechtian distantiation, provides a case in point. Roundly denouncing films which elicit strong audience identification, denouncing, in other words (Didi-Huberman's), an "excess of mimesis" on the part of film spectators, Willemen praises Sirk because by "intensifying" the rules of the melodramatic genre, he managed to produce a Brechtian distance from its conventions and clichés, clichés that are the stuff of, precisely, "the stories in women's weeklies."[19] Note that the process Willemen detects in Sirk is analogous to the process I have been outlining in this analysis. Sirk immerses himself in the feminine element—the "weepie" genre, which supposedly involves spectators in hysterical "overidentification"—in order to master and control it, and to enable the spectator to do the same.[20] Similarly, for Willemen and many of the *Screen* theorists, Brechtian theater became the "theater against hysterical theatricality," invoked to discredit the genre which has traditionally appealed to women and has elicited "feminine" modes of response—the surrender to the elements abhorred by Nietzsche. I will turn to a consideration of this genre in the next chapter.

That neither film art nor film theory can ever wholly extricate itself from "femininity"—any more than could Charcot and his colleagues—is an important assumption of the present work. Thus, although many writers, including feminists, canonize Hitchcock only insofar as they see him producing a distance between the spectator and the film spectacle, I would argue that one of Hitchcock's main interests for feminism lies in the way his films show the desire for distance itself to be bound up with the male's insistence on his difference from woman. Throughout his work Hitchcock reveals a fascinated and fascinating tension, an oscillation, between attraction to the feminine—his identification with women observed in the previous chapter—and a corresponding need to erect, sometimes brutally, a barrier to the femininity which is perceived as all-absorbing. This dialectic becomes in the course of Hitchcock's career a kind of frenzied *surenchère*, or upping of the stakes, which appropriately culminates in the director's late film, *Frenzy*.

All of this is not to say that we must choose one or the other side of the truth/illusion dichotomy (it is not a matter of now championing narrative cinema over avant-garde practices, for example). Rather, the strategy must be to understand what lies behind the need to achieve, in Willemen's words, a "totally anti-illusionist mode of representation."[21] As Luce Irigaray writes, we should begin to question "who or what *profits*" by this "*hierarchy* of values," what "has *been forgotten*, not about a truer truth, a realer real, but *about the profit that underlies the truth/fantasy pair.*"[22] And not only "who profits?" but, I would add, at whose expense?

# 3
# Woman and the Labyrinth
*Rebecca*

In what is perhaps the most perceptive full-length study of Hitchcock yet written, Robin Wood dismisses Hitchcock's first American film, *Rebecca* (1940), with these words: "the film fails either to assimilate or to vomit out the indigestible novelettish ingredients of Daphne du Maurier's book."[1] Hitchcock's own dismissal of the film contains a definition of this term, "novelettish": "Well, it's not a Hitchcock picture," he remarked to Truffaut; "it's a novelette, really. The story is old-fashioned; there was a whole school of feminine literature at the period, and though I'm not against it, the fact is that the story is lacking in humor."[2] So the "novelettish" aspect of the work is its "feminine" aspect, a femininity that remains alien and disturbing, neither expelled nor "digested" in the course of the film. In light of Wood's remarks, it is especially interesting to note how Hitchcock intended to supply the humor he found lacking in this piece of "feminine literature": the original script provided for two scenes of vomiting on boats, one of them to be provoked by Maxim's cigar smoking on board a passenger ship.[3] The film's producer, David O. Selznick, however, was outraged by these scenes, as well as by other changes Hitchcock had made, and he insisted that Hitchcock delete the offensive scenes to remain true to what he considered the feminine spirit of the book. In one of his famous memos he wrote:

> [Every] little thing that the girl does in the book, her reactions of run-
> ning away from the guests, and the tiny things that indicate her nervous-
> ness and her self-consciousness and her gaucherie are all so brilliant in
> the book that every woman who has read it has adored the girl and has
> understood her psychology, has cringed with embarrassment for her, yet
> has understood exactly what was going through her mind. [Your
> changes in the script] have removed all the subtleties and substituted big
> broad strokes which in outline form betray just how ordinary the plot is
> and just how bad a picture it would make without the little feminine
> things which are so recognizable and which make every woman say,
> "I know just how she feels … I know just what she's going through … "[4]

The struggle between the two men over the script of *Rebecca* (and here we encounter yet another triangular structure) was clearly the result of a disagreement about the extent to which it should adhere to the feminine discourse of du Maurier's Gothic novel. If Hitchcock failed to subvert this discourse by vomiting out the book's "novelettish" elements, with the result that many male critics find the film distasteful, it's not because he didn't, almost literally, try.

The connotations of cannibalism lurking in our discussion thus far—the implications of eating, and digesting or vomiting out, femininity—provides us with a clue to the obsession in Hitchcock films with dismembering and devouring the (usually female) body. There is a scene in *Rear Window*, for example, in which L.B. Jeffries (Jimmy Stewart) tries to eat bacon and eggs while Stella (Thelma Ritter) wonders how the murdered woman's body was cut up and worries that the trunk in which the body appears to be hidden might begin to leak. And in *Frenzy*, a film about a man who rapes and murders a woman and then stuffs her body into a potato sack, a running gag involves the police inspector whose wife serves him food that vaguely resembles human body parts. A full discussion of this concern with cannibalism will be reserved for a later chapter, where I will relate it to the question of identification. However, an analysis of *Rebecca*, which is all about a woman's problems of "overidentification" with another woman, places us in an excellent position for understanding the stakes of the later films. As we shall see, for all Hitchcock's desire to repudiate it, *Rebecca* remains very much a "Hitchcock picture": it is that feminine element in the textual body that is unassimilable by patriarchal culture and yet cannot be "vomited out."

As the passage quoted above suggests, Selznick believed his production of *Rebecca* would appeal especially to women, who he expected to identify strongly with the main character ("I know just how she feels; I know just what she's going through"). His emphasis on the female audience's potential to empathize closely with the heroine coincides with the culture's view—discussed at the end of the last chapter—of women as closer to the (textual) body than men and thus ready to surrender themselves freely to the fantasies offered by the "woman's film."[5] What is interesting about *Rebecca* in this context is that it makes the tendency of women to merge with other women, the tendency taken for granted by Selznick, its chief "problem," the solution to which it shows to be extremely difficult to achieve. This same tendency has been seen as a problem by psychoanalysis as well, and in fact, *Rebecca* offers a striking instance of a film that follows quite closely the female oedipal trajectory outlined by Freud.

In offering this thesis I am taking exception to the notion of the influential French film theorist Raymond Bellour that all Hollywood narratives are dramatizations of the male oedipal story, of man's entry into the social and Symbolic order.[6] In rejecting Bellour's thesis and arguing that there is at least one film dealing with woman's "incorporation" into the social order (to reinvoke Wood's metaphor), I do not mean to suggest that *Rebecca* is thereby a "progressive" film for women; the social order is, after all, a patriarchal order. I do, however, maintain that all kinds of interesting differences arise when a film features a woman's trajectory and directly solicits the interest of a female audience. Besides, as I have said, I do not believe the assimilation of femininity by patriarchy can ever be complete. My own analysis is dedicated to tracing the resistances that disturb the text.

In *Rebecca*, a young woman (Joan Fontaine), never named throughout the film, comes to Monte Carlo as a companion to a vulgar American woman, Mrs. Van Hopper (Florence Bates). There she meets Maxim de Winter (Laurence Olivier), a handsome, wealthy, older man with an air of mystery about him that seems to be connected to his late wife, Rebecca, who, we soon learn, has drowned at sea. Maxim takes an interest in the young woman and proposes marriage to her when he discovers she is on the verge of leaving for America with Mrs. Van Hopper. After a hasty wedding, the two go to his imposing country estate, Manderley, where the heroine is intimidated by the wealth and magnitude of the place. Soon she begins to feel overshadowed by the memory of Rebecca: Maxim appears to be obsessed with thoughts of his first wife; mementoes of Rebecca's past life are everywhere (her initial is embroidered on napkins, handkerchiefs, pillowcases); and Rebecca's former servant, Mrs. Danvers (Judith Anderson), dedicates herself to making the heroine feel inadequate in relation to "the first Mrs. de Winter."

After affording the audience numerous opportunities to "cringe with embarrassment" for her, the heroine finally stands up to Mrs. Danvers and asserts her authority as mistress of the house. She then persuades Maxim to give a costume ball at Manderley and proceeds to search for an appropriate costume with which to surprise her husband. Assuming a friendlier attitude toward the heroine, Mrs. Danvers suggests that she dress up in the costume of Lady Caroline De Winter, whose portrait hangs in the hall. The night of the ball, the heroine descends the great staircase radiantly dressed in a lavish white gown, only to be greeted by her horror-stricken husband, who, in a cruel reversal of the Cinderella myth, orders her back to her room to change her dress. It turns out that Rebecca had worn the same costume at a previous masquerade ball. The anguished heroine runs up to Rebecca's room, where Mrs. Danvers nearly persuades her to commit suicide, but just then fireworks signal a shipwreck and the heroine breaks out of her trance and runs to see what is the matter.

In the process of rescuing the ship, Rebecca's boat is discovered with Rebecca's body in it. This causes consternation, since Maxim had already identified Rebecca's body, which presumably is buried in the family vault. Maxim and his wife have a discussion in which she tells him how difficult life has been for her, knowing how much he still loves Rebecca. He is very shocked by her words, and reveals, to the audience's surprise and the heroine's great joy, that he hated Rebecca, that from the beginning of their marriage she lived a life of "filth and deceit," and continually mocked her husband with her infidelity. On the night she died she had laughingly revealed that she was pregnant with another man's child, and he had struck her; she stepped forward, fell, and hit her head on a piece of ship's tackle, killing herself. Maxim put the body in her boat, sank it, and identified as his wife's another body that conveniently washed up ashore some distance away.

The remainder of the film deals with the investigation into the circumstances of Rebecca's death, as her cousin and lover, Jack Favell (George Sanders), tries to implicate Maxim in her murder. At the end, the men visit the doctor who had secretly treated Rebecca and discover that Rebecca had been told she was suffering from cancer. Since this provides a motive for Rebecca's suicide, Maxim is cleared. He, however, now understands that Rebecca had told him that she was pregnant precisely in order to goad him into murdering her. After the visit to the doctor, Maxim and his estate manager, Frank Crawley (Reginald Denny), drive home to find that Mrs. Danvers has set fire to Manderley. As Maxim embraces his wife, we see Mrs. Danvers through the window being burned alive, and then the camera tracks in for a close-up of a flaming pillowcase with an embroidered "R" on it.

As this outline of the plot suggests, *Rebecca* is the story of a woman's maturation, a woman who must come to terms with a powerful father figure and assorted mother substitutes (Mrs. Van Hopper, Rebecca, and Mrs. Danvers). That *Rebecca* is an oedipal drama from the feminine point of view has been noticed by Raymond Durgnat: "For the heroine fulfills the archetypal female Oedipal dream of marrying the father-figure, who has rescued her from the tyranny of the domineering old woman (i.e., mother). But in doing so she has to confront the rival from the past, the woman who possessed her father first, who can reach out and possess him once again."[7] Actually, Durgnat is here describing not the female oedipal drama, but the long discredited "Electra complex"; nevertheless, his insights contain a great deal of validity and can be brought into line with more recent thinking about feminine psychology and feminist film theory.

*Rebecca* more or less explicitly declares itself to be a kind of feminine "family romance."[8] For example, the film emphasizes the heroine's childishness, contrasting her youth with her husband's age. Throughout the film Maxim continually orders her about, telling her to finish her breakfast "like a good girl," to stop biting her nails, to wear a raincoat ("you can't be too careful with children"), and, ludicrously enough, "never to wear black satin or pearls, or be thirty-six years old." By the end of the film, however, she has grown up, in spite of his professed wishes. "Ah, it's gone forever," he laments, "that funny, young, lost look I loved. It won't ever come back. I killed that when I told you about Rebecca. It's gone … in a few hours. … You've grown so much older." In addition, the film repeatedly stresses the heroine's total incompetence, this time contrasting her to the *"mother"* (i.e., Rebecca), who was all efficiency and control. When the heroine enters the morning room at Manderley, she sees proofs of Rebecca's industry everywhere and is herself at a loss for anything to do. At the luncheon table, Maxim's brother-in-law, Giles (Nigel Bruce), quizzes her about her abilities and succeeds only in establishing that, unlike Rebecca, she doesn't ride, doesn't dance, and doesn't sail.

*Mise-en-scène* and camerawork collaborate with the script to convey the heroine's sense of her own insignificance: she is continually dwarfed by the huge halls in which she wanders, and even the doorknobs are placed shoulder-level so that the viewer receives a subliminal impression of her as a child peeking in on or intruding into an adult world that provokes both curiosity and dread. A characteristic camera movement in the film begins with a close-up of the heroine receiving a bit of unwelcome news about Rebecca's superiority and then tracking out to a long shot in which she seems small, helpless, and alone. The culminating instance of this backward movement occurs when Mrs. Danvers attempts to persuade her to jump out the window to her death, and the camera, placed outside the window, begins to move away as if inviting and luring her to her doom.

The heroine is also shown to be extremely clumsy, tipping things over, tripping, breaking a china Cupid in Rebecca's "morning room" and then fearfully hiding the pieces in the back of a desk drawer. This inept behavior—her clumsiness, her bewildered wanderings through the labyrinthine mansion—presents a marked contrast to the actions of Rebecca's former maid, Mrs. Danvers, whose movements were very deliberately limited and controlled by Hitchcock:

> Mrs. Danvers was almost never seen walking and was rarely shown in motion. If she entered a room in which the heroine was, what happened is that the girl suddenly heard a sound and there was the ever-present Mrs. Danvers, standing perfectly still by her side. In this way, the whole situation was projected from the heroine's point of view; she never knew when Mrs. Danvers might turn up, and this, in itself, was terrifying. To have shown Mrs. Danvers walking about would have been to humanize her.[9]

In psychoanalytic terms, the heroine might be said to be at the Imaginary stage of development—a time when the child's motor control is not yet fully developed, and the mother's, by contrast, seems superhuman in its perfection. Further, the mother's appearances are terrifying because they are so unpredictable, a situation which, as Freud has documented, results in an intolerable feeling of helplessness on the part of the child.[10]

The Imaginary stage is the same for both boys and girls. For males, however, it eventually becomes possible to deny the mother's physical superiority by asserting their anatomical difference from her, a denial which is enacted in many Hollywood films, perhaps most emphatically in *films noir*, the project of which, as has amply been documented, is to bring the woman under the hero's visual and narrative control. By contrast, the female, who is anatomically similar to the mother, has difficulty assuming such control: thus, rather than appropriating the power of the look, as the male does, the female allows herself to be determined by it. In the words of Eugénie Lemoine-Luccioni:

> She prefers to tip over into the image guaranteed for her (as she believes) by the quite as captive look of the mother and later, by the all-powerful look of the father. She prefers to believe in that image. She believes she is herself. ... In so doing, she substitutes for the person of the mother crucial in the fort/da game her own person figured by her body in the specular image; an image that the mother's look brings out, "causes."[11]

This passage remarkably and quite literally sums up the plot of the film. For one thing, the heroine continually attempts to take the place of Rebecca in the specular image. From the film's outset, as the camera dissolves from a tracking movement to the right through the ruined Manderley estate of the heroine's dream to a leftward pan over the waves crashing ashore at Monte Carlo, and tilts up to an extreme long shot of Maxim staring out at a sea that is metonymically and metaphorically associated with Rebecca and her lawless sexuality, the project of the film is to get Maxim to turn his gaze away from Rebecca and toward the heroine.

In addition, Mrs. Danvers's gaze continually places the heroine in a sort of hypnotic trance, in which the heroine seems compulsively to act out the wishes of the older woman. And while, on the manifest level, it appears that Mrs. Danvers wants the heroine to feel the full force of her difference from—her inferiority to—Rebecca, it becomes clear that Mrs. Danvers is really willing her to *substitute her body for the body of Rebecca.* In one of the film's most chilling scenes, Mrs. Danvers shows her around Rebecca's room and forces her to gaze upon Rebecca's most intimate possessions (the underwear "made especially for her by nuns in a convent in St. Clare"). Then the heroine is actually put through Rebecca's motions, as she sits in Rebecca's chair while Mrs. Danvers pretends to brush her hair and repeats former conversations between Rebecca and herself. Thus, throughout the film, the heroine's body becomes the site of a bizarre fort/da game which reaches its climax when, at Mrs. Danvers's suggestion, she unknowingly dresses up exactly like Rebecca for the costume ball. At this moment, to repeat Lemoine-Luccioni, "she thinks she is herself." But her husband's angry reaction tells her otherwise, and her happiness gives way to horror.

Hitchcock, of course, pulls out all the stops in this scene to elicit audience identification. Thus, the camera insists on the heroine's point of view as she descends the stairs looking at the people—Maxim, his sister, and Frank—standing at the bottom with their backs turned away from her, and it continually cuts back to her smiling face, radiant with the anticipation of her husband's approval. When he turns to face her, becomes angry, and orders her to take off the costume, the interchange is filmed with progressively tighter close-ups suggesting the claustrophobia experienced by the heroine, who seems unable to escape possession by Rebecca. These shots draw us into the heroine's despair, which is so extreme that she nearly acquiesces when Mrs. Danvers tries to persuade her to leap to her death. It might thus be said that the *spectator* is here forced to undergo an experience analogous to that of the heroine: both she and we are made to experience a kind of annihilation of the self, of individual identity, through a merger with another woman; in this respect, the film appears to have more than fulfilled Selznick's desires for it on behalf of a female audience.

The horror of the moment of the masquerade ball derives from the fact that though the woman substitutes her body for her mother's she must believe, as Lemoine-Luccioni puts it, "she is herself." Neither hero nor heroine (not to mention spectator) must become aware that in presenting herself the woman does nothing but re-present another woman, the mother. The film, however, not only announces the submergence of the heroine's identity into that of the "mother's" but twice equates her predicament with death. The first incident occurs when she answers the telephone and says, "I'm sorry, Mrs. de Winter has been dead now for over a year." In not recognizing herself as the one addressed, in announcing the mother's death, the heroine simultaneously declares her own nothingness. The second episode occurs when she almost commits suicide after dressing up like Rebecca. Fortunately, Rebecca's body is discovered at this moment, and the discovery paves the way for an open discussion between the heroine and Maxim, in which her difference finally seems assured.

But what does this "difference" amount to? We are made to believe that the heroine is superior to the "mother" precisely because she has no self, no distinguishing characteristics. In contrast to Rebecca, we are told, she lacks "breeding, beauty, and brains." This is a reflection of the classic psychological dilemma for women, who allegedly remain forever outside the Symbolic: whereas the boy's entry into the Symbolic is effected by his perception of his (anatomical) "superiority" to the mother, the girl, with every attempt she makes to despise and hence distance herself from the mother, implicates herself in the devaluation of her sex. Thus the heroine, actively desiring the process by which all of Rebecca's apparently positive attributes are proved to be worthless, can offer the male nothing more than a vacuous self. In the film's fantasy, a *woman's* fantasy par excellence, the hero highly prizes the woman's insignificance.

In contrast to what Raymond Bellour claims is the classic scenario of American cinema, in which the hero must come to "accept the symbolization of the death of the father, the displacement from the attachment to the mother to the attachment to another woman,"[12] *Rebecca* shows the *heroine's* attempt to detach herself from the mother in order to attach herself to a *man*. In order to do so, it is true, she must try to make her desire mirror the man's desire, and in this respect the ideological task of the film is similar to that which Bellour sees at work in other Hitchcock films (most notably in *Marnie).*[13] Yet the film makes us experience the difficulties involved *for the woman* in this enterprise. In order for her to mold her image according to the man's desire, she must first ascertain what that desire *is*. And given the complex and contradictory nature of male desire, it is no wonder that women become baffled, confused. Feminist critics have noted, for example, the conflicting attitude toward the female expressed in film noir: on the one hand, the domestic woman is sexually nonthreatening, but she is boring; on the other hand, the *femme fatale* is exciting, but dangerous. From the woman's point of view, then, man becomes an enigma, his desire difficult to know. Although women have not had the chance to articulate the problem as directly as men have, they could easily ask Freud's question of the opposite sex: what is it men want?

In *Rebecca*, the question is posed at the very first view of Maxim de Winter, staring out at the ocean but clearly "seeing" something that we don't see. Interestingly, the system of suture is here reversed. This system typically works by presenting the woman as the object of the look of an implied character—the "absent one" who is made present in the reverse shot, and thus shown to be the possessor of the former image.[14] However, in this scene from *Rebecca*, the woman (Rebecca), the implied *object* of the look, is the "absent one." The effect is unsettling and stimulates our desire to see the heroine become a suitable object of the male gaze. And this, as I have said, is exactly what the heroine attempts throughout the film—to remold her image according to the (incorrect) solution to the enigma: Maxim "sees," is desiring, a beautiful, sensual, worldly woman. The rivalry which is thus set up between "mother" and daughter can only lead to one paradoxical result: all women become one woman, the girl becomes the mother. This paradoxical situation is reflected everywhere in our culture: in dividing women against themselves, in stimulating competition among women, the culture forces them to shape themselves according to a single standard (the fashion model, for example, whose "look"—in the dual sense of the term—determines the feminine image).

But there is something more at stake here, something potentially more subversive, though it is treated by the film, as it is treated by psychoanalysis, as a "problem": that is, the desire of women for other women. Freud himself was forced to reject the notion of an Electra Complex, according to which the young girl experiences her mother primarily as an object of rivalry, and to admit the importance of the young girl's early desire for her mother.[15] Moreover, he recognized how frequently this desire persists throughout the woman's life, influencing her heterosexual relationships, as well as her relationships with other women. In *Rebecca* the heroine continually strives not only to please Maxim, but to win the affections of Mrs. Danvers, who seems herself to be possessed, haunted, by Rebecca and to have a sexual attachment to the dead woman. Finally, it becomes obvious that the two desires cannot coexist: the desire for the mother impedes the progress of the heterosexual union. Ultimately, then, the heroine disavows her desire for the mother, affirming her primary attachment to the male. When the heroine stands up to Mrs. Danvers, who has been incessantly reminding her of the rule of the former Mrs. de Winter, and forcefully announces, "*I* am Mrs. de Winter now," the spectator experiences a sense of relief. Significantly, however, it is *after* this declaration that she follows Mrs. Danvers' advice about what to wear for the costume ball. Significantly, too, she has made a great point to Maxim about choosing a costume all by herself, a costume which she thinks will surprise and delight him. Thus, just when she believes she has succeeded in pleasing the man, in making her desire the mirror of his, it is revealed that she has not succeeded at all, but is still attached to the "mother," still acting out the desire for the mother's approbation. As she preens herself before the mirror on the night of the costume ball, the heroine is blithely unaware of how thoroughly she is conforming to the mother's image—very much as women can be said to "dress for other women" though they may be consciously motivated solely by the wish for masculine approval.

Finally, there is nothing left for the heroine but to desire to kill the mother off, a desire which, as we have seen, entails killing part of herself, for she cannot, like the male, project the woman as "other," as difference, thereby seeming to establish a secure sense of her own identity.

Of course, psychoanalysis tells us that a secure sense of identity is also illusory on the part of the male and that it is woman who poses the threat to masculine identity. Employing a strict psychoanalytic model, Laura Mulvey has analyzed how woman functions in narrative cinema as bearer of the lack, the sight of her serving to provoke castration anxiety in the male, anxiety that he (too) might lack unity and integrity. While in the previous chapter it was suggested that the notion of the castrated woman was a male projection, this projection nevertheless comes back to "haunt" the male subject. Hence, the "castrated woman" serves as a perpetual reminder to him of an undesirable situation he had hoped to ward off by imputing it to the woman in the first place.

As is well known by now, Mulvey considers two options open to the male for warding off castration anxiety: in the course of the film the man gains control over the woman both by subjecting her to the power of the look and by investigating and demystifying her in the narrative.[16] In *Rebecca*, however, the sexual woman is never *seen*, although her presence is strongly evoked throughout the film, and so it is impossible for any man to gain control over her in the usual classical narrative fashion. I have discussed how, in the first shot of

Maxim, the system of suture is reversed. This is of utmost importance. In her discussion of the system, Kaja Silverman notes, "Classic cinema abounds in shot/reverse shot formations in which men look at women."[17] Typically, a shot of a woman is followed by a shot of a man—a surrogate for the male spectator—looking at her. This editing alleviates castration anxiety in two ways: first, the threat posed by the woman is allayed because the man seems to possess her; secondly, the "gaze within the fiction" conceals "the controlling gaze outside the fiction"—that of the castrating Other who lurks beyond the field of vision.[18] But in *Rebecca*, the beautiful, desirable woman is not only never sutured in as object of the look, not only never made a part of the film's field of vision, she is actually posited within the diegesis as all-seeing—as for example when Mrs. Danvers asks the terrified heroine if she thinks the dead come back to watch the living and says that she sometimes thinks Rebecca comes back to watch the new couple together. (In this respect, it is interesting to compare the film to another from the same period that deals with the threat posed by a dead woman. In the *film noir, Laura,* the heroine, who is thought to have been murdered, is not only visually present in the portrait that dominates the *mise-en-scène,* but is seen in numerous flashbacks, and, finally, is "brought back" to life and subjected to an investigation on the part of the film's detective/hero.)

In "Film and the Labyrinth," Pascal Bonitzer equates the labyrinth with suspense and notes the power of off-screen space or "blind space" to terrorize the viewer: "Specular space is on-screen space; it is everything we see on the screen. Off-screen space, blind space, is everything that moves (or wriggles) outside or under the surface of things, like the shark in *Jaws.* If such films 'work,' it is because we are more or less held in the sway of these two spaces. If the shark were always on screen it would quickly become a domesticated animal. What is frightening is that it is not there! The point of horror resides in the blind space."[19] Similarly, Rebecca herself lurks in the blind space of the film, with the result that, like the shark and unlike the second Mrs. de Winter, she never becomes "domesticated." Rebecca is the Ariadne in this film's labyrinth, but since she does not relinquish the thread to any Theseus, her space, Manderley, remains unconquered by man.

In one of the film's most extraordinary moments, the camera pointedly dynamizes Rebecca's absence. When Maxim tells the heroine about what happened on the night of Rebecca's death ("She got up, came toward me," etc.), the camera follows Rebecca's movements in a lengthy tracking shot.[20] Most films, of course, would have resorted to a flashback at this moment, allaying our anxiety over an empty screen by filling the "lack." Here, not only is Rebecca's absence stressed, but we are made to experience it as an active force. For those under the sway of Mulvey's analysis of narrative cinema, *Rebecca* may be seen as a spoof of the system, an elaborate sort of castration joke, with its flaunting of absence and lack.

It is true, however, that in the film's *narrative*, Rebecca is subjected to a brutal devaluation and punishment. Whereas the heroine, throughout most of the film, believes Rebecca to have been loved and admired by everyone, especially by Maxim, she ultimately learns that Maxim hated his first wife. "She was," he says, "incapable of love or tenderness or decency." Moreover, the film punishes her for her sexuality by substituting a cancer for the baby she thought she was expecting, cancer being that peculiar disease which, according to popular myth, preys on spinster and nymphomaniac alike. In addition, Mrs. Danvers receives the usual punishment inflicted on the bad mother/witch: she is burned alive when she sets fire to the Manderley mansion.

The latter part of *Rebecca*, concerned with the investigation, can be seen as yet another version of the myth of the overthrow of matriarchy by a patriarchal order.[21] After all, Rebecca's great crime, we learn, was her challenge to patriarchal laws of succession. The night of her death she goaded Maxim into hitting her when she told him that she was carrying a child which was not his but which would one day inherit his possessions. Even more importantly, after Rebecca's death her "spirit" presides and its power passes chiefly down the *female* line (through Mrs. Danvers). Rebecca's name itself (as well as that of the house associated with her) overshadows not only the name of the "second Mrs. de Winter" but even the formidable one of the patriarch: George Fortesquieu Maximillian de Winter.

Ultimately, the male authorities must step in and lay the ghost of Rebecca to rest once and for all (and true to Hollywood form, the point of view is eventually given over to Maxim while the heroine is mostly out of the picture altogether). Nevertheless, despite this apparent closure, the film has managed in the course of its unfolding to hint at what feminine desire might be like were it allowed greater scope. First, it points to women's playfulness, granting them the power and threat of laughter. Over and over, Rebecca's refusal to take men seriously is stressed, as when Mrs. Danvers tells Maxim, Jack Favell, and Frank Crawley (another victim of Rebecca's seductive arts) that "she used to sit on her bed and rock with laughter at the lot of you." Even after the investigation, Maxim becomes upset all over again at the memory of Rebecca on the night of her death as she "stood there laughing," taunting him with the details of her infidelity.

Moreover, Rebecca takes malicious pleasure in her own plurality. Luce Irigaray remarks, "the force and continuity of [woman's] desire are capable of nurturing all the 'feminine' masquerades for a long time."[22] And further, "a woman's (re)discovery of herself can only signify the possibility of not sacrificing any of her pleasures to another, of not identifying with any one in particular, of never being simply one."[23] Rebecca is an intolerable figure precisely because she revels in her own multiplicity—her remarkable capacity to play the model wife and mistress of Manderley while conducting various love affairs on the side. Even after Rebecca's death, the "force of her desire" makes itself felt, and, most appropriately, in light of Irigaray's comments, during a *masquerade* ball, in which the heroine dresses up like Rebecca, who had dressed up as Caroline de Winter, an ancestor whose portrait hangs on the wall. And all this occurs at the instigation of Mrs. Danvers, another character who is identified with Rebecca, but to whom Rebecca is not limited. The eponymous and invisible villainess, then, is far from being the typical femme fatale of Hollywood cinema brought at last into the possession of men in order to secure for them a strong sense of their identity. Occupant of patriarchy's "blind space," Rebecca is, rather, she who appears to subvert the very notion of identity—and of the visual economy which supports it.

It is no wonder that the film is (overly) determined to get rid of Rebecca, and that the task requires massive destruction. Yet there is reason to suppose that we cannot rest secure in the film's "happy" ending. For if death by drowning did not extinguish the woman's desire, can we be certain that death by fire has reduced it utterly to ashes?

Despite the fact that producers of "women's films" expected to attract a large female audience, it seems reasonable to suppose that these films were by no means attended exclusively by women. It is interesting to speculate on men's relation to the woman's film—something film theory has rarely considered, though it has exhaustively analyzed women's relations to "men's" films, like *film noirs*. For example, in scenes like the one at the costume ball in *Rebecca*, insofar as the film elicits identification on the part of *all* viewers, it is the male spectator who becomes the "transvestite," to recall Doane's term, a being not unlike Handel Fane or Norman Bates. In this way *Rebecca* constitutes a challenge to the male spectator's identity. No doubt, the fact of the viewer's unmediated experience of identification with a woman who herself has profound identity problems accounts for some of the masculine dislike of this film.[24]

It seems fair to say, however, that despite this critical disdain, Hitchcock would develop from his work on Rebecca both a method—for drawing the audience into a close, even suffocating identification with his characters—and a subject: the perils and ambivalences involved in the very processes of identification. For while, as Jean Laplanche and J.-B. Pontalis note, "it is by means of a series of identifications that the personality is constituted and specified," there is a danger that the other with whom one identifies may usurp and annihilate the personality—a danger which is especially keen when the other is a woman and hence serves as a reminder of the original (m)other in whom the subject's identity was merged.[25]

That *Rebecca* was a milestone in Hitchcock's work was actually pointed out by Truffaut: "The experience [of making *Rebecca*], I think, had repercussions on the films that came later. Didn't it inspire you to enrich many of them with the psychological ingredients you initially discovered in the Daphne du

Maurier novel?"[26] Such are the paradoxes of auteurship: by being forced to maintain a close identification with du Maurier's "feminine" text to the point where he felt that the picture could not be considered his own ("it's not a Hitchcock picture"), Hitchcock found one of his "proper" subjects—the potential terror and loss of self involved *in* identification, especially identification with a woman.

*Rebecca* thus provides one final ironic instance of the notion that the feminine is that which subverts identity—in this case, the identity of the auteur, the Master of the labyrinth himself.

# 4

# The Woman Who Was
# Known Too Much
*Notorious*

Throughout the 1940s (and, indeed, to some extent in the 1950s), Hitchcock would continue to rework the genre of the "female Gothic," which features women who fall in love with or marry men they subsequently begin to fear; the plots typically involve women's investigation of their victimization by the men they love.[1] For example, in *Suspicion* (1941), a film made shortly after *Rebecca*, the heroine Lina (Joan Fontaine) marries the charming but unreliable Johnny (Cary Grant), despite the prohibition of her father, General McLaidlaw (Sir Cedric Hardwicke). Johnny turns out to be a gambler, a liar, and a thief, and after the death of her father, Lina begins to suspect her husband of plotting her murder—a suspicion that the film, in a highly unsatisfactory ending, proves to be unfounded. *Spellbound* (1945) and *Shadow of a Doubt* (1943) are also about women whose lives appear to be endangered by the men they love: in *Spellbound* the man is a female doctor's psychiatric patient who poses as the head of a mental institution and who believes himself to be a murderer; in *Shadow of a Doubt* he is a beloved uncle who murders wealthy widows. *Notorious* (1946) depicts a woman, Alicia Huberman (Ingrid Bergman), menaced by *both* her lover, Devlin (Cary Grant), and her husband, Nazi Alex Sebastian (Claude Rains), whom she marries in order to spy on him for an American intelligence agency.

In a way, *Notorious* reverses the situation developed in *Suspicion*: Lina is the daughter of an upstanding military officer, whereas Alicia is the daughter of a traitor (each father dies rather early in the film). In both films, the Cary Grant character is the antithesis of the father—in *Suspicion*, Johnny is lawless and irresponsible; in *Notorious*, Devlin is a representative of the law, forcing Alicia to atone for the sins of the guilty father. Further, Lina's "frigidity" and fear of her husband are linked to her father's repressive attitude (he claims she is not the type to marry); and her suspicions of Johnny seem to be linked to her violation of the *Non du Père*, which in this case coincides literally with the *Nom du Père* (McLaidlaw).[2] Alicia, on the other hand, traces her promiscuity to the discovery of her father's traitorous behavior: "When I found out about him, I just went to pot: I didn't care what happened to me." Thus, in both films, the father's position with respect to the law decisively determines the daughter's (aberrant) sexuality. In the one instance, the father's excessive severity in laying down the law results in his daughter's lack of sexuality, and in the other instance, the father's lack of fidelity to the law causes his daughter's excessive sexuality. In *Notorious,* it is only through allowing this sexuality to be placed *in the service of* a harsh and unbending law (that is, through becoming a Mata Hari for callous American agents) and nearly dying the same death as her father—death by poison—that Alicia can expiate her own sins and those of the father. This certainly does not sound like a promising narrative from a feminist point of view. As we shall see, however, in the process of working out the dialectics of excess and lack in relation to female sexuality and male law, a film like *Notorious* begins to expose some of the problems of women's existence under patriarchy.

After a title reading, "Miami, Florida. Three-twenty P.M., April twenty-fourth, nineteen forty-six," *Notorious* begins with a scene in which John Huberman is being sentenced for treason against the United States. Later that night after a wild party at her home, Huberman's daughter Alicia goes for a drive in her car with Devlin, who has been brought by one of the party guests. A policeman on a motorcycle stops them because Alicia is driving with drunken recklessness, but when Devlin shows him an identification card, the policeman salutes him and rides off. Realizing that Devlin is a federal "cop," Alicia begins to fight with him to make him get out of the car, but he overpowers her and knocks her out. The next day, when Alicia wakes with a hangover, Devlin tells her that the federal agents want her to infiltrate a Nazi ring working in Rio de Janiero because she is acquainted with one of the leaders, Alexander Sebastian. At first she refuses, but after Devlin plays a recording of a conversation between her and her father in which she repudiates the latter's traitorous activities, she agrees.

On the plane over to Rio, Devlin informs Alicia that her father has committed suicide by taking a poison capsule in his prison cell. Alicia explains how her discovery of her father's traitorous activities led to her loss of self-respect and to her "notorious" behavior. When they get to Rio, Alicia and Devlin begin an affair, although he continues to make nasty remarks to her about her past behavior. In the middle of a lengthy shot of the two of them embracing in her apartment, Devlin receives orders on the phone to come to the American Embassy, where he is informed of her assignment: to pretend to fall in love with Alex Sebastian, who had fallen in love with *her* some years ago. When Devlin returns to Alicia's apartment, his behavior is cold and forbidding, and Alicia is surprised and hurt that Devlin did not turn down the assignment on the grounds that the "new Alicia Huberman was not the girl for such shenanigans."

The next day, the two go out to meet Sebastian, who is taking his daily ride, but when they slowly ride past on their horses, Alex fails to recognize her.

Devlin gives Alicia's horse a kick, and Sebastian, who proves to be far more gallant and kind than Devlin, rides to the rescue. Alicia now renews her relationship with Alex, who invites her home to meet his mother at a small dinner party. During the dinner, Alicia witnesses a scene in which one of the men, Emile Hupka, points to a wine bottle and becomes extremely agitated. Over brandy the men have a conference and decide that Emile has become dangerously untrustworthy and must be eliminated.

In a scene at the races, Alicia reports to Devlin the incident with the wine bottle, and she also tells him that he "can add Sebastian" to her "list of playmates." He is furious, and as the film progresses, he continues to treat her with icy sarcasm. One day, Alicia makes a surprise visit to the embassy to inform the agents that Alex has proposed marriage, a proposition she agrees to accept when Devlin remarks that he thinks it is "a useful idea." After the honeymoon, Devlin tells Alicia to persuade her husband to throw a party so that Devlin can come and investigate the wine cellar. The night of the party Alicia manages to get the key to the wine cellar from Alex's key chain, and, despite the jealous eye her husband keeps on her and Devlin, passes it on to Devlin, who sneaks off with her to the wine cellar. While Devlin is looking over the stock, a bottle falls off the shelf and breaks, spilling some kind of "vintage sand." He tries to hide the evidence of the breakage, and as the two prepare to leave the cellar, Alex, coming down the stairs to get more champagne, discovers their presence. Devlin grabs Alicia and kisses her, so that Alex will think they are in the cellar for a love tryst rather than for the purpose of espionage. Soon after, Alex and his servant return for the champagne, but Alex realizes his key is missing. Later that night, after the key has been put back on his chain while he pretends to sleep, he explores the wine cellar and finds that the "sand" (which turns out to be uranium ore) has been discovered.

Defeated, Alex goes to his mother, whom he had defied in marrying Alicia, to plead for her help. She devises a plan to poison Alicia slowly, a scheme which nearly succeeds, partly because Alicia, rather than admitting that she is sick, defiantly pretends to have a hangover during her usual meeting with Devlin. Eventually Alicia becomes aware of the plot against her, but it has proceeded so far that she is helpless to run away, and is taken to her bed by Alex and his mother. Meanwhile, Devlin suspects that something is amiss and pays a visit to the Sebastian household. At long last avowing his love for Alicia, he helps her from her room and they descend the stairs accompanied by Alex and his mother, who are powerless to stop them because to do so would alert the other Nazis present in the house to the fact that Alex is married to an American agent. Claiming that they are taking Alicia to the hospital, Alex walks out of the house with Devlin and Alicia, but is locked out of the car by Devlin, who thereby leaves Alex to face certain death at the hands of his compatriots.[3]

As its title suggests, an issue of knowledge lies at the heart of the film. But although the term "notorious" alludes primarily to the idea of woman as sexually known and therefore held in contempt, the film is also concerned with other problems of knowledge and sexual difference. First, in the course of the film, as is the case in many Hollywood narratives, the woman becomes an object of man's sexual investigations. Secondly, however, the woman is *also* cast in the active role of knowledge seeker: in her capacity as spy she becomes an investigator, attempting to wrest the (literal) keys to the mystery from her jealous mother-in-law and her husband. Hence, one of the main interests of the film lies in the way it combines elements of *film noir,* an essentially male genre, in which man is the active investigator of woman, and of the female Gothic, in which woman is assigned an investigative role.

Alicia is positioned at the outset of the film as object of man's curiosity and voyeurism. After the title announcing the time, date, and place of the narrative, the film begins with a closeup shot of a reporter's camera and then tracks along a row of reporters waiting outside a courthouse. A point of view shot of a man spying on the courtroom proceedings follows this initial shot, and then the man exclaims, "Here she comes." Alicia emerges with the crowd while flashbulbs go off in her face, and the male reporters crowd in on her with their probing questions. The shot ends with one detective telling another to make sure that she doesn't leave town, and when the second one goes off, the first is shown in closeup looking after. Following a couple of shots of Alicia's house taken from across the street, the film dissolves to the interior, where a party is taking place. In an extraordinarily long take, we see Alicia standing in bright light drinking and bantering with the other guests, while in the shadowy foreground is a silhouette of the back of the head of a clearly identifiable Cary Grant; Alicia addresses him a few times ("I like you … you're my kind of guy"), but he remains perfectly still and unresponsive—exhibiting the wooden behavior that will characterize him physically and emotionally throughout the film until its climax.

After setting the woman up as an object of male desire and curiosity, the film proceeds to submit her to a process of purification whereby she is purged of her excess sexuality in order to be rendered fit for her place in the patriarchal order. She is, as the critics say, "redeemed by love." Hitchcock accomplishes this purification largely through visual means: in the party sequence, Alicia, photographed in a long shot and standing in a bright, harsh light, is wearing a bold striped blouse with a bared midriff (which, in a highly symbolic and repressive gesture, Devlin will cover when they go out to the car), and she exudes a kind of animal sexuality that is in keeping with her attire (later, Devlin will make a cynical remark about a woman's inability to "change her spots"—thereby equating female sexuality with animality). By the end of the film, however, when Alicia is on the verge of dying, she is etherealized and spiritualized until she becomes practically bodiless. Whereas in an earlier scene in bed, Alicia's voluptuous body had been emphasized when she woke up, hung over, still wearing the suggestive blouse, and turned slowly over onto her back, in this later scene Hitchcock shoots entirely in closeup and utilizes low-key backlighting for a kind of halo effect. In the climactic staircase sequence, Hitchcock continues to shoot predominantly in closeup, and even when he cuts to a medium or a long shot, Alicia's body, draped around Devlin, is entirely obscured by a loose, dark coat draped around *it*.

Not only does the film disembody the sexual woman, it also continually impairs her vision (something that Hitchcock films do to women with alarming frequency), thus ensuring that man remains in sole control of the gaze—and hence of the knowledge and power with which vision is always associated in the cinema. The threat inherent in Alicia's role as a Mata Hari may account for the severity of the punishment she undergoes and for the need to disable her vision. As the work of feminist film criticism has shown, sexuality and knowledge are usually mutually exclusive qualities in movie heroines, and in 1940s films they are kept separated by genre: in *noir* films, woman is typically eroticized and made the object of the male gaze and of narrative investigation, whereas in the Gothic film, she becomes the subject of the investigative gaze, but is characteristically de-eroticized in the process: masochistic fantasy comes to substitute for sexual fantasy.[4] One might speculate, then, that the situation in which woman becomes a Mata Hari, "making love for the papers," as Alicia comments, is extremely threatening to men because it involves women *exploiting* their sexuality to gain knowledge and power. Thus, despite the fact that Alicia's point of view is stressed once she gets inside the Sebastian house and begins searching for clues, the film takes care to maim her vision on several occasions. Early in the film, for example, when she is driving the car recklessly and drunkenly, a shot of the road taken from her point of view is obscured by her hair hanging down over her eyes. "This fog gets to me," she complains. The next morning she wakes up with a hangover, and another point of view shot reveals Devlin looming in the doorway in a canted frame; as he walks toward her, the camera turns until he is shown standing upside down. Later, at the moment she realizes she is being poisoned, her vision becomes totally blurred as she walks toward the silhouetted figures of Mother and Alex, who merge into a single shadow. And finally, in the climactic scene when Devlin takes her down the stairs, she keeps her gaze averted from the action, and it is Devlin's watchful point of view that the camera stresses.

In a typical *noir* move, then, the film displaces the center of interest from Alicia as an object of curiosity in relation to her father's espionage activities to Alicia as an object of male sexual desire who must be tortured for and purified of her sexual past—and nearly blinded and killed in the process. In effecting this displacement, the film collapses two very different registers—the realm of politics (espionage activities, postwar fascism, the beginnings of cold-war paranoia) and the realm of private life (sexuality and romance)—into one. The fact that the political elements in the film get reduced to the status of a MacGuffin has generally been celebrated by critics. For example, Donald

Spoto writes, "Although *Notorious* seems to be a spy melodrama, in fact it is not. The espionage activities are really Hitchcock's MacGuffin, his ubiquitous pretext for more serious, abstract issues. Here, the serious issue is one of common humanity—the possibility of love and trust redeeming two lives from fear, guilt and meaninglessness."[5]

Certainly Spoto's analysis is accurate at the level of description. For example, during the suspenseful scene at Sebastian's party, a drama of sexual jealousy coincides with the "spy melodrama": various point of view shots show Sebastian jealously watching Devlin and Alicia to determine the nature of his wife's feelings for this man (Alicia has persuaded Sebastian to give the party so that Devlin may be cured of his supposed one-sided passion for Alicia by seeing how happy she is with her husband); meanwhile, Devlin watches Sebastian watching them and waits for the moment he might slip off unseen to the wine cellar. At the same time, however, the viewer is aware that Devlin is also jealous of *Sebastian* and conscious of Sebastian's glances at the two of them as signs of his possessive attitude toward his wife. Thus, the entire drama of seeing and being seen is here and elsewhere motivated by the men's desire to know the real feelings of the woman and the nature of her relation to the other man in the triangle.

But while we might accept Spoto's description of how the "political" becomes the "personal" in this film, feminists certainly have less reason to celebrate the merger of these two realms, given the way in which the displacement makes the woman (rather than the uranium) into the object of man's epistemological quest. Instead, feminists might want to ask how it is that a collapse of these separate registers is so frequently and so facilely accomplished in the Hitchcock text (and in *noir* films in general). We might speculate that there is something in the nature of male modes of knowing in patriarchy that allows for the kinds of slippages I have been discussing. Jean-Paul Sartre's description of the search for knowledge—by which he means even scientific knowledge—as bound up with male vision and masculine sexual desire certainly suggests that this is the case. Sartre writes:

> [T]he idea of discovery, of revelation, includes an idea of appropriative enjoyment. What is seen is possessed; to see is to *deflower*. If we examine the comparisons ordinarily used to express the relation between the knower and the known, we see that many of them are represented as being a kind of *violation by sight*. The unknown object is given as immaculate, as virgin, comparable to a *whiteness*. It has not yet "delivered up" its secret; man has not yet "snatched" its secret away from it.[6]

We can readily understand from this passage why a "notorious" woman is a disturbance to the order of things from a male perspective, and why it is important for a film like *Notorious* to render the woman virginal even if it nearly kills her. Further, in Sartre's grotesque insistence on the extreme of masculine sexuality—rape and violation—as the model and motor force of all enterprises of discovery, the language clearly excludes women from such enterprises, and implies that they are even denied the pleasures of cinema itself: for to see is to deflower. But whether Sartre is describing the *only* way of knowing or only one, male, way of knowing remains to be investigated. For now suffice it to point out that Sartre's discussion, which stresses the appropriative, phallic nature of *every* kind of knowledge, indicates how political intrigue and sexual desire can easily merge into a single hermeneutic.

Contemporary theory is largely in agreement with Sartre's view of discovery and revelation as masculine activities, considering narrative itself to be based on male sexuality and tracing its pleasures to the Oedipus complex. Hence Roland Barthes, speaking of the pleasures of the text, writes: "the entire excitation takes refuge in the *hope* of seeing the sexual organ (schoolboy's dream) or of knowing the end of the story (novelistic satisfaction). Paradoxically (since it is mass-consumed), this is a far more intellectual pleasure than the other: an Oedipal pleasure (to denude, to know, to learn the origin and the end)."[7] Thus, narrative for Barthes is simply a reenactment of the child's investigations into his mother's sexuality and hence into his own origins: "seeing" and "knowing," regardless of *what* is seen or known, are equated with male sexual desire.

Barthes is clearly referring as much to Sophocles' drama of Oedipus Rex as he is to the Freudian myth. And what is interesting about the Sophocles work, from the point of view of the present discussion, is the way in which the great political enigma which that text poses—what is the origin of the plague?—finds its answer in the personal history of Oedipus Rex. The cause of the plague lies in Oedipus's crimes against the family: killing his father and committing incest with his mother. If it is not quite correct to see the plague as a MacGuffin in the Sophoclean text, it is, I think, at least fair to say that in this murder mystery (the investigation into the death of Laius), the personal and political realms are coextensive and congruent—Oedipus's drive to know the secret that plagues the state leads to the discovery of his private sexual and familial history. Similarly, though the process is reversed, this congruency may be seen in the Freudian use of the myth: the boy's drive to know the secret of his origin, his investigations into sexuality, ultimately result in his assuming a place in the social and Symbolic order—the world of culture and the fathers.

In *Notorious,* the male oedipal logic on which narrative is supposedly based may also be traced in the stories of Alex and Devlin—both variants of *the* story, which, as we saw in the last chapter, Raymond Bellour claims is continually told in Hollywood film: the hero must "accept the symbolization of the death of the father, the displacement from the attachment to the mother to the attachment to another woman." Alex's story, of course, represents the failure of Oedipus, since he is unsuccessful at effecting the displacement described by Bellour—hence, the little drama around keys in the film: Alex (whose very name, "a-lex," suggests his place outside the law) asserts himself in order to obtain the keys to the house from his mother, only to deliver them over to a woman who proceeds to betray him, personally and politically, thus forcing him into a renewed dependency on Mother. For Devlin, however, the outcome is very different. Bellour notes that the woman, who represents "lawless sexuality" in the classic film, serves as "the very image of castration" (like the mother in the oedipal scenario) and so she must give way to the heroine "who reverses the image, through whom the masculine subject will find … the positivity of a regulated sexuality, … the woman who permits the fixation of his desire … through the conjunction of his entry into the social order and the internalized, finally bearable image of his own castration."[8] We have seen that Alicia represents both types of woman successively in the film, that she herself must reverse the initial image of her "lawless sexuality" (a lawlessness or "a-licit-ness" suggested by *her* name) in order for the couple to be formed, and for the social order to be ratified and fascism to be vanquished. Facism here, in another collapse of the personal and the political, is represented by the mother who abuses maternal power (Mrs. Sebastian). Alicia is made to atone for *her* as well as for the father, with the result that Devlin finds in "the second Mrs. Sebastian" the good, domesticated, and eventually powerless German woman.

Drawing on the work of Jurij Lotman, Teresa de Lauretis writes of the way narrative works to produce Oedipus, and she observes, "plot (narrative) mediates, integrates, and ultimately reconciles the mythical and the historical, norm and excess, the spatial and temporal orders, the individual and the collectivity."[9] However, de Lauretis argues, no such integration is possible for women, whose lives in patriarchy are riven by contradiction. We might say, following on de Lauretis's insight, that women's experience in patriarchy is expressed not in the oedipal tragedy, nor in any myth which functions to "reconcile the individual and the collectivity," but rather in a more Hegelian conception of tragedy—of narrative in general—which stresses conflict and the *irreconcilability* of various imperatives facing the individual. It is interesting that Hegel's model for tragedy was *Antigone*, a play about *another* woman whose sufferings are required as atonement for the crimes of her father—in this case, the sins of Oedipus himself. Antigone, who insists on burying her brother against the decree of Creon, defies the laws of the state in the name of a higher law, which demands respect for the dead, and in the name of the "sacredness of kinship." Most of all, Antigone offends because she leaves the private sphere, to which as a woman (and therefore a slave) she is confined, to take up a public role. Similarly, in *Notorious,* the main dilemma facing Alicia is that she can perform her patriotic, public duty only by violating the private sexual code. Defending her in her absence after one of the agents snidely alludes to her sullied reputation (the only time he *does* come to her rescue until the climactic rescue scene itself), Devlin perfectly articulates the double bind in which Alicia is placed: "Miss Huberman is first, last, and always not a lady. She may be risking her life, but when it comes to being a *lady,* she doesn't hold a candle to your wife, sir, sitting in Washington and playing cards with three other ladies of great honor and virtue." Here we find a true instance of the "love vs. duty" theme which Hitchcock had elaborated in his discussion of *Blackmail* and which we saw could be applied with much more justice to the situation of women than to men.

A "conflictual" narrative of the sort I have been describing functions not to integrate the individual into the social order, but to express women's experience of lived contradiction in patriarchy, and thus is likely to elicit the kind of "dialectical" response that several feminist film theorists have insisted is characteristic of the female spectator at the cinema. It is in terms of this alternative notion of narrative that we may understand the impossible positions of the heroines in many, if not most, Hitchcock films, of which *Notorious* seems to me in this respect exemplary—perhaps because it is a film made shortly after the war ended. In his in-depth study of 1940s films, Dana Polan has shown how wartime narratives were forced to confront a basic contradiction between Hollywood ideology, which tended to submerge the political into the personal, and the ideology of the war years, which stressed the necessity of the individual's subordinating himself and his personal desires to the larger war effort.[10] Even women were expected to contribute to this effort—an expectation that, in its countermanding of traditional notions about woman's place, would only exacerbate the pull of contradiction in these films.

To answer the question posed earlier, then, about women's modes of knowing in patriarchy, we can say that this knowledge has to do with an awareness of contradiction, and that Hitchcock's films, in their preoccupation and identification with women as victims, reinforce that knowledge in the female spectator. Throughout the film, Alicia is shown to be the locus of the crisscrossing of various desires and duties that seem to conspire in her downfall (an apt image is that of the tiled floor over which Alicia moves like a pawn in the games of men).[11] Like *Blackmail,* which it resembles in some crucial respects, the film offers several striking shots that emphasize the woman's status as victim: the shot in which Devlin passes his identification card across her body to hand to the police officer on the motorcycle; the one in which a closeup shows his foot kicking her horse so that Sebastian will ride to her rescue; the one in which Alicia lies frozen in terror on her bed framed by the profiles of Alex and his mother looking at one another; and, finally, the ones at the end in which Alicia is half-carried down the stairs between Devlin and the Sebastians, the two forces—of law and order on the one hand, and of fascism on the other—having unwittingly colluded in her torture and near death.

As he had done in *Blackmail,* Hitchcock privileges the woman's consciousness—even as he makes her into an object of male investigation—so that *all* spectators are encouraged to identify with her in her plight. It is important not to allow this crucial point to be obscured by the fact that the film depicts male oedipal dramas and rivalries. For example, a recent "Bellourian" analysis of the film insists, quite wrongly I think, that our identification must be with Devlin:

> The second term of the romantic triangle to be introduced is Dev ... with whom a strong identification is immediately mobilized. If, so far, Alicia is defined as the object of the gaze, it is Dev who is encoded as the source of the look. In our first view of him, he is seated in the left foreground with his back turned to the camera, silent and in silhouette, while all others in the frame are bright and animated. This inert character *is* the spectator ...[12]

Now, one might very well question whether the film's spectator is more likely to establish a "strong identification" with a silent, "inert" character who shows us only the back of his head, or with characters who are humanized by being presented as "bright and animated."[13] If it is indeed correct to see an analogy between Devlin and the film's spectator—and I believe it is—surely this analogy is meant to be perceived *critically* by the viewer: spectatorship is here shown to be a somewhat shady activity—and more than a little menacing. From this shot onward, *Notorious* encourages us to condemn Devlin in his role as withdrawn judgmental spectator, and it draws us into an intimate identification with the vulnerable and increasingly helpless heroine: for example, insofar as the film uses point of view shots to convey Alicia's impaired vision, it forces us all to share in her disablement. Here, it would seem, is a classic example of a situation in which both male and female spectators occupy a primarily masochistic position.

As I have already had occasion to note, film theory has most frequently assigned the masochistic position to the female spectator. In an article on "the woman's film" of the 1940s, Mary Ann Doane has argued that this type of film mimes "a position which can only be described as masochistic, as the perpetual staging of suffering"; female fantasy is presented as preoccupied with notions of "persecution, illness and death."[14] In the chapter on *Blackmail,* I suggested that Doane neglects the important possibility that women's response to the depiction of feminine victimization and suffering is likely to be one of anger. Now, in light of *Notorious,* I would like to go even further and argue that female suffering may *itself* be an expression of anger. Alicia's self-destructive behavior is from the beginning shown to be simultaneously aggressive and hostile: her excessive drinking and her promiscuous behavior are an angry response to her father's criminality, and when she is driven by Devlin's sadistic treatment of her to renew her notorious ways (e.g., to drink too much), contempt and defiance are strongly marked in her voice and manner. "What a rat you are, Dev," she says in reply to one of his barbed remarks and orders the second drink she has just refused.

In her article, "Theorising the Female Spectator: Film and the Masquer-ade," analyzed in the chapter on *Blackmail*, Doane proposes that the only way for the female spectator to gain the appropriate distance from patriarchal cinema and the images of victimized, suffering womanhood is to adopt an ironic distance from them. This strategy, in Doane's view, would amount to performing a feminine masquerade—exaggerating the traits of femininity so as to call their "naturalness" into question. Doane offers the notion of masquerade as an alternative to the masochistic "overidentification" to which she considers the female spectator especially prone. I believe, however, that film theorists like Doane have erred in considering the psychic phenomenon of masochism to be a simple entity (consisting of pure pleasure in pain), rather than a complex process that may even be composed of ideas and emotions unacceptable in women in patriarchal society.

In this regard, it is interesting to note that in his impressive study, *Masoch-ism in Modern Man*, Theodor Reik considers masquerade to be the *essence* of female masochism. He writes: "Female masochists exaggerate their femininity. They display an ultrafemininity."[15] Analyzing the masochistic fantasies of his female patients, Reik observes that the "female situation is not only shown or acted out in the phantasy, the degrading and humiliating element not only demonstrated but these are the features which are even exaggerated." Reik concludes that the fantasy does not point to an "acceptance of femininity"; it is meant to expose the position of women in patriarchal society in such a way as to express contempt for it. The fantasy "mock[s] at the man's conception of the female role" (p. 237).

We must therefore not be misled by the submissiveness seemingly implied in Alicia's "ultrafeminine" traits: her "ecstatic weakness" (in Spoto's words); her soft, feminine gestures; and especially the "clinging kisses" so strongly emphasized in the early sequence shot when she and Dev kiss and talk about dinner in her apartment—the same "clinging kisses" referred to in anguish by Sebastian after he becomes aware of her betrayal.[16] As Reik observes of those theorists who emphasize "the dependence of masochistic characters," they overlook "the fact that one can draw somebody down by clinging to him" (p. 159). It is not only that the "clinging kisses" bring down Sebastian and the house of Nazis; Alicia's suffering also, eventually, causes Devlin to come round and admit his *own* pain and suffering. One might speculate that the appeal of *Notorious* as a woman's film is directly related to the way in which Alicia's tribulations force Devlin to acknowledge his vulnerability and his error: in this way, Alicia's "persecution, illness, and [near] death" may be said to provide an outlet for the female spectator's anger.

If Alicia appears in the film to be the perfect masochist, Devlin appears to be the quintessential sadist—stern, remote, and punishing, always in com-mand of himself and the woman who nearly dies for love of him (even in their poses, gestures, and clothing, the sharp contrasts between the two suggest the gendered binary oppositions of much feminist film theory). In the sequence following her party when the two are in her car, Devlin's control is stressed in a variety of ways, although Alicia is the one in the driver's seat. Several times the camera shows a closeup of his hand, ready to take hold of the wheel should a steady grasp be required. Even his expression conveys his *sang-froid*, so much so that Alicia deliberately begins to speed in order "to wipe that grin" off his face and break down his self-possession. Finally, in a very shocking incident, he knocks her out with a sharp punch to the jaw when she begins to fight him after discovering he is a "cop." Devlin's power and control continue to be stressed in the next scene, when he stands menacingly in the doorway and forces her to drink the cure for her hangover that is in a glass looming in the foreground of the image—a shot which rhymes with those of the poison coffee cups later. In making this connection, the film clearly links Devlin to the Nazis—to the father who killed himself with poison as well as to the Sebastians, who try to murder Alicia. To be sure, Devlin believes he is administering a *cure,* but as Alicia's face suggests when she drinks down the liquid, and as the entire narrative shows, his is a cure that nearly kills.

As the film progresses, Devlin steadfastly maintains his air of command and continually allows Alicia to be placed in compromising or dangerous circumstances; often, of course, he actually *places* her in these circumstances—for example, when he kicks her horse and then watches intently and impassively while Sebastian rides to the rescue. It is noteworthy that while, in ways we have already discussed, Devlin's trajectory involves an oedipal progression, in another way, we might say that he is fixed at a pre-oedipal moment—that moment analyzed by Freud in the child's fort/da game. According to Freud, the child gains symbolic mastery over the mother and her movements with a little object on a string that he makes disappear and reappear. For Freud, the game is ultimately a "sadistic" one, in that its object is to gain power over another. Recently, theorists have challenged Freud's interpretation, however, and have suggested that the game really points to a fundamentally *masochistic* inclination on the part of the child. Thus, as I pointed out in the introduction, Kaja Silverman insists on the importance of the fact that the child much more frequently sends the object away than brings it back, and seems to take more satisfaction in its disappearance than its reappearance.

Leo Bersani also notes the implications of the fort/da game for a theory of masochism, writing in terms which strikingly recapitulate Devlin's situation with respect to Alicia:

> The child enjoys the fantasy of the mother suffering the pain of separation which she originally inflicted on him. And to say this is to be reminded that revenge here must include the avenger's own suffering; by making his mother disappear, the child has just as effectively deprived himself of her presence as he has deprived her of his. But the

child's suffering is now inseparable from two sources of pleasure: his representation of his mother's suffering, and what I take to be the narcissistic gratification of exercising so much power. In reality, there is no sequence here; rather, there is a single, satisfying representation of a separation painful to both the mother and the child. In other words, mastery is simultaneous with self-punishment; a fantasy of omnipotence and autonomy (the child both controls the mother's movements and doesn't need her) is inseparable from a repetition of pain.[17]

That both hero and male spectator derive a great deal of "narcissistic gratification" from exercising—directly or vicariously—power over the female subject is one of the basic assumptions of feminist film theory. That the exercise of this power and the witnessing of a "satisfying representation" of the woman's suffering may be *painful* to the male subject has not been sufficiently considered. And yet, in *Notorious*, Devlin's position as passive spectator is clearly one which causes him a great deal of anguish—an anguish which he nevertheless seems determined to intensify on a number of occasions. It is almost as if he sends Alicia into the arms of Sebastian for the *purpose* of watching her, as if he stages her suffering so that he can increase his own distress. At the end of the film, Devlin makes explicit the idea that "mastery is simultaneous with self-punishment" when he apologizes for his cruelty to her and explains, "I couldn't see straight; I was a fat-headed guy filled with pain."

But if it is important for feminist film theory to recognize the masochistic urge at the heart of man's relation to his mother and to his subsequent love objects (and it is part of my project in this book to argue that it is), we must not suppose that there is the equality in suffering that Bersani's text seems to imply ("a separation painful to both the mother and the child"): if Devlin *says* he couldn't see straight because he was in such pain, it is Alicia's vision that the film consistently *shows* to be distorted, partly as a result of her self-destructive masochistic activities (her drinking) and partly as a result of other people's destructive treatment of her. If Devlin is "filled with pain," she is filled with pain *and* poison.

For Oedipus *does* finally intervene. The fact is, Devlin has the full power of the law behind him, as Alicia has not. The inequality of power relations means that, as I argued in the introduction, the man—hero or spectator—gets to displace his masochistic urges onto a female victim and can therefore maintain a mastery which enables him to deny his suffering while at the same time safely indulging it. For this reason, it is obviously absurd to replace the feminist emphasis on male sadism in film narrative with a "masochistic aesthetic." If *Notorious* suggests the importance of recognizing male masochism, it equally demonstrates the ease with which this masochism may be repudiated, and, most importantly, it reveals the potentially dire consequences for women of this repudiation. It is for *this* reason that a notion of male masochism must be factored into feminist theories of narrative and spectatorship and *not* in order to depoliticize the issues by pronouncing suffering to be part of the human condition—something we all do and enjoy equally.

Similarly, feminist theory must challenge the idea that femininity is a simple matter of (simple) masochism, of pleasure in one's objectification. Again, *Notorious* suggests the extent to which female masochism embodies and expresses hostile and subversive impulses. Of course, it is crucial to recognize that these impulses are aimed at the self as well as at the oppressor; but it is equally important to understand that they exist at all and are not simply the prerogative of the feminist critic who consciously and ironically distances herself from the images on the patriarchal screen.

My analysis of *Notorious* may stand, then, as a kind of prolegomenon to a *politicized* deconstruction of the binary oppositions informing feminist film theory: those oppositions clustered around the constellations male/subject/knower/sadist, woman/object/known/masochist. On the one hand, women at the movies are already engaged in an active, knowing and rebellious activity of spectatorship; and, on the other hand, as Hitchcock never ceases to fear, men are constantly in danger of having their power undermined—of being deprived of the keys to their secrets by women who, though notorious, can never be completely subdued or fully known.

# 5
# The Master's Dollhouse
*Rear Window*

In "Visual Pleasure and Narrative Cinema," Laura Mulvey uses two Hitchcock films to exemplify her theory. According to Mulvey, both *Rear Window* (1954) and *Vertigo* (1958) are films "cut to the measure of male desire"—tailored, that is, to the fears and fantasies of the male spectator, who, because of the threat of castration posed by the woman's image, needs to see her fetishized and controlled in the course of the narrative.[1] Certainly, these two films appear to support perfectly Mulvey's thesis that classic narrative film negates woman's view, since each of them seems to confine us to the hero's vision of events and to insist on that vision by literally stressing the man's point of view throughout. The film spectator apparently has no choice *but* to identify with the male protagonist, who exerts an active controlling gaze over a passive female object. In *Rear Window*, Mulvey writes, "Lisa's exhibitionism [is] established by her obsessive interest in dress and style, in being a passive image of visual perfection; Jeffries's voyeurism and activity [are] established through his work as a photojournalist, a maker of stories and captor of images. However, his enforced inactivity, binding him to his seat as a spectator, puts him squarely in the phantasy position of the cinema audience."[2]

This last observation connects Mulvey to a tradition of criticism of the film that begins with the work of the French critic Jean Douchet and that sees the film as a metacinematic commentary: spectators identifying with the chairbound voyeuristic protagonist find themselves in complicity with his guilty desires.[3] Because of Hitchcock's relentless insistence on the male gaze, even critics like Robin Wood who are anxious to save the film for feminism, restrict themselves to discussing the film's critique of the position of the hero and, by extension, of the *male* spectator whose "phantasy position the hero occupies."[4] But what happens, in the words of a recent relevant article by Linda Williams, "when the woman looks"?[5] I shall argue, against the grain of critical consensus, that the film actually has something to say about this question.[6]

*Rear Window* is the story of photojournalist L.B. Jeffries (James Stewart), who, as a result of an accident on the job, is confined to a wheelchair in his apartment, where he whiles away the time spying on his neighbors. These include a middle-aged alcoholic musician with composer's block; a newlywed couple who spend all their time in bed behind closed shades; a childless couple who sleep on the balcony at night and own a little dog; a voluptuous dancer, "Miss Torso," who practices her suggestive dance routines as she goes about her daily chores; "Miss Lonelyhearts," who fantasizes about gentlemen callers; and Lars Thorwald, a costume jewelry salesman with a nagging invalid wife.

The film opens with the camera panning the courtyard of a Lower East Side housing development and then moving back through a window, where we see L.B. Jeffries asleep, his chair turned away from the window, beads of sweat on his face. There is a cut to a thermometer, which registers over ninety degrees, and then the camera tilts down Jeffries' body to reveal that his leg is in a cast. The camera proceeds to explore the apartment, calling our attention to some smashed camera equipment, a photograph of a car accident, some other photographs Jeff has taken in his travels, and, finally, a negative of a blonde woman's face followed by a "positive" photograph of her on the cover of *Life* magazine. When Jeff wakes up, he begins to observe his neighbors and then complains on the phone to his editor that if he doesn't get back to the job soon, he's going to do "something drastic like get married." While he speaks of the horrors of marriage, we watch from his point of view as Thorwald (Raymond Burr) returns home to be greeted by a nagging wife.

Soon after, Stella (Thelma Ritter), the insurance company nurse, comes in to give Jeff a massage. She immediately begins to scold him for being a Peeping Tom, and tries to persuade him to marry Lisa Freemont, claiming that his lukewarm attitude to the woman he claims is "too perfect" is abnormal. Later that evening, Lisa (Grace Kelly) comes to visit, dressed in an $1100 gown and accompanied by a waiter from the Twenty One Club who is delivering their dinner. Lisa and Jeff have an argument as he tells her that marriage to him, given his grueling life style and her pampered one, is out of the question. When she goes home, Jeff begins to watch the neighbors again and observes some strange movements on the part of Lars Thorwald. Eventually Jeff falls asleep, and we see Thorwald and a woman leaving Thorwald's apartment. The next day Jeff notices that Mrs. Thorwald has gone, and he becomes convinced that Thorwald has murdered his wife—a conviction that becomes more and more obsessive as the film progresses—to the point where he uses first binoculars and then a huge telephoto lens to see more closely. He attempts to persuade Lisa, Stella, and his friend policeman Tom Doyle (Wendell Corey) of his interpretation of the events across the way. Though Doyle remains skeptical, the women eventually come to accept Jeff's view and actually go looking for clues.

Lisa is caught by Thorwald as she searches his apartment for the wedding ring that will prove Jeff's theory, and Jeff is forced to look helplessly on as Thorwald pushes her around. Jeff warns the police, whom he has just contacted on the phone to alert them that Miss Lonelyhearts is about to take an overdose of pills. The police arrive in time to prevent any harm from befalling

Lisa, and they take her to jail. After Jeff sends Stella off with the bail money, he finds himself face to face with the guilty Thorwald, who asks, "What is it you want of me?" and steps forward menacingly. Jeff tries to keep him at bay by popping off flashbulbs in his face, but Thorwald manages to grab him and, during a struggle, Jeff falls to the ground from a window ledge.

The film ends with another pan around the courtyard. The various plots featuring the neighbors have been resolved: workmen are repainting the bathroom of Thorwald's apartment, where blood had splattered when Thorwald murdered his wife and cut her up in pieces; Miss Lonelyhearts, whose suicide was prevented when she heard the musician's beautiful song, has formed a relationship with the musician; Miss Torso's little soldier boyfriend Stanley arrives and asks what's in the refrigerator; the childless couple, whose dog was murdered by Thorwald because it was digging in the flower garden where evidence was buried (the dog who "knew too much," as Lisa puts it), have gotten another dog; and the newlywed wife is nagging her husband because he has lost his job. The camera tracks back into the window to show L.B. asleep, as before, only this time both his legs are in casts. The camera movement ends on a medium shot of Lisa lying on Jeff's bed in pants and shirt, and reading a book entitled *Beyond the High Himalayas*. She steals a glance at Jeff to make sure he is still asleep, puts down the book, and picks up a copy of *Harper's Bazaar*. On the soundtrack is the musician's song, "Lisa," finally completed, like the narrative itself.

A number of critics, most of whom center their analyses around the film's critique of voyeurism, have pointed out that the film's protagonist is fixated at an infantile level of sexual development and must in the course of the narrative grow into "mature sexuality": "Jeffries's voyeurism goes hand in hand with an absorbing fear of mature sexuality. Indeed, the film begins by hinting at a serious case of psychosexual pathology. The first image of Jeffries, asleep with hand on thigh is quietly masturbatory, as if he were an invalid who had just abused himself in the dark."[7] By the end of the film Jeff has supposedly learned his lesson and "has realized the corollary psychic costs of both voyeurism and solitude": he is now ready for the marriage he has all along resisted and for the "mature" sexual relation that this implies. Yet there is a sense in which the image of Lisa in masculine clothes, absorbed in "masculine" interests only places Jeff—and the audience—more squarely than ever in the Imaginary. For as the narrative proceeds, the sexuality of the woman, which is all along presented as threatening, is first combated by the fantasy of female dismemberment and then, finally, by a remembering of the woman according to the little boy's fantasy that the female is no different from himself.[8]

Jeff claims that Lisa is "too perfect." On the face of it, of course, this reason for resisting marriage is patently absurd, as Stella does not fail to point out. (This absurdity leads one critic to argue that the project of the film is to stimulate the audience's desire for the couple's union by inducing frustration at

"Jeff's indifference to her allure."[9]) But, while it may indeed be "unrealistic" that any red-blooded man would reject Grace Kelly, there is a certain psychological plausibility in Jeff's fear of Lisa's "perfection"—a fear that is related to man's fear of women's difference and his suspicion that they may not, after all, be mutilated (imperfect) men, may not be what, as Susan Lurie puts it, *men* would be if they lacked penises—"bereft of sexuality, helpless, incapable."[10] Lurie's words certainly describe the situation of Jeff, whose impotence is suggested by the enormous cast on his leg and his consequent inability to move about, so that ultimately he is unable to rescue the woman he loves from danger. By contrast, Lisa Freemont is anything but helpless and incapable, despite Mulvey's characterization of her as a "passive image of visual perfection"—and this is where the "problem" lies.

In our very first view of her, Lisa is experienced as an overwhelmingly powerful presence. Jeff is asleep in his chair, the camera positioned over him, when suddenly an ominous shadow crosses his face. There is a cut to a close-up of Grace Kelly, a vision of loveliness, bending down toward him and us: the princess-to-be waking Sleeping Beauty with a kiss. These two shots—shadow and vibrant image—suggest the underlying threat posed by the desirable woman and recall the negative and positive images of the woman on the cover of *Life*. When Jeff jokingly inquires, "Who are you?" Lisa turns on three lamps, replies, "Reading from top to bottom, Lisa … Carol … Freemont," and strikes a pose. While the pose confirms the view of her as exhibitionist, her confident nomination of herself reveals her to be extremely self-possessed—in contrast to the man who is known by only one of *his* three names. The two engage in small talk as Lisa sets about preparing the dinner brought in from the Twenty One Club, and Jeff makes continual jibes about married life. Lisa ends the conversation by claiming, "At least you can't say the dinner's not all right," and over a shot of a very appetizing meal, Jeff replies, exasperated, "Lisa, it's perfect, as *always*." In the meantime, we have witnessed Thorwald taking dinner in to his wife, who pushes it from her in disgust and flings away the rose he has placed on the tray.

Important parallels are thus set up between Lisa and Thorwald on the one hand, and Jeff and the wife on the other. Critics have seldom picked up on this parallelism, preferring instead to stress a symmetry along sexual lines—that is, Jeff's similarity to Thorwald and Lisa's resemblance to the blonde wife. Interestingly, Hitchcock himself was quite explicit about the gender reversal: "The symmetry is the same as in *Shadow of a Doubt*. On one side of the yard you have the Stewart-Kelly couple, with him immobilized by his leg in a cast, while she can move about freely. And on the other side there is a sick woman who's confined to her bed, while the husband comes and goes."[11] Raymond Bellour has shown how in classic cinema a binary opposition between movement and stasis generally works to establish male superiority in classical narrative cinema.[12] In *Rear Window*, however, the *woman* is continually shown to be physically superior to the hero, not only in her physical movements but also in her dominance within the frame: she towers over Jeff in nearly every shot in which they both appear.

Given this emphasis on the woman's mobility, freedom, and power, it seems odd that an astute critic like Mulvey sees in the image of Lisa Freemont only a passive object of the male gaze. Mulvey bases her judgment on the fact that Lisa appears to be "obsessed with dress and style," continually putting herself on visual display for Jeff so that he will notice her and turn his gaze away from the neighbors.[13] (In this respect, the "project" of the film resembles that of *Rebecca*, which also deals with a woman's efforts to get the man she loves to look at her.) It is important, however, not to dismiss out of hand Lisa's professional and personal involvement with fashion but to consider all the ways this involvement *functions* in the narrative. This is no simple matter. For if, on the one hand, woman's concern with fashion quite obviously serves patriarchal interests, on the other hand, this very concern is often denigrated and ridiculed by men (as it is by Jeff throughout the film)—thus putting women in a familiar double bind by which they are first assigned a restricted place in patriarchy and then condemned for occupying it. For feminist criticism to ignore the full complexity of woman's contradictory situation is to risk acquiescing in masculine contempt for female activities. In *A Room of One's Own,* Virginia Woolf suggested that a necessary, if not sufficient, feminist strategy must be to reclaim and revalue women's actual experience under patriarchy. The example Woolf gives of the double literary standard operating against this experience is telling, and relevant to our discussion here: "Speaking crudely, football and sport are important, the worship of fashion, the buying of clothes trivial, and these values are inevitably transferred from life to fiction."[14] Certainly these two sets of values are counterpoised in the fiction of *Rear Window* (Jeff has, after all, broken his leg at a *sporting* event, where he stepped in front of an oncoming race car to get a spectacular photograph) and are the source of the couple's quarrels. Jeff dwells on the hardships of his manly life style and belittles Lisa's work when she enthusiastically describes her day to him. In the film, then, "fashion" is far from representing woman's unproblematic assimilation to the patriarchal system, but functions to some extent as a signifier of feminine desire and female sexual difference.

Throughout the film, Lisa's exquisite costumes give her the appearance of an alien presence in Jeff's milieu, more strange and marvelous than the various exotic wonders he has encountered in his travels—a strangeness that is fascinating and threatening at the same time. The threat becomes especially evident in the sequence in which Lisa boldly acts on her desire for Jeff and comes to spend the night with him. Significantly, this is the night when she becomes convinced of the truth of Thorwald's guilt. Jeff has just observed Thorwald talking on the phone and sorting through some jewelry, which includes a wedding ring, in his wife's purse. In Hitchcock's films, women's purses (and their jewelry) take on a vulgar Freudian significance relating to female sexuality and to men's attempts to investigate it. One might think, for example, of the purse in the opening close-up shot of *Marnie* (1964) that contains Marnie's "identity" cards and the booty of her theft from patriarchy. In *Rear Window*, Lisa concludes that Mrs. Thorwald *must* have been murdered rather than, as Tom Doyle believes, sent on a trip because no woman would leave behind her favorite purse (to say nothing of her wedding ring). As she muses, Lisa picks up her own designer purse, which we discover is a kind of "trick" purse; it is really a tiny suitcase, and in one of her many lines that sound like sexual double entendres (this one unwittingly echoing the Freudian notion of male and female sexuality, but reversing their values since it takes the latter as the standard), she says, "I'll bet *yours* isn't this small." When she opens the case, an elaborate and expensive negligee comes tumbling out, along with a pair of lovely slippers. The purse connects Lisa to the victimized woman, as does the negligee, since the invalid Mrs. Thorwald was always seen wearing a nightgown; but it also, importantly, connects her to the criminal, Lars Thorwald, and so is an overdetermined image like the images in the Freudian dreamwork. Thus, when Tom Doyle comes to Jeff's apartment later in the evening, he keeps casting meaningful glances at the nightgown as if it were an incriminating object; when Jeff asks why Thorwald didn't tell his landlord where he was going, Doyle looks at the suitcase and asks pointedly, "Do you tell *your* landlord everything?" After Doyle has gone, Lisa picks up the suitcase, offering Jeff a "preview of coming attractions," and as she goes into the bathroom to change, she asks, "Do you think Mr. Doyle thought I stole this case?"

Lisa's aggressive sexuality, which is thus humorously labelled "criminal," would seem to provoke in Jeff and the male spectator a retaliatory aggression that finds an outlet in Thorwald's acts of murder and dismemberment. The interpretation of *Rear Window* which critics like Robin Wood take to be primary—that Lars Thorwald's murder of his wife enacts a wish on the part of Jeff to be rid of Lisa—is persuasive as far as it goes, but this wish may further be analyzed as a response to the male fear of impotence and lack. Jeff's impairment—his helplessness, passivity, and invalidism—impel him to construct a story that, in the words of Kaja Silverman (describing the male's psychic trajectory), attempts to "resituate ... loss at the level of the female anatomy, thereby restoring to the [male] an imaginary wholeness."[15] Hence the fantasy of female dismemberment that pervades the film: not only are there many gruesome jokes about Lars Thorwald's cutting up his wife's body, but Jeff also names the women across the way according to body parts: Miss Lonelyhearts and Miss Torso—yet another decapitated woman.[16]

This response is a psychic consequence of Jeff's placement at the mirror stage of development, a placement that, as critics like to point out, makes him very much like Christian Metz's cinematic spectator, who occupies a transcendent, godlike position in relation to the screen.[17] To some extent, however, this analogy between the windows across the way and the cinema screen is misleading, since it is the very *difference* between the world observed by Jeff and the larger-than-life-world of most films that accounts for the strong effect of transcendence evoked by *Rear Window*. For Jeff's world is a miniature one, like a dollhouse—a world, as Susan Stewart writes, "of inversion [wherein] contamination and crudeness are controlled ... by an absolute manipulation of space and time."[18] "Resembling other fantasy structures, ... even sleep, the miniature," according to Stewart, "tends toward tableau rather than narrative" and "is against speech, particularly as speech reveals an inner dialectical, or dialogic, nature . ... All senses are reduced to the visual, a sense which in its transcendence remains ironically and tragically remote" (pp. 66–67).[19] It is significant that in *Rear Window* only little snatches of conversation may be heard across the way; generally the events proceed mutely, with diegetic noises and music filling the soundtrack (one song even proclaims the primacy of the visual: Bing Crosby's "To See You is to Love You," playing, ironically, while Miss Lonelyhearts entertains a phantom lover). Moreover, the tableau-like spaces of the microscreens across the way find their temporal equivalent in the device of the fade, which punctuates the film, likewise creating a sense of a sealed-off fantasy world impervious to the dialogic, "contaminated" world of lived experience.

Just as the cinema, in its resemblance to the mirror at the mirror stage, offers the viewer an image of wholeness and plenitude, so too does the dollhouse world of the apartment buildings Jeff watches. In fact, one of the reasons the miniature is so appealing is that it suggests completeness and "perfection," as in the description of Tom Thumb quoted by Stewart: "No misshapen limbs, no contorted features were there, but all was sweet and beautiful" (p. 46; unlike, say, Gulliver's ugly Brobdingnagians, whose every imperfection is magnified a hundredfold). But just as this passage must raise the specter of physical mutilation in order to banish it, the mirror phase—the phase at which the child first "anticipates ... the apprehension and mastery of its bodily unity"—evokes retroactively in the child a phantasy of "*the-body-in-pieces.*"[20] This fantasy, according to Lacan, corresponds to the autoerotic stage preceding the formation of the ego (precisely the stage evoked by the "quietly masturbatory" image of the "mutilated" Jeff at the film's opening).[21] On the one hand, then, there is the anticipation of bodily "perfection" and unity which is, importantly, first promised by the body of the woman; on the other hand, the fantasy of dismemberment, a fantasy that gets disavowed by projecting it onto the body of the woman, who, in an interpretation which reverses the state of affairs the male child most fears, eventually comes to be perceived as castrated, mutilated, "imperfect."

Similarly, Jeff's interpretation of the events he sees across the way—his piecing together the fragments of evidence he observes in the Thorwald apartment into a coherent narrative—is designed to reverse the situation in his own apartment, to invalidate the female and assure his own control and dominance. It is not enough, however, for him to construct an interpretation that victimizes woman; for patriarchal interpretations to work, they require her assent: man's conviction must become woman's conviction—in a double sense. Those critics who emphasize the film's restriction of point of view to the male character neglect the fact that it increasingly stresses a *dual* point of view, with the reverse shots finding *both* Jeff and Lisa intently staring out the window at the neighbors across the way. It seems possible, then, to consider Lisa as a representative of the *female* spectator at the cinema. And through her, we can ask if it is true that the female spectator simply acquiesces in the male's view or if, on the contrary, her relationship to the spectacle and the narrative is different from his?

From the outset, Lisa is less interested than Jeff in spying on the neighbors and adopting a transcendent and controlling relation to the texts of their lives; rather, she relates to the "characters" through empathy and identification. Early in the film, Jeff jokingly points out a similarity between her apartment and that of Miss Torso, who at the time is seen entertaining several men. Jeff says, "she's like a queen bee with her pick of the drones," to which Lisa responds, "I'd say she's doing a woman's hardest job—juggling wolves." Miss Torso accompanies one of the men onto the balcony, where she kisses him briefly and tries to go back inside while he attempts to restrain her. Jeff says, "she sure picked the most prosperous looking one," and Lisa disparages this notion, claiming, "she's not in love with *him*—or with any of them for that matter." When Jeff asks her how she can be so certain, she replies, "you *said* it resembled my apartment didn't you?" Later, the same man forces himself on Miss Torso, who has to fight him off, and still later—at the end of the film—Miss Torso's true love, Stanley, will come to visit her. Thus, despite critics' emphasis on the film's limited point of view, Lisa and Jeff have very *different* interpretations about the woman's desire in this scene fraught with erotic and violent potential, and it is *Lisa's* interpretation, arrived at through identification, that is ultimately validated.

Whereas Jeff sees Miss Torso as "queen bee," Lisa significantly changes the metaphor: Miss Torso is prey to "wolves." In fact, Lisa's increasing absorption in Jeff's story, her fascination with his murderous misogynist tale, is accompanied by a corresponding discovery of women's victimization at the hands of men. At one point in the film, Lisa can be seen staring even more intently than Jeff: that is, when Miss Lonelyhearts picks up a young man at a bar and brings him home, only to be assaulted by him. As Lisa stares and Jeff looks away in some embarrassment, the song "Mona Lisa" is heard, sung by drunken revelers at the musician's party. The title of the song suggests an important link between the two women ("is it only cause you're *lonely*, Mona *Lisa*"), and between the male fantasies that are projected onto woman ("Mona Lisa, Mona

Lisa, men have named you"; and "many dreams have been brought to your doorstep") and the brutal reality of male violence to which women are frequently subjected.

Of course, the most brutal act of all is Thorwald's butchering of his wife's body—an act devoutly desired by Jeff—and later, by Lisa herself. At one level, *Rear Window* may be seen as a parable of the dangers involved for women of becoming invested in male stories and male interpretations. Or perhaps we should say "overinvested"—unable, as Mary Ann Doane maintains, to adopt, as men do, the appropriate, voyeuristic distance from the text.[22] Rather, women supposedly "enter into" films so thoroughly that they tend to confuse the very boundary between fantasy and reality—like Lisa crossing over and merging into the "screen" opposite Jeff's window. This merger is a logical extension of her ready identification with the victimized woman, an identification that actually leads to the solution of the crime. Lisa is able to provide the missing evidence because she claims a special knowledge of women that men lack: the knowledge, in this case, that no woman would go on a trip and leave behind her purse and her wedding ring. Lisa appeals to the authority of Stella, asking her if she would ever go somewhere without her ring, and Stella replies, "They'd have to cut off my finger."

Embarking on a search for this incriminating ring, Lisa becomes trapped in Thorwald's apartment when he returns unobserved by Stella and Jeff, who have been preoccupied by the sight of Miss Lonelyhearts about to kill herself. Jeff alerts the police and then watches in agonized helplessness as Lisa is flung about the room by Thorwald. The police arrive in time to prevent another woman from being cut up, and as Lisa stands with her back to the screen—caught, like so many Hitchcock heroines, between the criminal and the legal authorities—she points to the wedding ring on her finger. Francois Truffaut has admired this touch:

> One of the things I enjoyed in the film was the dual significance of that wedding ring. Grace Kelly wants to get married but James Stewart doesn't see it that way. She breaks into the killer's apartment to search for evidence and she finds the wedding ring. She puts it on her finger and waves her hand behind her back so that James Stewart, looking over from the other side of the yard with his spyglasses, can see it. To Grace Kelly, that ring is a double victory; not only is it the evidence she was looking for, but who knows, it may inspire Stewart to propose to her. After all, she's already got the ring.[23]

Thus speaks the male critic, who has habitually considered the film to be a reflection on marriage from the man's point of view. A female spectator of *Rear Window* may, however, use her special knowledge of women and their position in patriarchy to see another kind of significance in the ring; to the woman identifying, like Lisa herself, with the female protagonist of the story, the episode may be read as pointing up the victimization of women by men. Just as Miss Lonelyhearts, pictured right below Lisa in a kind of "split screen" effect, has gone looking for a little companionship and romance and ended up nearly being raped, so Lisa's ardent desire for marriage leads straight to a symbolic wedding with a wife-murderer. For so many women in Hitchcock—and this is the point of his continual reworking of the "female Gothic"—"wedlock is deadlock" indeed.[24]

But it is not only the female spectator who is bound to identify with Lisa at this climactic moment in the story—the moment which seems actually to be the point of the film. Jeff himself—and, by extension, the male film viewer—is forced to identify with the woman and to become aware of his *own* passivity and helplessness in relation to the events unfolding before his eyes. Thus, all Jeff's efforts to repudiate the feminine identification the film originally sets up (Jeff and Anna Thorwald as mirror images) end in resounding failure, and he is forced to be, in turn, the victim *of Hitchcock's* cinematic manipulations of space and time. In a discussion with Truffaut about his theory of suspense, Hitchcock uses this scene with Grace Kelly as his chief example of how to create "the public's identification" with an endangered person, even when that person is an unlikable "snooper." "Of course," he explains, "when the character is attractive, as for instance Grace Kelly in *Rear Window,* the public's emotion is greatly intensified" (p. 73). The implication here is that in scenes of suspense, which in Hitchcock films, as in other thrillers, usually take woman as their object as well as their subject, our identification is generally with the imperiled woman. In this respect, we do in fact all become masochists at the cinema—and it is extremely interesting to note that Theodor Reik considered suspense to be a major factor in masochistic fantasies.[25]

Suspense, Truffaut has claimed, "is simply the dramatization of a film's narrative material, or, if you will, the most intense presentation possible of dramatic situations"; suspense is not "a minor form of the spectacle," but *"the spectacle in itself"* (p. 15). Granted this equivalence between suspense and *"the* spectacle," *the* narrative, might we not then say that spectatorship and "narrativity" are themselves "feminine" (to the male psyche) in that they place the spectator in a passive position and in a submissive relation to the text? Robert Scholes has observed that "narrativity"—the "process by which a perceiver actively constructs a story from the fictional data provided by any narrative medium,"[26] (the process, that is, which is inscribed in *Rear Window* through the character of Jeff)—is a situation of "licensed and benign paranoia" in that "it assumes a purposefulness in the activities of narration which, if it existed in the world, would be truly destructive of individuality and personality as we know them" (p. 396).[27] Narrativity involves, in Scholes' words, a "quality of submission and abandon" (we may recall the paranoid Dr. Schreber's attitude of "voluptuousness" toward God's grand narrative, which featured a plot to impregnate the feminized doctor). This quality once noted by Scholes leads him to call for stories which reward the "most energetic and rigorous kinds of narrativity" as a means of exercising control over the text that seeks to manipulate and seduce its audience (p. 397). Of course, it is precisely Jeff's suspicion that there is a "purposefulness" to the activities across the way that impels him to adopt an "energetic and rigorous"—i.e., controlling, transcendent, and, above all, *"masculine"*—narrativity.

At this moment in the film the camera traces a triangular trajectory from Jeff's gaze at the ring to Thorwald, who sees the ring and then looks up at Jeff, returning the gaze for the first time. And then Thorwald proceeds to complete the "feminization" process by crossing over to Jeff's apartment and placing Jeff in the role previously played by Mrs. Thorwald and then by Lisa—that of victim to male violence. Jeff's "distancing" techniques, of course, no longer work, and the flashing bulbs only manage to slow Thorwald down a bit. Like Lisa, Jeff finally becomes a participant in his story, though *his* identification with the female character is involuntary, imposed on him by Thorwald, whose visit comes like the return of the repressed.

Although Jeff's interpretation of the Thorwald story has been validated by the end of the film, Jeff himself remains *invalided,* ending up with *two* broken legs, the body less "perfect" than ever, while Lisa, lounging on the bed, has become the mirror image of the man—dressed in masculine clothes and reading a book of male adventure. No longer representing sexual difference, nominating herself and speaking her own desire, Lisa is now spoken *by* the male artist—by the musician, whose completed song "Lisa" plays on the soundtrack ("men have named you," indeed), and ultimately by Hitchcock himself, who earlier made his appearance in the musician's apartment. More clearly than most, the film's ending and its "narrative image" of Lisa in masculine drag[28] reveals the way in which acceptable femininity is a construct of male narcissistic desire, despite Freud's claim that women tend to be more narcissistic than men, who supposedly possess a greater capacity for object love.[29] The film has consistently shown the opposite state of affairs to be the case, and in particular has revealed Jeff to be unable to care for Lisa except insofar as she affirms and mirrors him: significantly, he becomes erotically attracted to her only when she begins to corroborate his interpretation of the world around him (the first time he looks at her with real desire is not, as Mulvey claims, when she goes into the Thorwald apartment and becomes the object of his voyeurism, but when she begins to supply arguments in favor of his version of events).

One of the most highly reflexive of films, *Rear Window* indicates that what Jean-Louis Baudry has argued to be characteristic of the cinematic apparatus as a whole—and in particular of *projection*—is also true at the level of narrative, which functions as masculine fantasy *projected* onto the body of woman. Baudry maintains that because film projection depends on negation of the individual image as such "we could say that film … lives on the denial of difference: the difference is necessary for it to live, but it lives on its negation."[30]

Similarly, much narrative cinema negates the *sexual* difference that nevertheless sustains it—negates it in the dual sense of transforming women into Woman and Woman into man's mirror. (Thus Baudry's analogy between cinema and woman is more revealing than he seems to know: speaking of our tendency to "go to movies before deciding which film we want to see," Baudry writes that cinéphiles "seem just as blind in their passion as those lovers who imagine they love a woman because of her qualities or because of her beauty. They need good movies, but most of all, to rationalize their need for cinema."[31] Any woman, like any movie, will do to fulfill man's "need." Put a paper bag over their heads and all women are like Miss Torso or the headless "Hunger" sculpture of the female artist in Jeff's courtyard, both of whom function, like the cinematic apparatus itself, to displace male fears of fragmentation. "What might one say," Baudry asks, "of the function of the head in this captivation [of the spectator at the movies]: it suffices to recall that for Bataille materialism makes itself headless—like a wound that bleeds and thus transfuses."[32])

That "difference is necessary" for cinema to live and therefore can never be destroyed, but only continually negated, is implied by the ending of *Rear Window*. Jeff is once again asleep, in the same position as he was at the film's opening, and Lisa, after assuring herself that he is *not* watching her (in contrast to former times when she had worked so hard to attract his gaze), puts away his book and picks up her own magazine. As important as this gesture is, even more important is the fact that the film gives her the last look. This is, after all, the conclusion of a movie that all critics agree is about the power the man attempts to wield through exercising the gaze. We are left with the suspicion (a preview, perhaps, of coming attractions) that while men sleep and dream their dreams of omnipotence over a safely reduced world, women are not where they appear to be, locked into male "views" of them, imprisoned in their master's dollhouse.

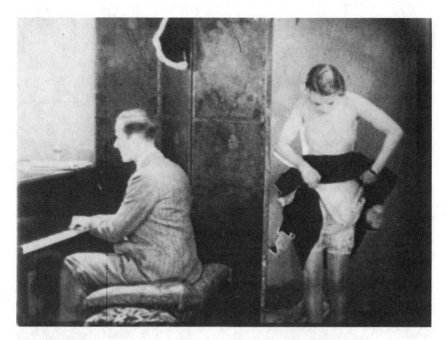

1. Crewe and Alice.

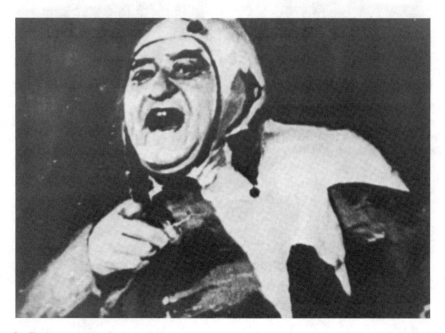

2. The jester.

*Blackmail:* an elaborate joke on woman.

3.   Fane in *Murder!*

In Hitchcock films man is continually haunted by his similitude to woman—"by the fear of becoming like his sexual other."

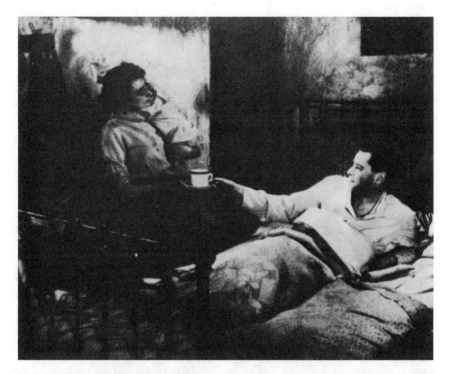

**4.** Sir John Menier in *Murder!*

**Domestic space.**

**5.** Mrs. Danvers and the "second Mrs. de Winter."

*Rebecca* **as a female oedipal drama.**

**6.** Mrs. Danvers and the "second Mrs. de Winter."

**Mrs. Danvers wills the heroine to substitute her body for the body of Rebecca.**

7. Alicia and Devlin.

In *Notorious* spectatorship is a "shady," morally dubious activity.

8. Alicia and Devlin.

If Alicia appears to be the perfect masochist, Devlin appears to be the perfect sadist—stern, remote, and punishing.

**9.** Mrs. Sebastian, Alicia, and Alex.

**Alicia's "purification."**

# 6
# Femininity by Design
## *Vertigo*

Masochism is characterized as a species of vertigo, vertigo not before a precipice of rock and earth but before the abyss of the Other's subjectivity.

Jean-Paul Sartre, *Being and Nothingness*

In criticism of *Vertigo* (1958), as in that of *Rear Window*, one repeatedly encounters the assertion that "the spectator constructed by the film is clearly male."[1] My analyses of Hitchcock have in part been meant to demonstrate that this male spectator is as much "deconstructed" as constructed by the films, which reveal a fascination with femininity that throws masculine identity into question and crisis. This fascination opens a space for the female spectator of the films, providing for a more complicated relation to the texts than has generally been allowed in contemporary film criticism. As I hope to have made clear by now, the questions relating to spectatorship and identification, despite the difficult theoretical language in which they are often couched, have often been posed too simply. Take, for example, Mulvey's contention that *Vertigo*, like all narrative films, is "cut to the measure of male desire" because it is from the male point of view: "In *Vertigo*, subjective camera predominates. Apart from one flashback from Judy's point of view, the narrative is woven around what Scottie sees or fails to see."[2] What Mulvey dismisses as an aberration, an exceptional instance that proves the rule (of Hollywood cinema as male cinema), has been seen by at least one critic—quite rightly, I think—as a privileged moment, the flashback producing "a spectator position painfully split between Scotty and Judy for the rest of the film."[3] Thus identification is, in the words of Robin Wood, "severely disturbed, made problematic."[4] My analysis will suggest, however, that identification is "severely disturbed" long before this moment and that the film may indeed be taken as a kind of "limit text" in its treatment of the problematics of identification first introduced in the film *Rebecca*.[5]

Vertigo begins with the credits shot over an extreme close-up of a woman's face; spiral shaped figures emerge from her eye and form themselves into the names of the credits, and then the camera moves directly into the eye as the spirals continue to shape themselves into words. At the end of the sequence, the camera returns to the eye and the final credit emerges from it: "Directed by Alfred Hitchcock." Immediately, we are placed into a state of anxiety: a man is being chased across some rooftops in San Francisco by two men, one in police uniform and the other—the Jimmy Stewart character, Scottie Ferguson—in plain clothes. In a leap from one building to another, Scottie loses his footing and winds up hanging precariously from the edge. The man in uniform abandons his pursuit to help Scottie but slips and falls; the sequence ends with Scottie clinging for his life to the gutter of the roof.

After the fade, Scottie is shown in the apartment of Midge (Barbara Bel Geddes), a woman to whom he was once briefly engaged. One of the more benign of Hitchcock's many bespectacled female characters, Midge is a "motherly" type, as the film continually emphasizes, too prosaic for Scottie's romantic imagination. Scottie explains that he has quit the police force because he is suffering from vertigo as a result of his recent traumatic experience. He says he has received a message from an old schoolmate of theirs, Gavin Elster (Tom Helmore), who, when Scottie visits him, says that he wants Scottie to follow his wife to find out why she has been behaving peculiarly. Scottie at first resists the idea of doing detective work, but soon finds himself lured into it by the mystery of Elster's beautiful wife, Madeleine (Kim Novak), with whom he rapidly becomes obsessed. In his investigation of the woman, he follows her around San Francisco and learns that she appears to be "possessed" by an ancestor from the past, Carlotta Valdez, whose portrait hangs in the art gallery in the Palace of the Legion of Honor. In order to find out more about this mysterious figure, Scottie asks Midge to take him to Pop Liebl (Konstantine Shayne), a bookstore owner conversant with San Francisco lore. According to Pop Liebl, Carlotta Valdez was the beautiful mistress of a wealthy and influential man who at length wearied of her and "threw her away," keeping their child. "A man could do that in those days," says Pop Liebl reflectively. "They had the power, and the freedom." The woman pined away for her lost child, becoming first "the sad Carlotta," and then at length "the mad Carlotta," stopping strangers in the street to ask, "Have you seen my child?" and eventually committing suicide.

One day, in an apparent suicide attempt, Madeleine jumps into the bay, and Scottie rescues her, brings her to his home, and puts her into his bed. Soon after, they go "wandering" together, and Scottie learns of Madeleine's hallucinations of death, her vision of walking down a long corridor that ends with the sight of an open grave. He becomes desperate to solve the mystery, and when she visits him one night to tell of a recurring dream she has had of a Spanish mission where she believes she lived as a child, he joyfully tells her that her dream has a basis in reality. The next day he takes her to the mission in order to convince her that she has been to the place before. She, however, becomes distraught and runs into the tower. He tries to follow her up the stairs, but his vertigo prevents him from reaching her before she falls.

After an inquest, which reaches a verdict of suicide, Scottie is placed in an asylum where Midge attempts to get him to respond by playing Mozart records, but Scottie is inconsolable. Later we see him walking the streets, becoming upset when he sees Madeleine's car, which has been sold, and mistaking various women for Madeleine. Then he spots a woman who looks uncannily like Madeleine and follows her to her hotel. At first the woman is annoyed at being importuned by a stranger, but then she relents and allows him to come inside her room, where she shows him her identity cards to persuade him that she really is Judy Barton from Salina, Kansas, rather than the woman he seems to be mistaking her for. When he leaves, the camera for the first time deserts Scottie and stays with the woman. A flashback and a letter Judy writes and then tears up tell the whole story: Scottie was part of Gavin Elster's plan to murder his wife, Madeleine. Elster had made up Judy, his mistress, to look like his wife, in order to get Scottie to witness Madeleine's "suicide." Knowing that Scottie's vertigo would prevent him from reaching the top of the mission tower Elster had waited that day for Judy to ascend the stairs and then had flung his own wife from the roof.

Out of love for Scottie Judy decides not to run away, but to stay and try to make him love her for herself. He, however, becomes obsessed with recreating Madeleine, and he dresses Judy in the same clothes and shoes Madeleine had worn and even has her hair dyed and restyled. One night at her hotel room, while they are preparing to go out for dinner, Judy puts on the necklace worn by Carlotta in the portrait and Scottie suddenly understands everything. He forces Judy to go back with him to the mission and to climb the stairs while he relates the events of Madeleine's death. Cured at last of his vertigo, he makes it to the top and the panic-stricken Judy tries to convince him that they can still go on together. As they begin to embrace, a dark shape suddenly looms up at the top of the stairs and Judy screams at this apparition—which turns out to be a nun—and falls from the tower. The last shot of the film shows Scottie emerging from the arched door of the tower onto the roof as he looks blankly downward, arms slightly extended.

If in *Rear Window* the hero continually expresses a masculine contempt for the feminine world of fashion (while the film itself exhibits and elicits a near obsessional interest in what Grace Kelly is wearing), this is hardly the case with *Vertigo's* hero, Scottie.[6] In attempting to re-create Judy as Madeleine, Scottie displays the most minute knowledge of women's clothing, to the point where the saleswoman twice remarks on how well the gentleman knows what he wants. To reinvoke the metaphor central to my analysis of *Rear Window*, the female character, Madeleine/Judy, is like a living doll whom the hero strips and changes and makes over according to his ideal image.

Indeed, it might be said that the film's preoccupation with female clothing borders on the perverse. Midge's job as a designer in the female "underwear business" has gone largely unremarked in criticism of *Vertigo*, perhaps because it is felt to be unworthy of the film's great theme of love and death, a theme which places it in the tradition of Tristan and Isolde. (In fact, critics tend to slight all those parodic elements of the film which work against the serious- ness of the "love theme," and in this they reveal themselves to be like Scottie, who rejects Midge's demystificatory act of painting her own face into the Car- lotta portrait as "not funny.") In the early scene in Midge's apartment she is shown sketching a brassiere that is prominently suspended in the air from wires. Scottie is attempting to balance a cane in his palm, and as it falls he utters an exclamation of pain and then speaks his first line in the film: "It's this darned corset—it binds." Midge replies, "No three-way stretch? How very unchic." From the outset, then, with his failure to perform his proper role in relation to the Symbolic order and the law, Scottie is placed in the same position of enforced passivity as L.B. Jeffries, a position that the film explicitly links to femininity and associates with unfreedom: "Midge," Scottie asks a moment later, "do you suppose many men wear corsets?" He is elated because tomorrow is "the big day" when "the corset comes off" and he will be a "free man."

Shortly thereafter he spots the brassiere, walks up to it and points to it with his cane. "What's this doohickey?" he asks, and Midge answers, "It's a brassiere; you know about such things, you're a big boy now." And she pro- ceeds to describe it as the latest thing in "revolutionary uplift," explaining that it was designed by an aircraft engineer down the peninsula, who built it on the "principle of the cantilever bridge." Now, given the prominence in the film's *mise-en-scène* of high places—the Golden Gate Bridge, for example—and given the association of these places with Scottie's vertigo,[7] it seems clear that the film is humorously linking his condition to femininity, a relation that later sequences will treat with deadly seriousness. (An association between female- ness and fear of heights may also be found in *North by Northwest* [1959]. Roger O. Thornhill [Cary Grant] claims that Eve (Eva Marie Saint) uses sex "like some people use a fly-swatter," and throughout the film we see him performing a human fly act, hanging over precipices, scaling walls, and clinging, as it were, to nothing as he attempts to gain possession of the woman, who is mistress to the villain.)

It is as if at this early moment in *Vertigo*, the film is humorously suggesting that femininity in our culture is largely a male construct, a male "design," and that this femininity is in fact a matter of external trappings, of roles and mas- querade, without essence. This is an idea that the film will subsequently evoke with horror. For if woman, who is posited as she whom man must know and possess in order to guarantee his truth and his identity, does not exist, then in some important sense he does not exist either, but rather is faced with the pos- sibility of his own nothingness—the nothingness, for example, that is at the heart of Roger O. Thornhill's identity ("What does the 'O' stand for?" Eve asks, and he answers, "Nothing"). In this respect, it is possible to see the film's great theme of romantic love as something of a ruse, a red herring—and Hitchcock, of course, was master of the red herring. Hélène Cixous writes, "the spirit of male/female relationships … isn't normally revealed, because what is normally revealed is actually a decoy … all those words about love, etc. All that is always just a cover for hatred nourished by the fear of death: woman, for man, is death."[8] Certainly these words have a strong resonance in relation to *Vertigo*, since the source of the man's fascination with the woman is her own fascination with death, with the gaping abyss, which she hallucinates as her open grave and which is imaged continually in the film in its many arch-shaped forms of church, museum, cemeteries, mission.

But for this moment at least, the film is lighthearted; and the "hatred nourished by fear" will be suppressed until later in the film. Until that point the film will only be concerned to arouse in us as spectators a curiosity about and desire for the woman as idealized object of romantic love. When Scottie goes to see Gavin Elster, a shipbuilding magnate from the east, Elster articulates a longing for the past which will eventually be Scottie's own, and he speaks of the old San Francisco as a place where men had "freedom" and "power," terms that Pop Liebl will later echo. As in *Marnie,* with which *Vertigo* in some ways invites comparison, the film first presents the woman as object in a dialogue between men, creating the triangle on which desire so frequently depends. Then, as in *Marnie,* the camera itself takes over the enunciation: in Ernie's Restaurant it first shows Scottie sitting at a bar and then detaches itself from his searching gaze to conduct its own search for the woman through the restaurant.[9] Finally, it comes to rest in a long shot of a woman seated with Elster at a table, with her back to the camera. Romantic music emerges slowly on the soundtrack, and the camera moves slightly forward. It cuts back to Scottie looking and then to a point of view shot of Madeleine, who gets up from her chair and walks into a close-up shot of her profile. Only much later will we be able to see her entire face and only at that time will we get to hear her speak; for much of the first part of the film she will be the mute, only half-seen object of man's romantic quest: the eternal feminine.

When Scottie starts to follow Madeleine in her car, she leads him in a downward spiral—a typical trajectory of Hitchcock heroines—to a back alley, gets out of her car and disappears into a building. Scottie follows her through a dark back room, with the camera insistently wedding our subjectivity to his through point of view shots. Then the door is slowly opened in a very striking point of view shot, the romantic strains of the love theme again come on the soundtrack, and a long shot reveals Madeleine standing with her back to the camera amid an array of flowers and bathed in soft light. The *mise-en-scène* at once conveys the woman's ideality and links her to death, the flowers adding a distinctly funereal touch. Madeleine turns around and comes toward the camera, and with the cut we expect the reverse shot to show that, as is usual in classical cinema, the man is in visual possession of the woman. Quite startlingly, however, it turns out that the door has a mirror attached to it, so this shot shows both Scottie, as he looks at Madeleine, *and* Madeleine's mirror image. Donald Spoto says of this shot, "by implication he (and we) may be seen as her reflection."[10] Spoto, however, does not pause to note the extraordinary significance of this observation, which suggests that identification is "disturbed, made problematic" *at the very outset* of Scottie's investigation—just as we saw his identity as a man thrown into doubt with his very first words. The shot is in many ways prophetic: despite all his attempts to gain control over Madeleine, Scottie will find himself repeatedly thrown back into an identification, a mirroring relationship, with her and her desires, will be unable to master the woman the way Gavin Elster and Carlotta's paramour are able to do.

It is as if he were continually confronted with the fact that woman's uncanny otherness has some relation to himself, that he resembles her in ways intolerable to contemplate—intolerable because this resemblance throws into question his own fullness of being. Sarah Kofman puts it this way: "men's fascination with [the] eternal feminine is nothing but fascination with their own double, and the feeling of uncanniness, *Unheimlichkeit,* that men experience is the same as what one feels in the face of any double, any ghost, in the face of the abrupt reappearance of what one thought had been overcome or lost forever."[11] These words poetically capture the spirit of *Vertigo,* the way in which Woman keeps uncannily returning, keeps reminding man of what he in turn keeps trying to overcome, to master. And it captures as well the "ghostliness" of the figure of woman in *Vertigo* (Hitchcock's famous discussion of the theme of necrophilia notwithstanding), as she is photographed through diffusion filters, shot in soft light, dressed in a white coat, and accompanied by haunting music on the soundtrack.

The uncanniness of woman for man is also rendered in a lengthy dreamlike sequence in the middle of the film after Madeleine has been at Scottie's house. He is following her in his car, and she leads him on an especially circuitous route, while the camera, continually cutting back to his face, emphasizes his increasing perplexity. To his great surprise and puzzlement, they wind up back at his house, where she has come to deliver a note. Scottie's pursuit of the mysterious other, then, inevitably takes him to his own home, just as Freud has shown that the uncanny, the *unheimlich,* is precisely the "homelike," the familiar which has been made strange through repression.[12]

As for Madeleine, she herself becomes the very figure of identification, which here is realized in its most extreme and threatening form in the idea of possession. Hitchcock draws once again on the du Maurier plot, the Gothic plot he disparaged in his discussion with Truffaut, to tell Madeleine's story, a story of a woman who appears to be so obsessed with a female ancestor that she actually *becomes* that other woman from the past and finds herself compelled to live out the latter's tragic fate. It is ironic that the woman whose initials are M.E. (like those of Marnie Edgar) is a person with no identity, not only because Madeleine's persona has been made up by Elster in imitation of his wife, whom he murders, but also because Madeleine continually merges into the personality of Carlotta Valdez, who has committed suicide and who, we are led to believe, attempts to repeat the act through Madeleine (so much is death, and woman's association with death, overdetermined in this film). Madeleine represents the lost child whom "the mad Carlotta" had sought everywhere to no avail. A powerless and pitiful figure when she was alive, Carlotta becomes on her death a figure of terror and omnipotence. In contra-distinction to the Lacanian scenario, according to which the dead *father* is endowed with an omnipotence that "real" fathers lack, Hitchcock presents us (not for the first or the last time), with the imago of a mother who assumes unlimited power in death.[13] Dispossessed in life, discarded by her lover, who also takes their child, the dead woman wields this new power in acts of psychic possession, thereby avenging her losses on patriarchy.

Scottie becomes progressively absorbed in Madeleine's situation, and we as spectators are made to share in his absorption, as the camera continually works to draw us into a closer and closer identification with the woman and her story. When Scottie enters the museum where Madeleine sits before the portrait in a hypnotic trance, the camera shows a close-up of the bouquet placed beside Madeleine, then tilts up and tracks forward into a close-up of the bouquet in the portrait. A similar movement begins with a shot of the spiral-shaped knot of hair at the back of her head, and then the camera tracks into a close-up of Carlotta's hair. These constant forward tracking shots do more than simply trace Scottie's observations; in their closeness and intensity they actually participate in his desire, which, paradoxically, is a desire to merge with a woman who in some sense doesn't exist—a desire, then, that points to self-annihilation. As a result of this threat posed by the figure of woman before the portrait, Scottie is driven to break the spell she exerts by competing with Carlotta for possession of Madeleine. As Kofman writes, "Because with 'woman' men never know for sure *with whom* they are dealing, they try to overcome her lack of 'proper' nature and propriety by making her their property."[14] When Madeleine jumps into the bay, Scottie rescues her and brings her home, later indicating that by saving her he now has a claim over her: "You know, the Chinese say that once you've saved a person's life, you're responsible for it forever." At one point he kisses her feverishly, insisting, "I've got you now"; during another embrace he urgently declares, "No one possesses you"—no one, the implication is, but himself. The more Scottie finds himself absorbed by this fascinating woman, the more he resorts to a rather brutal interrogation of her in his search for the "key" to her mystery.

At the heart of *Vertigo* lies the lure and the threat of madness. As Scottie desperately searches for the key to Madeleine's strange behavior, she says, "If I'm mad, that would explain everything." He looks horrified, and then pursues her when she runs from him in order to grasp her ever more tightly. It is crucial for Scottie that he convince Madeleine of her sanity so that he can be assured of his own, and thus it is imperative that he make her *recognize* him, force her to turn her inward gaze away from the "mother" and to acknowledge his presence and his supremacy. "Where are you now?" he keeps asking, and she answers, not very convincingly, "Here with you." It might be said that Scottie's project is to reverse the state of affairs at the beginning of their relationship, and from being a reflection of the woman, to use Spoto's observation, he needs to make her a reflection of himself. In an essay on "Women and Madness," Shoshana Felman argues that man needs woman to be his mirror in order to insure "his own self sufficiency as a subject."[15] This requires removing the "mad" woman from the realm of the "supernatural" and the "unreal" to which patriarchal "reason" consigns her. "Woman," says Felman, is "the realistic invisible" (or as I put it in a previous chapter, she is occupant of patriarchy's "blind space"), that which "realism is inherently unable to see" (p. 6).

Scottie's "cure" for Madeleine involves bringing her to the scene of her dream in order to convince her of the "reality" of the place and to force her to remember a previous visit there. Scottie counters his truth—which is the law of representation and verisimilitude—to hers, which appears to masculine "reason" as mad and supernatural. Throughout the film Scottie will be concerned with staging these representations in order to gain mastery over them: at the end, for example, he forces Judy to return to the tower and reenact the occurrences of the day Madeleine supposedly died. But in trying to effect the woman's cure, Scottie only realizes the "tragic outcome ... inscribed ... from the outset in the very logic of representation inherent in the therapeutic project" (Felman, p. 9). The woman will die. The very effort to cure her, which is an effort to get her to mirror man and his desire, to see (his) reason, destroys woman's otherness.

Scottie's failure to cure Madeleine deals a mortal blow to his masculine identity, as the dream that he has shortly after Madeleine's presumed death indicates. The dream begins with a close-up of Scottie's face, over which flashing lights of various colors are superimposed. A cartoon image of Madeleine's bouquet is seen disintegrating and then the camera tracks into an extreme close-up of the necklace in Carlotta's portrait and we see Carlotta come "alive" standing between Elster and Scottie. Scottie's "beheaded" face (castration has been "in the air" since the credit shots[16]) is superimposed over a "vertigo" shot of vertical lines on a purple background, and he walks forward toward an open grave into which the camera descends. Finally, there is a cartoon-like image of Scottie's silhouette falling first toward the red tiles of the mission roof and then into a blinding white light, an image of nothingness, of infinitude. What is most extraordinary about this dream is that Scottie actually *lives out Madeleine's hallucination,* that very hallucination of which he had tried so desperately to cure her, and he *dies Madeleine's death*. His attempts at a cure having failed, he himself is plunged into the "feminine" world of psychic disintegration, madness, and death. Even the form of the dream, which is off-putting to many viewers because it is so "phoney," suggests the failure of the "real" that we have seen to be the stake of Scottie's confrontation with Woman.

Looking for the source of this renewed identification with the woman implied by the dream, we find a clue in Freud's important paper "Mourning and Melancholia." According to Freud, melancholia, the state of inconsolability for the loss of a loved person, differs from mourning in part because the former involves "an extraordinary diminution in [the sufferer's] self-regard, an impoverishment of his ego on a grand scale. In mourning," says Freud, "it is the world which has become poor and empty; in melancholia it is the ego itself."[17] Freud attributes this diminution in self-regard to the fact that the melancholiac internalizes the loved object, who had been the source of some disappointment to the subject and who henceforth becomes the object of severe reproaches which, as a result of internalization, appear to be self-reproaches (it might be said that the judge at the inquest who speaks so harshly of Scottie's "weakness" utters the reproaches that later get internalized). In effect, says Freud, "an *identification* of the ego with the abandoned object" is established. "Thus," he continues, rather poetically, "the shadow of the object fell upon the ego, and the latter could henceforth be judged by a special agency, as though it were an object, the forsaken object" (p. 249).[18] This identification with the lost object that Freud takes to be characteristic of melancholia involves a regression to an earlier narcissistic phase, that same phase evoked in the film in the mirror image of Madeleine at the florist shop. "This substitution of identification for object-love ... represents ... a *regression* from one type of object-choice to original narcissism. [Identification] is a preliminary stage of object-choice, ... the first way—one that is expressed in an ambivalent fashion" (p. 249). The shadow of the object having fallen upon him, Scottie not only identifies with Madeleine in his dream, but becomes caught up in the very madness he had feared in her. In his quest for his lost Madeleine, he becomes like "the mad Carlotta," who had accosted strangers in the street as she desperately sought the child that had been taken from her: after the dream we see Scottie wandering around the city and repeatedly mistaking other women for Madeleine, approaching them only to be bitterly disappointed at his error. Importantly, the film at this point emphatically *discredits* his vision—and by extension, *our* vision—on several occasions. On each of these occasions it sets us up for one of the point of view shots Hitchcock has employed throughout the first part of the film to draw us into Scottie's subjectivity, and then it reveals the sight to have been deceptive. In a way, we experience through Scottie the split that Freud says is characteristic of melancholia: on the one hand we identify with him as before, but the repeated disqualification of his vision makes us wary; we become more judgmental than we had previously been. Further, Scottie's faulty vision provides additional proof that he now occupies a *feminine* position, in that Hitchcock frequently impairs the vision of his female protagonists in one way or another.[19]

Finally, Judy appears walking down the street with some other women. A brunette dressed in a cheap green tight-fitting dress and wearing gaudy makeup, she is not, as Truffaut observes (without, however, recalling the early scene in Midge's apartment), wearing a brassiere.[20] Though we have not yet been apprised of the situation, Judy is the "original" woman, who will soon be remade (for the second time) into the fully fetishized and idealized, "constructed" object of male desire and male "design." The camera lingers on her profile as she bids her friends goodbye, and the romantic music once again is heard on the soundtrack. But it doesn't altogether work. Not only are we wary of this "apparition" because of all the previous faulty point of view shots, but she looks "wrong," a disappointing counterfeit of the beautiful Madeleine. That Woman seems to become at this point in the film a debased version of her former self is not surprising. The melancholiac's disappointment in the love object results, says Freud, in hatred coming to the fore: "the hate comes into operation on [the] substitutive object, abusing it, debasing it, making it suffer and deriving sadistic satisfaction from its suffering" (p. 251). Before this sadism receives complete release, however, Scottie tries to restore the lost object by making Judy over into Madeleine—forcing her to wear the same clothes, shoes and makeup and to change her hair color and style.

But by this time we have been let in on the secret and we know that Judy was a tool of Gavin Elster's nefarious plot to murder his wife. This knowledge makes us much more sympathetic toward the woman, who finds herself continually negated and manipulated by men, and it contributes as well to our increasing tendency to condemn Scottie for having become, in Hitchcock's word, "a maniac."[21] As if to emphasize a shift in interest and point of view, Hitchcock includes a scene in Judy's hotel room, which at the beginning shows her in profile, the camera tracking forward in a shot which resembles the subjective shots of Madeleine that predominated in the first part of the film. By the end of the scene, however, Hitchcock has changed camera positions and placed the camera in front of her while Scottie remains to one side, so that we are made to see a part of her that he in his obsession cannot see. As a result of the expanded sympathetic consciousness Hitchcock arouses in the spectator, we feel the full irony and poignancy of her situation—as when Scottie is begging Judy to let herself be made over and urges, "It can't matter to you." Judy acquiesces, in great anguish, out of love for Scottie.

When the process of makeover is complete, Madeleine emerges, ghostlike, into the room where Scottie awaits her; she walks slowly toward him, and the two embrace in a famous shot in which the camera circles around the couple who, in turn, are placed on an (unseen) revolving pedestal. The romantic music swells and the background, Judy's hotel room, metamorphoses almost imperceptibly into the livery stable of San Juan Bautista. Ironically, the place where Scottie had attempted to cure Madeleine's hallucination by restoring her to the real now returns to signal the triumph of *Scottie's* hallucination over the real.

But "real" women, it seems, are not so easily vanquished, and Judy gives herself away by putting on the necklace worn by Carlotta in the portrait. At this moment Scottie's sadism reaches its peak, for it becomes clear to him that he never was in possession of the woman, that she has always eluded his grasp. He forces her to return to the scene of the crime, his words as he drags her up to the tower making clear what has been at stake for him all along:

> You played the wife very well, Judy. He made you over didn't he? *He* made you over just like *I* made you over. Only better. Not only the clothes and the hair, but the looks and the manner and the words. And those beautiful phony trances. And you jumped into the Bay! I bet you're a wonderful swimmer, aren't you ... aren't you ... *aren't you*! And then what did he do? Did he *train* you? Did he *rehearse* you? Did he tell you exactly what to *do* and what to *say*? You were a very apt pupil, weren't you? You were a very apt pupil! But why did you pick on me? Why *me*? I was the set-up, wasn't I? I was the made-to-order-witness. This is where it happened. And then, you were his girl. What happened to you? Did he ditch you? Oh Judy, with all of his wife's money, and all that freedom and all that power ... and he ditched you.

Scottie's pain results not only—not even primarily—from discovering that Madeleine was a fraud, but from realizing that she had been made up by another man, who "rehearsed" and "trained" her in the same way that Scottie had rehearsed and trained Judy. Just when Scottie had thought himself to be most in control of the woman, to have achieved the "freedom" and "power" that he has been longing for and that the film associates with masculinity, he discovers that he is caught up in repetition, like Judy/Madeleine/Carlotta, repetition which, as Freud has shown, is linked to unfreedom, to masochism, and to death. Scottie must now confront the fact that, like a woman, he was manipulated and used by Gavin Elster, that his plot too had been scripted for him: "You were the victim," writes Judy in the letter she tears up—just as Judy and Carlotta and the real Madeleine Elster are all ultimately victims in the plots of men.

"Some portion of what we men call 'the enigma of woman' may perhaps be derived from [the] expression of bisexuality in women's lives," Freud wrote.[22] This bisexuality is attributable both to the fact that the little girl undergoes a "phallic phase"—an active phase, in contrast to the passivity typically associated with femininity—and that her first love object is the mother, just as is the male's. In order to achieve what Freud called "normal femininity," the female must turn away from her mother and shift her object of desire to the father—a trajectory we have seen is traced in the film *Rebecca*. As I noted in my chapter on that film, however, Freud was forced to recognize how frequently desire for the mother persists throughout the woman's life, affecting her heterosexual relationships as well as her relationships with other women. Woman is thus often caught up in a "double desire," and feminist film theory has tried to draw out the implications of this double desire for a theory of female spectatorship. Speaking of *Rebecca*, for example, Teresa de Lauretis argues that there are "two positionalities of desire that define the female's Oedipal situation."[23] In contrast to those feminists who claim that the situation of woman at the cinema is an either/or situation (either she is a masochist or she is a transvestite), de Lauretis believes that female identification is double: "This manner of identification would uphold both positionalities of desire, both active and passive aims: desire for the other and desire to be desired by the other."[24]

De Lauretis contrasts *Vertigo* unfavorably to *Rebecca* because for all their similarities, in *Vertigo* it is through the male protagonist that we experience events. As I observed at the outset, however, the situation is considerably more complicated. There is first of all the "painful split" in identification between Judy and Scottie opened up by Judy's flashback and sustained throughout the last part of the film. But even before this point, we have seen how one of the major attractions of Scottie to Madeleine is his identification with her, an identification that the film works to elicit in the audience as well: we are identifying with Scottie identifying with Madeleine (who is identifying with Carlotta Valdez). Woman thus becomes the ultimate point of identification for *all* of the film's spectators. Not only is "a double desire" on the part of a female viewer not precluded by this setup, but it is possible to see the film as soliciting a masculine bisexual identification because of the way the male character oscillates between a passive mode and an active mode, between a hypnotic and masochistic fascination with the woman's desire and a sadistic attempt to gain control over her, to possess her. (Hence the aptness of the famous "vertigo shot," the track-out/zoom-forward that so viscerally conveys Scottie's feeling of ambivalence whenever he confronts the depths.) Of course, sadism wins the day, and the woman dies. "To make a dead body of woman," writes Sarah Kofman, speaking of Freud's "killing off" of woman at the end of his essay on "Femininity," "is to try one last time to overcome her enigmatic and ungraspable character, to fix in a definitive and immovable position instability and mobility themselves. ... For woman's deathlike rigidity ... makes it possible to put an end to the perpetual shifting back and forth between masculinity and femininity which constitutes the whole enigma of 'woman.'"[25]

The mother/daughter relationship central to the enigma of bisexuality is presented over and over again in Hitchcock films as the main problem.[26] No doubt this is partly because it signifies that woman never wholly belongs to the patriarchy. But perhaps too it is troublesome because it provides a model of "overidentification" in which the boundaries between self and other become blurred, and desire for and identification with the other are not clearly separable processes. This "boundary confusion" can be intimidating to the male who, unlike the female, appears to achieve his identity through establishing a firm boundary between himself and woman. But *Vertigo* shows just how precarious the boundary can be. As Freud noted in *Mourning and Melancholia*, it is always possible to "regress" to narcissistic identification with the object. And this is so because identification is "*a preliminary stage of object choice.*" Far from being opposed to object love, as Freud at times argued, narcissistic identification is in fact *constitutive* of it, and thus, he here implies, the boundaries between self and (m)other tend to be more fluid for the male than is sometimes supposed.

Hitchcock himself provides us with an illustration of the fluidity of these boundaries in his explanation of how he came to construct *Vertigo* the way he did, in particular of how he came to give away the secret of the film before the end:

> Though Stewart isn't aware of it yet, the viewers already know that Judy isn't just a girl who looks like Madeleine, but that she *is* Madeleine! Everyone around me was against this change; they all felt that the revelation should be saved for the end of the picture. I put myself in the place of a child whose mother is telling him a story. When there's a pause in her narration, the child always says, 'What comes next, Mommy?' Well, I felt that the second part of the novel was written as if nothing came next, whereas in my formula, the little boy, *knowing* that Madeleine and Judy are the same person, would then ask, 'And Stewart doesn't know it, does he? What will he do when he finds out about it?'[27]

Hitchcock here imagines himself in the double role—a bisexual role—of the little boy (the audience) who listens to a story and the mother (the director) who tells it. Interestingly, despite Hitchcock's implication that the focus remains on the Stewart character, this appropriation of the mother's story, her authority, means that Hitchcock defies all expectations to give the *female* point of view, to make us privy to Judy's thoughts and feelings. It may be possible to argue, then, that "Mother wins," that woman's story gets out, though weakened and distorted in the process. However much we may be invited to condemn her as duplicitous in her "double desire," we must also see the way she is used and cast aside or tortured and finally killed off, as man desperately tries to sustain a sense of himself that necessitates the end of woman.

7

# Rituals of Defilement
## *Frenzy*

Food in *Frenzy* is a basic visual metaphor for the devouring abuses of man-against-man.

Donald Spoto, *The Art of Alfred Hitchcock*

Seeing a rotten fruit full of worms, Mair, the Urubu demiurge, exclaimed, "That would make a nice woman!" and straightaway the fruit turned into a woman . ... In a Tacana myth the jaguar decides not to rape an Indian woman after he has caught the smell of her vulva, which seems to him to reek of worm-ridden meat . ... Here again, then, we are dealing with stench and decay which, as has already been established, signify nature, as opposed to culture . ... And woman is everywhere synonymous with nature.

Claude Lévi-Strauss, *The Raw and the Cooked*

Curiosity in an animal is always either sexual or alimentary . ... In knowing, consciousness attracts the object to itself and incorporates it in itself . ... But this movement of dissolution is fixed by the fact that the known remains in the same place, indefinitely absorbed, devoured, and yet indefinitely intact, wholly digested and yet wholly outside, as indigestible as a stone.

Jean-Paul Sartre, *Being and Nothingness*

Having begun with a discussion of Hitchcock's *Blackmail,* this study ends appropriately with *Frenzy* (1972), which is concerned with many of the same issues as the early film. In particular, both films include a rape that has proven to be very problematic to Hitchcock's critics, though for opposite reasons: in *Blackmail,* the difficulty is that *nothing is shown* (only shadows of the characters projected onto the walls), whereas in *Frenzy* too much is shown, nothing is left to the imagination. In the later film, Hitchcock provides the kind of "incontrovertible evidence" of rape that Durgnat had found lacking in *Blackmail* and that enabled him to disqualify the heroine's view of her own experience.

Some critics have looked at the increasing use of graphic violence in Hitchcock films as evidence of a rather sick mind. For example, in his biography of Hitchcock, Donald Spoto has documented Hitchcock's obsession with filming a rape/murder and has condemned the director as something of a dirty old man. The way the biographer tells it, Hitchcock's career can be seen as one long frustrating bout with cinematic impotence until he managed finally to achieve full orgasmic satisfaction with *Frenzy:* "Unable to realize a rape in *No Bail for the Judge* he had hinted at it in *Psycho,* metaphorized it in *The Birds* and, against all advice, included it in *Marnie.* Now at last—encouraged by the new freedom in the movies—his imagination of this sordid crime could be more fully shown in all its horror."[1]

But precisely *because Frenzy* seems to take crimes against women to new lengths, and because it seems to be the culmination of an entire career, a lifetime of obsession, it provides a good occasion for us to reflect back on and draw together some of the themes that have been important in this study. At the same time, I will use this analysis as an occasion to say something about *Psycho* (1960), a film whose impact was such that no subsequent Hitchcock film can be talked about without reference to it. In a way, though, I have never really not been discussing *Psycho*—to my mind, the quintessential horror film.

After an opening sequence showing the discovery of a woman's body floating in the Thames, a necktie around her neck, *Frenzy* dissolves to a shot of the mirror image of the film's hero/antihero, Richard Blaney (Jon Finch), former Squadron Leader of the R.A.F., putting on a necktie exactly like the one used by the strangler. He goes into the bar where he works and has a drink, whereupon the proprietor, Felix Forsythe (Bernard Cribbins), enters and reprimands him for stealing. Blaney claims he was going to pay for the drink and is defended by the waitress, Babs Milligan (Anna Massey). From the altercation that ensues, we are made to understand that Forsythe is motivated by jealousy over the relationship between Blaney and Babs. The scene ends with Blaney's being fired and having to pay back a loan to Forsythe, so that he is left financially strapped.

Blaney runs into a friend, Bob Rusk (Barry Foster), owner of a wholesale fruit market. Bob is exceedingly friendly, offering money, a bunch of grapes, and a tip on a horse. Instead of betting on the horse, however, Blaney spends all his money on drink, and when he learns from Bob (leaning out over his apartment window to introduce his "old Mum") that the horse has actually won, he walks off in a rage, trampling on the grapes as he goes. He pays a visit to his ex-wife, Brenda Blaney (Barbara Leigh-Hunt), owner of a matrimonial agency, and picks a fight with her in her office. After they make up, she invites him to dinner at her club, where Blaney again becomes enraged at the thought of his bad luck in comparison to his wife's success. He apologizes for his temper when he breaks a brandy glass in his hand, and then the two take a cab to her house. Although Blaney clearly expects to spend the night, the next shot shows him sleeping at the Salvation Army, where an old man tries to steal money Brenda has slipped him on the sly.

In the next scene, Bob Rusk, alias Mr. Robinson, enters Brenda's office. He has clearly been here before, and Brenda, nervous as well as contemptuous, tells him that she cannot accommodate his desire for women who will submit to his "peculiarities." In this prolonged scene, Rusk first intimidates, then rapes, and finally strangles Brenda, the camera dwelling on every lurid detail of the latter action. The secretary, Monica Barling (Jean Marsh), returning from lunch, sees Blaney go by and after she discovers her employer's body, assumes that Brenda's former husband has committed the murder. Inspector Oxford (Alex McCowen) and his men from Scotland Yard begin investigating the crime, while Blaney, unaware of what has occurred, takes Babs to the fancy Hotel Coburn. After showing them to their room, the porter recognizes the description of Blaney in a newspaper and alerts the police, but the pair have seen the headlines in the newspaper put under their door and have escaped. They find temporary refuge with one of Dick's R.A.F. comrades, Johnny Porter (Clive Swift), whose wife, Hetty (Billie Whitelaw), is convinced of Blaney's guilt and reacts angrily at being forced to shelter him.

Babs returns to the bar the next day and quits after a quarrel with Forsythe. Rusk overhears the argument and offers to put Babs up for the night. They go to his apartment and the camera follows them just to the door and then slowly, silently moves back down the stairs and out into the street. That night Rusk puts Babs' body, stuffed into a potato sack, into a truck and returns home, where he discovers that his tie pin is missing and realizes that it is in the hand of the dead woman. He goes out to the truck, which starts moving after he climbs in, and he begins a frantic search amid the lurching and careening of the truck, until he finally reaches the pin clutched in the hand of the corpse. Rigor mortis at first prevents him from retrieving it, however, so he tries unsuccessfully to cut off a finger and then snaps the fingers open one by one to get at the pin.

Blaney's friends refuse to help him after Babs' murder, so he seeks out Rusk, who manages to frame him by hiding him in his apartment and alerting the police to his presence there, having first placed Babs's clothes in Blaney's suitcase. Blaney is found guilty and sent to prison, vowing all the way to avenge himself on Rusk. Meanwhile, the inspector has been discussing the case with his wife (Vivien Merchant) as she serves him grotesque meals she has learned to make at a school for continental cooking (soup with fish heads, pigs' trotters, etc.). Mrs. Oxford insists all along that Blaney is innocent of murdering his wife since a *"crime de passion"* after ten years of marriage seems unlikely. "Look at us, we've only been married eight years and you can hardly keep your eyes open at night." Evidence finally convinces the inspector of his error, but Blaney has in the meantime broken out of prison and returned to Rusk's apartment. He begins to beat the body lying in bed with a tire jack, but it turns out to be another strangled corpse. The inspector surprises Blaney, who for a moment believes himself to be further incriminated. Just then, a sound on the stairs causes the inspector to motion for silence, and Rusk enters the room pushing a heavy trunk. The inspector observes mildly, "Why, Mr. Rusk, you're not wearing your tie," the trunk falls, and the film ends.

Shot in London, *Frenzy* marks a return of the director to his roots, a move that was paralleled by one from the studio to the streets—and hence to a more "realistic" style of filmmaking. This return to London is emphatically signaled in the credit sequence when the camera (suspended from a helicopter) drifts over the Thames and under Tower Bridge. A dissolve reveals an overhead shot of a crowd gathered in front of some large buildings on the banks of the river. As the camera cranes down, the words of the politician haranguing the crowd (among whom stands Alfred Hitchcock in a bowler hat) gradually become audible. The politician is promising to restore the "ravishing sights" of London, to eradicate the "waste products of our society with which for so long we have poisoned our rivers." He continues, "Let us rejoice that pollution will soon be banished from the waters of this river." He is interrupted by one of the spectators, who yells out in alarm as the gaping crowd rushes forward to witness the sight of a naked female corpse floating face down in the Thames, a man's tie around her neck. The sequence ends with a male voice saying, "I say, that's not my club's tie, is it?"

This sequence is remarkable for many reasons. While on the one hand London is here and throughout the movie strongly evoked, Hitchcock exhibits the utmost contempt for tourism—and most especially for what one might call cinema as tourism (in this respect, the film is markedly different from *Vertigo*, which, as Virginia Wright Wexman has argued, indulges us in the tourist's view of San Francisco).[2] Later on, two doctors, well dressed and seemingly eminently civilized men, will reveal just what it is that the tourists crave. As they stand at a bar in a pub, one of them says that in one way he hopes the murderer, who rapes his victims and then strangles them with a necktie, won't be caught because "a good juicy series of sex murders" is "so good for the tourist trade." Foreigners, he observes, "expect the squares of London to be fog-wreathed, full of hansom cabs, and littered with ripped whores." As regards the third expectation, Hitchcock devotes himself with a vengeance to giving the tourists what they want—or at least, if it is not quite accurate to say that the film is "littered with ripped whores," nevertheless, the shots depicting sexual violence or the results of sexual violence are some of the most disturbing ever shown in the cinema. If many critics have found these images to be more palatable than they ought, this is surely at least in part a measure of the extent to which sexual violence is condoned in patriarchal society. As I argued at the outset of this study, whether a viewer endorses or condemns the sexual violence in the film is partly a matter of interpretation of the viewer's own predilections and experience. To use a metaphor suggested by the film itself, one man's meat may be another man's poison.

At the same time, although by the end of the film we might be inclined to agree with the porter who says, "Sometimes just thinking about the lusts of men makes me want to heave," and although, as Robin Wood has contended, the main female characters are more sympathetic than anyone else in the film, there is little doubt that part of what makes the crime Hitchcock depicts so repellent has to do with an underlying fear and loathing of femininity.[3] This paradoxical state of affairs is simply a more extreme version of the ambivalence toward femininity I have traced throughout this study. In *Frenzy*, ambivalence can be related to the polarity woman as food vs. woman as poison (source of "pollution," "waste-product" of society, to use the politician's words). To understand how woman functions throughout the film as both edible commodity and inedible pollutant (the stench of femininity alluded to in the myths studied by Lèvi-Strauss) helps us to achieve a deeper insight not only into this particular film, but of some of Hitchcock's major concerns throughout his career.[4]

That eating and copulating have frequently been posited as analogous activities in Hitchcock films has certainly not gone unremarked in the criticism. However, the tendency—most pronounced in the Spoto biography—has been to put this parallelism down to the imagination of an overweight pervert. Such a view has unfortunately obscured the extent to which Hitchcock films put into bold (and rather comic) relief an equation that seems to exist at the heart of patriarchal culture itself. As Lèvi-Strauss observes in *The Savage Mind*, there is a "very profound analogy which people throughout the world seem to find between copulation and eating. In a very large number of languages they are even called by the same term. In Yoruba 'to eat' and 'to marry' are expressed by a single verb the general sense of which is 'to win, to acquire,' a usage which has its parallel in French [and also in English], where the verb 'consommer' [to consummate] applies both to marriage and to meals."[5]

In *Frenzy*, when Bob Rusk, owner of a fruit market, forces himself sexually onto Brenda Blaney, he says, "There's a saying in the fruit business, we put it on the fruit: don't squeeze the goods until they're yours. I would never, never do that." (Of course, he proceeds directly to contradict himself and violate "goods" which are not his.) As he sits on her desk, Rusk comments on Brenda's "frugal" lunch, and then he begins to eat the (English) apple she has brought. When he is finished raping and strangling her, he spies the apple, resumes eating it, puts it down, picks his teeth with his tie pin, and again takes up the half-eaten apple (shown in close-up) as he leaves. Now, given the numerous references to gardens in the film (Forsythe sarcastically says to Babs and Blaney when they are talking outside the pub, "This is Covent Garden, not the Garden of Love"; Rusk tells Blaney that his "old mum" lives in Kent, "the Garden of England"; etc.), it seems plausible to argue that the Adam and Eve myth is being invoked, but that a deliberate reversal is effected: here the *man* eats the apple, "knows" the woman, and is responsible for her destruction.

In *The Savage Mind* Lèvi-Strauss suggests that the common cultural "equation of male with devourer and female with devoured" may be intended to reverse the situation man most fears. Lèvi-Strauss refers to the sexual philosophy of the Far East where "for a man the art of love-making consists essentially in avoiding having his vital force absorbed by the women [possessors of the *vagina dentata*] and in turning this risk to his advantage."[6] (We recall the analysis *of Murder!* in which the hero takes the risk of hystericization and feminization in order to achieve masculine control over the narrative.) Thus, it is possible to see in the film's brutality toward women still one more indication of the need expressed throughout Hitchcock's works to deny resemblance to—absorption by—the female, a need that for Lèvi-Strauss lies at the inaugural moment of culture and of myth (it is no accident that *The Raw and the Cooked* begins with several myths about the disorder introduced by boys who refuse to leave the world of women to enter the separate men's house and ends with a chapter entitled "The Wedding").[7] Yet, as we shall see, the identification of male with devourer and female with devoured may not always have the psychic effect of negating the imagined ability of the female to absorb the male, since food is frequently endowed with the power to transform the eater into its likeness.[8] You are, after all, what you eat.

Lévi-Strauss's linguistic analysis suggests once more the connection we have encountered so often between men's hostility to woman (the need to "win" or conquer her, to "acquire" possession of her) and fear of the female other. Behind all this fear and loathing of woman, this desperation to acquire mastery over her, lies the threat of the devouring mother, a familiar figure in Hitchcock—so familiar indeed that by the time of *Frenzy*, Hitchcock need do no more than place her picture prominently on display in the villain's apartment, have him quote her on several occasions, and get her to pop her head out the window in a cameo appearance. After *Psycho*, the public understands through these slight allusions and without the necessity of elaborate psychiatric explanations exactly who is responsible for the murderous "lusts of men." We might say (taking our cue again from Lévi-Strauss) that the film *knows so well* who the culprit is and what motivates the crimes that it can dispense with the full articulation of the theme. Traces of it remain, however, displaced into bit parts: for example, when Blaney first visits his wife he observes a brief Thurberesque vignette occurring between a newly paired couple, a large, loud, domineering woman and a meek, mousy, little man. The man suggests they go right for the marriage license, and the woman asks, "What's your hurry? We'll go to my place first." As the two descend the stairs to the street, the camera holds on them in a long take while she tells the man how her late husband used to get up every morning at 5:30 to clean house, a task which he had completed by 9:30 when he brought her her coffee in bed. And he was so quiet the whole time that in thirty years he never woke her once. "A neat man, was he?" her partner asks. "He liked a tidy place," she replies, "So do I, come to that."

It has been part of my task in this book to suggest how fear of the devouring, voracious mother is central in much of Hitchcock's work, even where it is not immediately apparent. By "voracious," I refer to the continual threat of annihilation, of swallowing up, the mother poses to the personality and identity of the protagonists. Far from being the mere gimmick criticism has tended to consider it, the mother's psychic obliteration of her child in *Psycho* is paradigmatic of the fear haunting many Hitchcock films, at least since *Rebecca.* Julia Kristeva has theorized that such a threat constitutes the very "powers of horror." In Kristeva's account, phobia and the phobic aspects of religion are all ultimately linked to matrophobia and are concerned with warding off the danger of contact with the mother: "This is precisely where we encounter the rituals of defilement ... which, based on the feeling of abjection and all converging on the maternal, attempt to symbolize the other threat to the subject: that of being swamped by the dual relationship, thereby risking the loss not of a part (castration) but of the totality of his living being. The function of these religious rituals is to ward off the subject's fear of his very own identity sinking irretrievably into the mother."[9] Drawing on the work of Mary Douglas, who considers defilement to be connected with boundaries and margins, Kristeva claims that the feminine/maternal is deemed a "pollutant" because it is experienced as subversive of male symbolic systems and masculine notions of identity and order. Kristeva's language in the above quote, describing feelings of being "swamped," of "sinking" into the morass of the maternal, uncannily captures the experience of *Psycho,* in which the response of Norman Bates (Anthony Perkins) to his "possessive" mother is to conduct his own ritual of defilement, murdering Marion Crane (Janet Leigh), meticulously cleaning the bathroom of her blood, throwing her body into the trunk of a car, and pushing it into the swamp, which slowly sucks it down. Thus do men's fears become women's fate.

It is commonplace, at least since Rohmer and Chabrol's study, to consider Hitchcock a Catholic director, especially insofar as he is concerned with the themes of guilt and original sin. It seems to me possible to deepen this insight of the religious nature of Hitchcock's work, endeavoring to get beyond the platitudinous to understand the strong hold Hitchcock has had on the public imagination right up to the present day. Thus, we may speculate that Hitchcock films enact "rituals of defilement," evoking and then containing the fear of women that lies at the heart of these rituals.

The association of women with defilement, with filth, is as strong in Hitchcock as it is in the "savage mind" analyzed by Lévi-Strauss. In *Psycho,* Marion Crane is identified with money ("filthy lucre"), bathrooms, toilets, blood, and, of course, the swamp.[10] In an earlier film, *Shadow of a Doubt* (1943), Uncle Charlie (Joseph Cotten), who murders wealthy widows, sees the world as a "foul sty," a "filthy, rotting place," and he delivers a speech (significantly, at the dinner table) in which he speaks of men who work hard until they die, leaving their wives to throw their money away: "Eating the money, drinking the money, … smelling of money . … Faded, fat, greedy women." In *Frenzy*, the association of women with pollution is made explicitly in the film's opening sequence, and the film is "littered" with shots of grotesque-looking female corpses (Hitchcock had been dissuaded from showing spittle dripping from the tongue of Brenda Blaney in the shocking close-up of her after the murder). Babs' body, dusted with potato flour, spills out of the truck and onto the road, and the potato dust which Rusk brushes off himself after the truck episode is the clue leading to his capture as the murderer. (Earlier, Blaney was incriminated for his wife's murder because traces of her powder were found on his money.) Finally, the body of Babs is paralleled with the repellent, virtually inedible food the inspector's wife gives him to eat, food like pig's feet, which the inspector nearly gags on while reconstructing the potato truck episode with his wife. He relates how the corpse's fingers had been snapped open to retrieve an incriminating object, and as he speaks of this, his wife snaps breadsticks in two and crunches on them.

The corpse of woman is a figure of extreme pollution. "Impure animals become even more impure once they are dead," writes Kristeva; "contact with their carcasses must be avoided" (p. 109). As if reversing the scene in *Psycho*, in which—to the audience's great satisfaction—Norman Bates painstakingly restores the bathroom to its pristine state after stabbing Marion Crane to death there, *Frenzy* shows its villain, who has neatly disposed of the body in the potato truck, returning to the corpse and grubbing around among the potatoes and the body parts, searching for the tie pin that might incriminate him. While critics have frequently noted Hitchcock's detachment in this late film, evidenced in his sparing use of point-of-view shots, it is important to note that this particular sequence employs several point-of-view shots, drawing us into an immediate experience of the man's grotesque encounter with death. The feeling is very much one of violating an ultimate taboo, of being placed in close contact with the most "impure" of "impure animals": the carcass of the decaying female. It is as if Hitchcock is punishing the spectator for years of guilty movie-going pleasures, as if the kick in the face Rusk receives from the corpse's foot is repayment for all the times cinema has fetishized the female body, dismembering it for the sheer erotic pleasure of the male spectator. When Rusk peels back the potato sack to get to the hands (he has, unfortunately, put the body into the sack head first), we are witness to a kind of macabre striptease, a complete deromanticization of the necrophilia that Hitchcock insisted was at the heart of *Vertigo*. Ultimately, the corpse gets its vengeance, since in spite of his efforts to clean himself, Rusk is unable to eradicate the pollution which has contaminated him. In this way, the film works yet another variation on Hitchcock's perennial theme of the powers of a dead woman.

These powers are also exerted on the chief inspector, whose wife forces him to partake of a symbolic feast of the corpse. The later scenes at the dinner table may be paralleled with and contrasted to the earlier one of the rape. In the first scene, Rusk sexually attacks a woman he likens to food; unable to achieve orgasm, he explodes in a murderous rage and strangles her. In the later scenes, the inspector eats food that is likened to a woman; and though he experiences great difficulty consummating *his* meals he remains civil to his wife. She, on the other hand, seems to be wreaking revenge on her husband because of his lack of sexual inclination (a deficiency in the "lusts of men"). In contrast to Rusk, then, who exerted brutal control over the woman, Oxford seems very much at the mercy of his wife.

The scenes at the dinner table, flirting as they do with connotations of cannibalism and hence of extreme pollution—i.e., the idea of feeding off the "carcass" of the dead woman—are the culmination of the motifs of food and filth pervading the film. According to Kristeva, dietary prohibitions are based upon the prohibition of incest (an analysis confirmed by Lévi-Strauss) and thus are part of the "project of separation" from the female body engaged in not only by the Biblical text, which Kristeva analyzes at some length, but by patriarchal symbolic systems in general. Speaking of nutritional prohibitions, Kristeva writes, "[T]he dietary, when it departs from the conformity that can be demanded by the logic of separation, blends with the maternal as unclean and improper coalescence, as undifferentiated power to be cut off" (p. 106). The inspector's cannibalization of the female would obviously be an extreme form of this unclean, improper coalescence, violating in the most immediate way the separation of female body and male law.

Here again Hitchcock makes rather extensive use of point-of-view shots, and in so doing it might be said that he forces the spectator into symbolically sharing the unholy feast with the inspector—metaphorically incorporating what he literally incorporates. Interestingly, in film theory, incorporation has been considered to be the basis for "secondary identification"—that is, identification with characters: "character representations are taken into the self and provide the basis for a momentary subjectivity."[11] According to Freud, incorporation may be seen as a preliminary stage of identification, one which expresses a fundamental ambivalence toward the object: "The ego wishes to incorporate this object into itself, and the method by which it would do so, in this oral or cannibalistic stage, is by devouring it."[12] The ambivalence is such that, on the one hand, the subject wishes by devouring the object to destroy it and, on the other hand, both to preserve it within the self and to appropriate its qualities (this is truly wanting to have one's cake and eat it too).[13] The cannibalism in *Frenzy* seems to me to be the ultimate expression of the ambivalence toward women we have seen to be operating in Hitchcock films, which seek with equal vehemence both to appropriate femininity and to destroy it—hence that curious mixture of "sympathy and misogyny" found in these films.

Kristeva speculates that "defilement reveals, at the same time as an attempt to throttle matrilineality, an attempt at separating the speaking being from his body. ... It is only at such a cost that the body is capable of being defended, protected—and also, eventually, sublimated. Fear of the uncontrollable generative mother repels me from the body; I give up cannibalism because abjection (of the mother) leads me toward respect for the body of the other, my fellow man, my brother" (pp. 78–79). At the end of *Frenzy* the film brings together for the first time the three male protagonists—villain, "wrong man," and officer of the law. The chief inspector speaks on behalf of propriety, civilization, and sublimation when he observes wryly, "Why, Mr. Rusk, you're not wearing your tie," thereby restoring us to a world in which men are in control of themselves and their "lusts." It is a world from which women are altogether excluded, having been expelled from it mostly by brutal means, their power throttled. Throughout the film, the specter of this power has been continually evoked and subsequently choked off. Babs Milligan is the sexually active woman, unrestrained by marriage (the inspector remarks to Forsythe, who wonders if she will return from her night with Blaney, "Don't worry, these days ladies abandon their honor far more readily than their clothes"). Other women, like Hetty, wife of Dick's R.A.F. buddy, are threatening because they dominate *within* marriage. Still others, like the bespectacled, prudish secretary, keep "a sharp eye on men" and seem to despise them altogether. Finally, Brenda Blaney, as head of a matrimonial agency, is an especially dangerous figure of female power because she has usurped male rights of exchange: no longer are women objects of exchange among men (as, for example they were in *Blackmail);* rather it is the woman who delivers men over to other women, who proceed to enslave them. Brenda passes some of the money she makes off this trade to her down-and-out husband, who is embittered because he is not as successful as she, and sends him off to spend the night at the Salvation Army, which he calls the "hotel for bachelors." The film suggests that Brenda's marital and sexual rejection of her husband is avenged by Rusk, since the shot of Dick sitting in the dirty Salvation Army bed holding up the money his wife has given him is immediately followed by the scene of Brenda's rape/murder. As he has done so often in the past, Hitchcock here plays on the notion of the transference or exchange of guilt, only by this point it is clear that such an exchange—the only kind seemingly now possible among men—is a result of women's having usurped male prerogatives and refused to allow themselves to serve as objects of exchange in the usual male rituals like marriage. Thus, extreme rituals of defilement become the last bleak hope for patriarchy.

That *Frenzy* is such an extreme film has generally been attributed to the loosening of censorship that was occurring in the movies at the time it was made and that presumably permitted Hitchcock greater scope for his prurient imaginings. It seems to me more useful, however, to consider *Frenzy* not simply as the reflection of the dirty mind of a frustrated old man nor even of a new "freedom" in sexual mores, but rather as a cultural response to women's demands for sexual and social liberation, demands that were, after all, at their height in 1972 when *Frenzy* was made. In this connection, Mary Douglas's observation about the kind of society in which ideas about sex pollution are likely to flourish is most illuminating. According to Douglas, sex is likely to be pollution-free in a society where sexual roles are secure and enforced directly. "When male dominance is accepted as a central principle of social organisation and applied without inhibition and with full rights of physical coercion, beliefs in sex pollution are not likely to be highly developed."[14] On the other hand, ideas about sex pollution tend to thrive in societies where male dominance is challenged or where other principles tend to contradict it. Douglas's insight is of enormous importance for feminists. It is not because male dominance is so firmly entrenched that ideas about women such as those found in *Frenzy* are held, but rather because it *isn't*. These ideas come about as a result of inroads made on the system by women who insist on crossing the borders designed to separate male and female spheres. The resultant "boundary confusion" is threatening to man's sense of social and personal identity, making him feel contaminated, unsafe. In other words, when men are no longer able to use women to consolidate their (oedipal) relations with one another and hence to ensure their separateness from the female, the kinds of psychological fears discussed throughout this chapter—fears of the "totality" of one's "living being" sinking "irretrievably into the maternal"—are aroused.

This is not to say that the film endorses all the violence it portrays, despite feminist analyses of *Frenzy* that assume Hitchcock's total approbation of his villain's behavior. I have argued in previous chapters that Hitchcock's fear and loathing of women is accompanied by a lucid understanding of—and even sympathy for—women's problems in patriarchy. This apparent contradiction is attributable to his profound ambivalence about femininity, ambivalence which, in *Frenzy*, reaches an extreme form that I have accounted for psychoanalytically by analysis of the cannibalism motif. In Freudian theory, as we have seen, the individual at the cannibalistic stage wants to destroy the object by devouring it, but he also wishes to preserve it and to assimilate it. To say, then, that Hitchcock films seek both to destroy *and* preserve femininity is not to admit to a failure to arrive at the correct interpretation of the films, an inability to decide once and for all whether or not Hitchcock is really a misogynist. Rather, it is to acknowledge how pervasive and how deep the ambivalence is in these films, and to begin to understand just why it is we *cannot* decide.

By this I do not mean to glorify the undecidability of interpretation the way certain varieties of deconstructionist criticism do. The consequences for women of the negative aspect of ambivalence are too dire. But I do mean to insist on the importance of the fact that woman is never completely destroyed in these films—no matter how dead Hitchcock tries to make her appear, as when he inserts still shots in both *Psycho* and *Frenzy* of the female corpse. There are always elements resistant to her destruction or assimilation. Thus, at the same time that *Frenzy* undoubtedly shares some of the contempt for and fear of women exhibited by the men in the film, it also portrays the main female characters more sympathetically than most of its male characters. Even more importantly, the film links the sexual violence it depicts to a system of male dominance rather than confining it to the inexplicable behavior of one lone psychopath: thus both Blaney and Oxford are shown at different points in the film wearing ties similar to that found on the neck of the corpse floating in the Thames; moreover, this tie appears to be the tie of a certain men's club, as the male onlooker in the opening sequence reveals. Finally, the ironic nature of this sequence, in which the corpse appears as if in response to the politician's remarks about the pollution of the rivers, enables us, if we choose, to take a distance from the equation of woman with pollution and even to see it as a male projection.

In fact, the film provides plenty of evidence of this kind of projection. When a female bartender asks the doctors who have been speaking of the murderer, "He rapes them first, doesn't he?" they reply, "Yes, well, it's nice to know that every cloud has a silver lining." At another point in the film Rusk says, "Mind you, there are some women who ask for everything they get." Yet in the very way it depicts sexual violence, the film belies the notion, common in patriarchy, that women actually want to be raped and either invite or deserve sexual victimization.

The graphic depiction of sexual violence in *Frenzy* has been the source of some critical controversy, as I mentioned earlier. Donald Spoto, we recall, castigated Hitchcock for showing the "sordid crime" in "all its horror." For Spoto, as for so many critics, much of Hitchcock's distinction had lain in the discretion with which he had treated such subject matter in the past (and notably in *Psycho*): "The act of murder in Alfred Hitchcock's films had always been stylized by the devices of editing and … photographic wizardry. [But in *Frenzy*] Hitchcock insisted on all the ugly explicitness of this picture, and for all its cinematic inventiveness, it retains one of the most repellent examples of a detailed murder in the history of film."[15] Of course, one might ask why, if a sordid crime like rape/murder is to be depicted at all, it should *not* be shown "in all its horror." In fact, it could be argued that the stylization and allusiveness of the shower scene in *Psycho* have provided critics with the rationale for lovingly and endlessly recounting all the details of its signification in the very process of self-righteously deploring its signified, the crime of rape/murder.[16] In *Frenzy*, by contrast, Hitchcock's use of graphic details, his casting of ordinary non-fetishized women in the various female roles, and his refusal to eroticize the proceedings as he had in *Psycho*—teasing viewers with shots of Janet Leigh in her brassiere and Janet Leigh stripping so that even while she is being stabbed to death we irresistibly wonder if we'll get a glimpse of her naked breasts—all this makes the crime he is depicting more difficult for the spectator to assimilate—more "repellent," in Spoto's word. In the assault scene in *Frenzy* the woman's anguish is stressed as the camera shows her in close-up uttering a psalm. These shots and her words clash grotesquely with those of Rusk, to whom the camera keeps cutting and who repeatedly utters the single word, "Lovely" (until, enraged by his own impotence, he yells, "You bitch," and begins to strangle her). In contrast to *Psycho*, which in promotions and in the film itself had titillated spectators with hopes of seeing Janet Leigh's breasts but which had withheld the full sight of the desired objects, *Frenzy* shows an extreme close-up of the woman's breast as she struggles to pull her bra back over it, all the while murmuring the words of the psalm. It is all anything but lovely; it is infinitely sad, pathetic, among the most disturbing scenes cinema has to offer.

The film, then, veers between disgust at the "lusts of men" and loathing of the female body itself, treated in several scenes as an object of ghoulish humor, so that many critics have justly pointed to the film's utter cynicism about sex and the relation between the sexes. This cynicism seems to provide some critics with a convenient excuse for not dealing with the issue of misogyny at all: the logic seems to be that since Hitchcock shows contempt for women *and* men, there is no reason to single out his treatment of women for special discussion—no reason, then, for considering why women are the exclusive objects of rape and mutilation in the film or why it is their "carcasses" that litter the film's landscape and not men's. The extreme of this blindness can be seen in statements like Spoto's about the "devouring abuses of man against man." For feminists there is an obvious need to keep the problem of violence against women at the center of the analysis (as it is at the center of the film); nevertheless, we cannot afford to ignore the full complexity of the film and its attitude toward women.

When Rusk comes to the matrimonial agency, he is, as we learn, in search of a woman—a "masochist," the inspector says—who will submit to his peculiar appetites. The film makes it quite clear that he does not find what he is looking for. At one point Brenda says, "All right, I won't struggle," and he tells her that he wants her to struggle, "some women like to struggle." As Rusk's reply suggests, and as the female spectator very well knows, Brenda's refusal to struggle is not the masochistic submission the man desires—not the acquiescence that in his eyes masquerades as resistance.[17] This is a small detail, perhaps, but it is significant. It provides yet one more indication of the fact that despite the considerable violence visited on women in the movies—and by proxy, women *at* the movies—their capitulation to male desires and expectations is never complete. Or, to put it another way, for a whole variety of reasons which it has been the task of this book to explore, we may suppose that, while women are important consumers of the films, the films themselves do not utterly consume women.

# Afterwords
## *Hitchcock's Daughters (1988)*

It's the scene of the crime the murderer returns to—not the theater.

Charlotte Inwood in *Stage Fright*.

A scene from *Stage Fright*, a film made in 1950 at the exact midpoint of Hitchcock's career, puts into play many of the ideas and themes that have concerned me in these pages. In this film, narrative disorder is introduced at the outset when a man opens a door and we get a shot of a woman (Marlene Dietrich), seen from the waist down, her skirt all bloodied. The woman, Charlotte Inwood, is tricked into betraying herself when the father (Alistair Sim) of the film's heroine, Eve (Jane Wyman), bloodies a doll's skirt and pays a little boy in a scout uniform to hold up to Charlotte this image of her guilty self as she sings on stage. The point is to get the police, who are looking on, to suspect her of the murder of her husband so that they will exonerate the man she appears to have framed. The father's trick thus sets into motion the machinery that eventually restores narrative and patriarchal order.

Up to this point, Charlotte has been the most self-possessed and self-obsessed of women. She is continually shown looking at herself in a mirror, even when she is talking to the other characters. While the prop of the mirror suggests the importance of performance in the film (and also, of course, points to the perennial classical-narrative theme of woman as duplicitous), it appears here to function primarily as an indicator of female narcissism. Charlotte is a woman in love with herself. In a passage that has attained a great deal of notoriety in recent years, Freud remarks on the charms of narcissistic women and makes some telling comparisons:

> The charm of a child lies to a great extent in his narcissism, his self-contentment and inaccessibility, just as does the charm of certain animals which seem not to concern themselves about us, such as cats and the large beasts of prey. Indeed, even great criminals and humorists, as they are represented in literature, compel our interest by the narcissistic consistency with which they manage to keep away from their ego anything that would diminish it.[1]

Analyzing this text at length, Sarah Kofman concludes that many of the other writings of Freud on femininity are meant to "cover over" the knowledge that he here briefly exposes. For, though the narcissistic woman may charm, she also, obviously, inflicts considerable damage on the male ego. To reduce woman to a castrated hysteric is a way of dealing with her "inaccessible," "enigmatic," "indecipherable" character.[2] Similarly, we might say that Hitchcock's text exposes for a brief moment the need of patriarchy to reduce the "great" female "criminal" to a frightened hysteric—bearer of the bleeding wound. In place of the mirror she would hold up to herself, patriarchy holds up a distorting mirror reflecting her as a defiled, mutilated, and guilty creature.[3]

Rather than the classical oedipal scenario, in which the sight of the mother instills horror in the child, we have here a scene that reveals father and little boy conspiring to instill horror in the woman by forcing her to recognize a repellent view of her formerly beautiful self. In this way, the scene seems to me to constitute a wonderful parable for patriarchal cinema and for the situation of the female spectator at the movies. Because Charlotte doesn't "know what fear is," as one of her lovers puts it, it becomes the job of the father and the representatives of the law to teach her. They accomplish this important task primarily by forcing her to internalize a view of herself as a monstrous and loathsome creature—just as Hitchcock films force us to shudder at the possibility of a resemblance between ourselves and the likes of such women as Mrs. Bates.

A full consideration of the female spectator, however, must also take into account the role of *Stage Fright's* other female character, Eve Gill, who investigates Charlotte Inwood by acting in the role of her maid. The person we identify with most closely in the film, Eve ardently desires the guilt of the woman to become manifest because she is in love with the man who has been accused of the crime. If Charlotte is—at least throughout most of the film—the figure of female resistance, Eve is the figure of female complicity with patriarchal law. Thus, after the film's climactic sequence, in which Eve finally confronts Charlotte and gets her to confess some of the truth, she is applauded by her father when she comes out on the stage of the theater. (The women's words have been overheard by the police, who have placed a microphone under a dress that hangs in Charlotte's dressing room—where else but under her skirts would we expect to find the evidence of woman's guilt?) Feminist criticism has frequently tended to see only one aspect of female spectatorship—either the complicity or the resistance; I have argued throughout this book, however, that woman's response is complex and contradictory and requires an understanding of woman's placement on the margins of patriarchal culture—at once inside and outside its codes and structures.

*Stage Fright*, like so many of Hitchcock's films, appears on one level to be centrally concerned with overcoming this duality in woman and subduing her resistance to being placed entirely within the boundaries of patriarchal law. In this respect, the film provides a version of the myth of patriarchy's overthrow of "matriarchy" (the latter equated with death, theater and spectacle, masquerade, disorder, defilement, and irrationality—this final trait most vividly exemplified by Eve's mother, played by Sybil Thorndike). As I have attempted to show with each film I have analyzed, however, the overthrow is never complete or final, for reasons which have to do, in part, with the nature of male desire itself. On more than one occasion I have quoted Jean-Paul Sartre, whose work seems to me to capture more than that of any other thinker the impossible dialectics of this desire. In a passage that could stand as the epigraph for many of Hitchcock's films, Sartre writes, "[T]he lover's dream is to identify the beloved object with himself and still preserve for it its own individuality; let the Other become me without ceasing to be the other. To know [the body of the other] is to devour it yet without consuming it." Given the fact that male desire and the texts which express that desire are, so to speak, divided against themselves, it is not surprising to find that occasionally the "individuality" of the Other decisively triumphs over the efforts to assimilate and destroy it. As a feminist critic, I find it crucial to identify and celebrate these triumphs, as, for example, in *Stage Fright,* when we discover that the really guilty person is not the sexual woman whom we have suspected all along, but the man who has appeared to be her victim. It turns out that he has smeared her dress with blood and marked her as a murderess precisely in order to cover up his *own* guilt. The duplicity that is habitually attributed to woman (since Eve) is reassigned to the male sex, and the entire story is shown to be founded on a male lie—precisely the lie about woman's guilt that fuels the machinery of patriarchal cinema. Charlotte is not, however, declared completely "innocent." Rather, the text never allows us to pin her down, to understand her motives or the extent to which she participated in the crime. When she is being watched by the policeman at the end, she remarks that he doesn't have everything down in his "little book." She proceeds, like the Sphinx, to speak in riddles, recounting the story of a dog that once bit her, and concluding, "When I give all my love and get treachery in return, it's as if my mother slapped me in the face." The final shot is an enigmatic high angle close-up of her wreathed in cigarette smoke and staring mysteriously off—once again, not returning man's gaze. The film, then, ultimately maintains the woman as inaccessible, indecipherable, and unknowable.

The text of *Stage Fright* at first participates in the guilty man's lie by presenting it in the form of a flashback at the beginning of the film.[5] Of course, critics have strenuously objected to this lying flashback—disturbed, no doubt, by the fact that the normal process of fetishized film-viewing—the easy coincidence between seeing and believing—is disrupted, with the result that the viewer finds *himself* drawn into the theatricalized space of deception. The stakes of this process are made painfully clear at the film's finale when the curtain descends in a murderous, castrating gesture onto the villain, whose point of view we assume just before the curtain cuts him in two.

In the chapter on *Murder!*, I dealt with another film in which the theatrical world is the scene of the crime, and I suggested that theatrical space was dangerous in the male Imaginary in that it draws man into a world of illusion and false or mixed identities: a world which threatens castration and feminization. It is not surprising, therefore, that a recent monumental study of the films of Hitchcock, William Rothman's *Hitchcock: The Murderous Gaze*, asserts strenuously and repeatedly Hitchcock's "masterful" control over theatricality. Indeed, for Rothman, this control precisely defines the true auteur and separates him decisively from the mere *metteur-en-scène*:

> We might distinguish those films that call upon the viewer to recognize their authors from those that do not. We might make the further distinction between those films whose authors present themselves only through a style, as it were *theatrically*, and those whose authors call for their work, and their humanity, to be authentically acknowledged. These last—and it is my premise that Hitchcock films are among them—are films that acknowledge their viewers' capacity for acknowledgement. In calling for acknowledgement of their authorship, they also acknowledge the viewer as their author's equal.[6]

Rothman proceeds to point out that "unread, its authorship unacknowledged," a theatrical film like *Murder!* is "seductive" and "treacherous," turning its viewers into "victims" and committing "symbolic murder" of those who refuse to give Hitchcock his due and pay obeisance to what Rothman continually refers to as his "godlike powers." On the face of it, it might seem difficult to reconcile the kind of power Rothman ascribes to the author with a notion of the viewer's equality. Indeed, one is continually struck in reading *Hitchcock: The Murderous Gaze* by Rothman's own submissive Schreber-like posture vis-à-vis the director (e.g., he writes in awestruck tones of the way Hitchcock "compels the blindest viewer to bow before the terrifying power his camera commands").[7] If ever a text confirmed the doctrine of male masochism, this book is it. But we must recall Eve Sedgwick's remarks about the "masculinizing potential" of submission to another man. Through this submission, paradoxically, it becomes possible for the male viewer to achieve a rough equality with the director.

But what about the female viewer? In acknowledging the "terrifying power" of the author, in performing the mirroring function Rothman recommends, does she not rather consent to the very eradication of her difference that the texts demand? It is not for her a question of attaining equality, but of being reduced to a sameness which, as the story of Lisa Freemont reveals, tames the threat posed by her otherness. If women in Hitchcock texts are routinely punished for their refusal to acknowledge male authority (and Rothman's universal "we" notwithstanding, women make up the overwhelming majority of victims in Hitchcock films), such acknowledgment only leads to a "symbolic murder" of woman *as* woman, as other.[8] If, then, we would seek to prevent being absorbed by male authority and male texts, we must risk punishment and withhold the authorial acknowledgment the texts exact. Feminist critics must refuse to bow before the camera's "terrifying power" and, instead, *affirm* the theatrical, "treacherous" aspects of these "seductive" texts—those parts which "know" more than their author, those moments I have stressed here when woman resists capitulation to male power and male designs.

It all comes down to a question of interpretation, which, as I suggested in the chapter on *Blackmail,* involves a struggle for survival. I want to stress this point again, because it has become fashionable in recent years to take a stand "against interpretation," or, in many cases, "beyond interpretation." In a review essay on Rothman's book, for example, Fredric Jameson addresses himself not to the correctness of any given interpretation, but to the issue of interpretation itself, challenging Rothman's emphasis on authorial mastery and interrogating his book for "what it can tell us about *interpretation* as such, its conditions of possibility, what must be left out in order to include what it does finally manage to include."[9] Jameson begins his essay with a quotation from Christian Metz's "The Imaginary Signifier" that appears to buttress this transcendent approach to art and criticism. Metz castigates those "theorists" of author aesthetics whose practice consists in rationalizing films that they have "first liked." Such "theories," says Metz, "may contain insights of considerable theoretical importance, but the writer's posture is not theoretical.... A simultaneously internal and external love object is constituted, at once comforted by a justificatory theory which only goes beyond it ... the better to surround and protect it, according to the cocoon principle."[10] Metz's words do indeed accurately describe the project of William Rothman (and even more so, perhaps, that of Robin Wood, in whose recent work feminism itself has become the "justificatory theory," which protects the loved objects and maintains the absolute mastery of their creator). And yet it is important to ask whether feminists ought to adopt the "theoretical posture" Metz endorses. Is not this posture usually a very *erect* one?

Jameson's own text certainly provides evidence that the theorist's attempt to gain a view of the dollhouse world of interpretation which would permit us to see *all* (all that a text leaves out "in order to include what it finally does include") is likely to fail. For instance, Jameson, in common with almost all other male commentators who have been quoted throughout this study, omits any discussion of Hitchcock's treatment of women, even though he refers to a "new interpretive task of discovering the meaning ... of the connection between murder and marriage." Jameson immediately proceeds to engage in a metacommentary on the the word "meaning" and never returns to elucidate the meaning of a connection which is, after all, a life and death matter to women. My task here has been to insist on interpreting such themes from the woman's point of view, the omission of which has surely constituted one of the primary "conditions of possibility" of male interpretations as well as male metacommentaries.

Interestingly, in calling into question Rothman's "organicist" author aesthetics, Jameson counterposes a notion of artistic and filmic fragmentation, which he puts into a "dialectical" theory of the fragmentation and discontinuity of American daily life. What is made possible by this move (and one might recall L.B. Jeffries, for whom fragmentation was also at stake) is a replacement of the older notion of the artist as master with one of the theorist as master: the man who is able to situate the fragmented, partial, decentered aspects of art and daily life into a historical totality. And this while ignoring the contributions feminism might be able to make to the understanding of such problematics.

My book has consisted of a series of readings that *are frankly* partial and "impure" (in that they allow art and theory to intermingle freely). Although many considerations went into determining the choice of films—not only did I want representative films from each period, I also sought a blend of canonical and noncanonical works and of texts that feature the male point of view and those that privilege the female point of view—they are all films I have "first liked." Indeed, this liking, which is shared by millions of women, seemed to me one of the key rationales for my undertaking. While it is not at all accurate to say that I wanted to "save Hitchcock," to recall the words of Robin Wood, I did indeed aim to save his female viewers from annihilation at the hands not only of traditional male critics but of those feminist critics who see woman's repression in patriarchal cinema as total, women's "liking" for these films as nothing but masochism. At stake, I felt, was the ongoing development of female subjectivity—a subjectivity that, if it reveals us all to be Hitchcock's daughters, also reveals this identity to be far from simple. Though our monstrous father may have made us fear our own image of ourselves, he has also (no doubt against his will) given us reason to hope that we will be able to survive patriarchy's attacks.

In this regard, I have always been intrigued by the fact that in *Strangers on a Train*, Hitchcock's own daughter appears in the role of a woman who "returns" to haunt the film's villain with her resemblance to the person he has strangled—the scandalously sexual and unfaithful woman. At one point in the film, the villain stares into Patricia Hitchcock's eyes (she is wearing the glasses Hitchcock associates with noncooperative women) and recollects the horrible crime he has perpetrated. This memory precipitates an incident that leads the film's heroine—sister of the Patricia Hitchcock character—to a knowledge of the man's guilt. Such knowledge, putting the blame for crimes against women where it belongs, is available everywhere in the Hitchcock text if one cares to look; it has been the task of my study simply to place this knowledge more securely than ever in the possession of women.

# Resurrection of a Hitchcock Daughter (2005)

In the 1988 version of *The Women Who Knew Too Much*, I noted that in Hitchcock's films, some of the most threatening female characters are likely to stage an uncanny return or even to appear to rise from the dead, usually with renewed power. It's 2005, and I write at a time when feminist critiques of Hitchcock and the concern with the female viewers of his films have been buried under other sorts of critiques. Hoping to restore the place of women and remind the public of the centrality of "marriage and murder" in Hitchcock's films, I, like some of the female figures in these films, rise again.[1]

I cannot truthfully say that my motives are entirely disinterested. It is a rare critic who would not feel miffed when, having written a book on Hitchcock, theory, and women, she finds herself unmentioned even in the "Works Consulted" pages of articles and books on the same or related topics. I hope the reader will be convinced, however, that I'm not undertaking this new afterword primarily for personal reasons, although in these reasons I believe there is a feminist issue at stake. One of my book's main theses was that the female Gothic, in particular Daphne du Maurier's *Rebecca*, was at the heart of the "Hitchcock picture," despite Hitchcock's repudiation of the film ("It's not a Hitchcock picture"). As author of *The Women Who Knew Too Much*, I wanted to throw in my lot with the likes of Rebecca and her creator and to undermine the claim to absolute mastery on the part of the ultimate patriarch of film, Alfred Hitchcock. So when I find myself unceremoniously cast into the company of the unnamed second Mrs. de Winter, I sense that something more than a snub to me personally is at stake.

Take for example, this statement, which appears in the introduction to the collection of essays titled, *Everything You Always Wanted to Know about Lacan (But Were Afraid to Ask Hitchcock)*, edited by a person whom we shall call the second Mr. Lacan:

> [It] should be clear how one should answer those who reproach Hitchcockian *aficionados* with the "divinization" of their interpretive object—with the elevation of Hitchcock into a God-like demiurge who masters even the smallest details of his work: such an attitude is simply a sign of transferential relationship where Hitchcock functions as the "subject supposed to know (sujet suppose savoir)"—and is it necessary

to add that there is more truth in it, that it is theoretically far more productive, than the attitude of those who lay stress on Hitchcock's fallibility, inconsistencies, etc.? In short, here, more than ever, the Lacanian motto "*Les non-dupes errent*" is in force; the only way to produce something real in theory is to pursue the transferential fiction to the end.[2]

Now, as far as I am aware, my book goes further than any other work in taking to task critics who deify Hitchcock. For example, in the "Afterword" to the 1988 edition, I showed to what lengths such idolatry could go by quoting William Rothman's remark that we should "bow before the terrifying power [Hitchcock's] camera commands." So "naturally" I figure the passage above is fingering me.

Despite believing myself to be targeted by these remarks, I would scarcely want to argue with all of them. How could I? Having titled the final pages of my work, "Hitchcock's Daughters," I too quite obviously wanted to point out the transferential relation between female viewers and the cinemaster par excellence. But my notion of transference is more complicated than the one invoked in the above quotation. True, the analyst in psychotherapy tends to be idealized, but in the course of therapy, the analysand works through all sorts of feelings (love, anger, envy, hate) in relation to "the one supposed to know." She, the analysand, might say, for example, "You're *supposed* to know, dammit"—supposed to know, say, that women shouldn't be gleefully brutalized. She will moreover be vigilant in looking for the evidence and meaning of the analyst's *counter-transference* (Marnie to Mark: "So what about *your* dreams, Daddy dear?"), looking, that is to say, for signs indicating the contents of *his* unconscious, as I did with Hitchcock. Once the therapy has been successfully terminated, the analyst can be seen for what he is—human and therefore, insofar as he appeared to us in the guise of Master, "an imposter," to adopt another favorite term of the second Mr. Lacan. In *The Women Who Knew Too Much*, I consider myself to have pursued the "transferential fiction' for quite a distance: I dealt with my love of the films (I've said it before: I am no non-dupe) and dealt with my anger. I hope to have enacted by proxy a similar process for some of my readers.

As is so often the case, then, the intent of the critic in question seems to be to "hystericize" the female critic, to refuse her a hearing. By not naming names, the writer gives himself deniability. When we consider the fact that in the relevant parts of *Everything You Wanted to Know about Lacan* male critics are not only frequently named but receive the highest of praises even when their work is at the other end of the political and philosophical spectrum from said critic's we are entitled to conclude that "Hitchcock *aficionados*"—many of them, at least—wish to keep women out of the club. Hom(m)osexuality reigns supreme.

In the pages that follow I want to look at how feminist scholarship on Hitchcock has fared, and to bring my own feminist scholarship to bear when it seems to me pertinent to other related issues recent critics have been addressing. As much as possible, I try to keep my ego to one side, but given that I am practically the only one to have written a full-length feminist study of Hitchcock's films, and the only one, I believe, who has been remotely antagonistic toward the notion of Hitchcock as God, I cannot keep myself out of the picture altogether.[3] Nor, given what I have just been discussing, do I think the female ego *should* always be suppressed. I will leave it to the reader to judge when I am indulging in *mere* egoism, and when I am, on the contrary, using myself effectively as an example to illuminate larger points.

But I'm not just dishing out criticism; I'm taking it too. I want to look at how recent criticism of Hitchcock films, especially that of psychoanalytic critics and of gay, lesbian, and queer critics, enables a more complete understanding than I had at the time of the various themes or obsessions in the films, especially as they relate to women. In certain cases I will be responding to direct criticisms of my work, some of which are well founded.

Over the years, particularly in recent years, there has been a great deal of fine work on the films of Alfred Hitchcock. I simply don't have the space to acknowledge it all, much less treat the criticism in depth. Thus, I will be looking at currents of thinking that seem most relevant to the ideas in *The Women Who Knew Too Much.*

I begin by looking at a text that seems to give feminist criticism pride of place in its account of the directions taken by Hitchcock critics throughout the years. In his very useful book, *Hitchcock: The Making of a Reputation*, Robert E. Kapsis shows how a cinematic master is, at least partly, constructed, not born. He traces the development of Hitchcock's career, citing reviews, conducting interviews, and uncovering evidence of Hitchcock's own efforts to be recognized and taken seriously as a film artist. One major chapter traces the shifting assessments of Hitchcock's work among academic critics, who were ultimately responsible for securing Hitchcock's reputation as a serious and important auteur. Writing in the early 1990s, when feminist interest in Hitchcock was at its height (or, perhaps, soon after it peaked), Kapsis devotes a significant portion of the chapter to summarizing various feminist analyses of the films—in particular, of *Marnie* and *The Birds.* The stakes for feminism in such a project like Kapsis's are high, since this sort of history may constitute the only exposure contemporary students will have to feminist Hitchcock criticism.

For much of the chapter Kapsis does give the reader a competent summary of what some of the debates were in the high theory days of feminist criticism. The first clue that such judiciousness is too good to be true, however, comes when Kapsis begins to deploy the old strategy of divide and conquer. He pits two pieces of feminist criticism dealing with the film *Marnie* against one another, finding one, Rebecca Bailin's "Feminist Readership, Violence and *Marnie*," to be true to the complicated "enunciatory" structure of the film, and the other, Michelle Piso's "Mark's Marnie," to be a "one-dimensional" study, lacking in subtlety and coming "dangerously close to presenting Hitchcock as a merciless and unrelenting critic of patriarchal and capitalist society."[4] What struck me most on reading this passage was the oddness of the word "dangerously." For the sake of argument, let's say Piso does misrepresent Hitchcock's intentions. Maybe she is wrong. But *dangerous*? If *Marnie* were in fact the kind of indictment Piso is supposedly reading into the film, and if Hitchcock actually intended such a critique, as Piso is alleged to be suggesting, I for one *would* be bowing before the camera. In my feminist view, what's really dangerous is the lethal misogyny often apparent in the director's work. After several readings of this section of the chapter, I concluded that the problem for Kapsis is that he doesn't see patriarchy and capitalism as *deserving* such a bleak indictment. But instead of coming right out and saying so, he brings in an article by a woman, Rebecca Bailin, to do the work of partly exculpating "patriarchal capitalism"—and yet a more unpropitious essay to enlist in such a project one would be hard put to find.

Bailin's insightful, compelling essay, "Feminist Readership, Violence and Marnie," studies the enunciation in *Marnie* to conclude that there is a woman's discourse at work in the film, one which recognizes the "violence against women in its more traumatic and sadistic forms."[5] Bailin labels the woman's discourse "progressive." Unfortunately, as she goes on to show at painstaking and convincing length, this voice is systematically undercut by the male enunciation—for example, by instilling doubt in the spectator about whether the traumatic event in Marnie's life stemmed from an act of child abuse on the part of a drunken sailor or whether, in fact, the sailor was simply trying to comfort a little girl terrified of a thunderstorm. A similar ambiguity is at play in the relationship between Mark and Marnie—most sinisterly during the rape scene in which Mark alternates between violence, as when he tears off her clothes, and tenderness, as when he apologizes (before going ahead with the rape) and partly covers her up with his robe.

Bailin notes that Mark seems to soften in his attitude toward Marnie at the end of the film, and so whatever negative views we might have had about him tend to be undermined. Furthermore, she writes, "This change in Mark erases the 'wrongness' in the patriarchal order that he has signified, because the 'cure' [note quotation marks] reasserts the patriarchal order. It is with the cure that the two enunciations, the patriarchal enunciation and the women's discourse, collide. The film recognizes women's oppression by violence but erases its own critique of patriarchal society by saying that the recognition is, in and of itself, enough. The patriarchal order is reborn as nonoppressive."[6] It ought to be clear even from the little I have quoted that Bailin sees the ending of

*Marnie* as a deplorable negation of the woman's point of view and a reassertion of an order in which men rule; nothing has really changed for the better as far as women are concerned. She is describing what we used to call "the film's ideological project," not stating her own convictions, when she says that "the patriarchal order is reborn as nonoppressive."

Now, throughout much of his discussion, Kapsis is faithful to Bailin's argument in his paraphrase of it, until suddenly he veers off course, and, while elsewhere complimenting Bailin for her employment of irony, uses her words quoted above unironically when he discusses another scene in the movie (one Bailin herself does not discuss) and ends by turning her argument on its head and chalking one up for patriarchy. Speaking of the party scene that occurs right after Marnie has been "psychoanalyzed" by her blackmailer husband, Kapsis notes that Marnie seems happier and more relaxed than we have ever seen her. According to Hitchcock himself, Kapsis says, Marnie's happiness at this point is "'real.'" For, "'she's recovered, you see. She *is* mistress of Wykwyn.'" (How Hitchcock loved the female Gothic!) Marnie's happiness dissipates with Strutt's appearance at the party. "Still," Kapsis concludes, the pleasure Marnie shows up to this point "can be viewed from Bailin's interpretive scheme as a sign that the patriarchal society can be 'reborn' as 'nonoppressive.' From this perspective the dinner-party scene functions to 'erase' some of the 'wrongness' of the patriarchal order which Mark's earlier entrapment of Marnie had signified."[7]

Bailin's point is totally upended; no longer is the film "progressive" because it gives voice to women's discourse. It is progressive, apparently, because a miraculously reformed patriarchy is reborn out of the ashes caused by its own destructiveness.

Kapsis does to Bailin exactly what she argues the film does to Marnie and the woman's discourse, appearing to give her/it a voice, but undercutting her/its indictment of a society in which violence against women is endemic and of a film that in the end "erases" its acknowledgment of this violence or renders it ambiguous.

As for Piso, I was stunned when Kapsis so cavalierly dismissed her work as one-dimensional. Significantly, he cites as an example of one-dimensionality the fact that she doesn't consider the events leading up to the rape scene in which "Mark is shown to have allowed Marnie to maintain her sexual independence."[8] He also finds her "unambiguous reading of Mark's rape of Marnie" a problem, apparently because it doesn't consider those shots which "suggest … the tenderness of Mark's lovemaking"![9] Kapsis harps on the "ambiguous" rape scene in his discussion of feminist readings of *Marnie* to the point where one must ask what is at stake for him. I would argue that, in contorting feminist interpretations of the film, he is giving us the postfeminist version of the tactics we saw operating in the prefeminist-male critics' treatment of rape in *Blackmail*—the knee-jerk attempts to "lighten up" the experience and meaning of the assault.

Michelle Piso's essay is anything but one-dimensional, even if it does call a rape a rape. When I first read her essay, "Mark's Marnie," I was bowled over by its rich analysis and its compassionate tone—compassionate toward Marnie and her mother, first and foremost, but, to an extent, toward Mark Rutland too. "*Marnie*," Piso contends, "is as much about a man's inability to free himself from the constraining ideology of his wealth, from the authority and certainty it confers, as it is about a woman's refusal to submit to that ideology."[10]

Piso writes (the quotation marks within the quotation are placed around Mark's own words), "His youth 'blighted, dragged down by money, ambition, noblesse oblige,' then bored by his corporate interests, a boredom only briefly relieved in the desire to escape the bourgeois world," Mark sees in Marnie a potential for escape from this world, represented by the "glass cage" of the Rutland office.[11]

> With her own private secret Marnie turns the profession of secretary on its head. Mark wants the outlaw, the criminal, the woman who can jam sociality and ridicule the routine of tea and classy talk … He loves her because, tumbling combinations, she dares to challenge the codes, to mimic them in her voice, her dress, her good manners, because perhaps she can smash the glass that surrounds his emotional and sexual desire and free him from the rut that is his life. Unfortunately for Mark, however, he is not Godard's perfect hero, always ready to flee the infinite net of the bourgeoisie. The net is of his own weaving, and with it he captures Marnie. Instead of stealing his property she becomes it.[12]

Obviously, the understanding Piso exhibits for a character like Mark, because it is inseparable from a larger critique based on class and gender, is not what Kapsis is seeking from feminist critics. Mark must not be cut down to size, portrayed as a man who has some of the right instincts but fails to make good on them because in the end he's dug his own rut and is comfortable with the power and privilege he possesses. Kapsis's Mark must turn out to be the hero, effecting on his own the cure not only of the woman who rebels against patriarchy but of *patriarchy itself*.

One suspects that the *coup de grâce* for Kapsis comes when Piso points out (and she does so more than once) that Marnie's mother Bernice is not the only prostitute in the movie. Mark himself has done a "bit of familial whoring," having married his first wife for the money that helps him to build up the family business.[13] Piso's poetic essay builds itself around such connections, in the process enacting a kind of grieving for the losses of a society in which collective life, privacy, rituals, and much else have lost their meaning or become debased. Attentive to film form, theoretically rich, building on Marxist theory, anthropological theory, feminist theory, and the works of Foucault and Sartre, the essay follows out the verbal and visual metaphors in the film and explores its many motifs. Focusing, for example, on the way gifts function in the film, Piso writes, "The most consequential act of degraded reciprocity is the mother's first sexual union." Bernice makes a trade with a boy named Billy—"his sweater for her virginity."[14] Later Piso invokes the sweater in discussing the rape: "Mark strips Marnie and then shields her nakedness with his robe, as if this covering, like the boy's sweater and the jacket that Mark will finally give to Marnie in the rain, were the male body's promise of protection. Yet Mark's is the gift that takes. Raping her, he breaks all promises."[15] I quote at length because the essay makes its points with a lyricism to which paraphrase simply can't do justice. It is one of my favorite pieces of film criticism.

To return to Kapsis: Fearing perhaps that he was too subtle in the way he subverted feminist criticism and made it speak with his voice, he comes right out and slaps feminist critics in the face. When he discusses *The Birds*, he remarks that that film has received less attention in recent years from feminists than a number of other Hitchcock films, and he speculates that articles on *The Birds* would not have furthered feminists' careerist ambitions! The reader may now guess that another quotation from a woman critic is forthcoming. And so it is. Kapsis quotes Janet Staiger at length from an essay in which she deplores the careerism of scholars and students who are encouraged "to make one's name with a new methodology." She nowhere mentions feminist critics. Nevertheless, Kapsis feels empowered. Noting that *The Birds* does not seem to lend itself the way *Marnie* does to psychoanalytic interpretations, he repeats his charge against feminist critics: "It is conceivable, following Staiger's reasoning, that feminist critics concluded that 'psychoanalyzing' Melanie Daniels would not be as effective a vehicle for advancing their academic careers as focusing on Marnie or some other complex Hitchcock heroine."[16] This gratuitous swipe at feminists is, "following Staiger's reasoning," wholly illogical, as psychoanalysis was the established methodology for feminist criticism at the time, and therefore could not have been that *new* methodology Staiger accused scholars of constantly trying to develop. Just for the record, I want to add that Kapsis accuses no other kinds of critics of being especially careerist.

### The Woman Who Claimed Not to Know Too Much

Certainly the articles written early on in the history of feminist film theory took *The Birds* as a crucial text in serving to illustrate the misogyny of narrative cinema. Raymond Bellour's analysis of the film was famously taken up by feminist critic Janet Bergstrom, and its theoretical premises later contested by Susan Lurie, whose article on the film had a major impact on feminist film theory. Margaret Horwitz's 1982 article, "*The Birds*: A Mother's Love," advanced a thesis that would later be promoted (without, needless to say, attribution) by Slavoj Žižek: that the birds represent a mother's wrath and a mother's vengeance on the woman she fears could steal away her son.

Indeed, given the intense feminist concerns expressed in the above-mentioned essays about the film's violence, a thinly veiled sexual violence, toward its main female character, recent analyses of *The Birds* can show us how far Hitchcock criticism has diverged from the marvelous militancy of those earlier works. Below, where I discuss Lee Edelman's reading of the film, we will see an ingenious example of how the suffering visited on Melanie Daniels, the film's heroine, is made magically to disappear. Here I would like to focus on another work by a woman who claims to write as a feminist and to make gender a central concern of her study: Susan Smith's *Hitchcock: Suspense, Humour, and Tone*. In many ways this book is a *tour de force* and in my opinion should be required reading in courses on Hitchcock. Smith looks at the formal and narratological aspects of Hitchcock's films and treats them in depth with great sophistication. Debunking the simple notion of "suspense" (as opposed to "surprise") advanced by the director himself and perpetuated by most critics who have rather uncritically accepted Hitchcock's observations of how suspense works to elicit audience identification with an imperiled character, Smith shows just how complex the question of identification is and how various forms of suspense work partly or wholly to complicate both identifications and identity itself. The range of examples Smith uses in making her points, particularly in the earlier chapters, is extraordinarily impressive—indeed, I know of no other work on Hitchcock that comes close to this book in demonstrating the complex relations between audience and characters capable of being charted throughout Hitchcock's oeuvre.

Smith's occasional attempts at feminist critique are at times felicitous as well—for example, when she quotes the sharp retort of Marnie's mother to Mark who says he is going to tell Marnie the whole story of what happened to her as a child, "Oh no you won't, mister, because you don't *know* the whole story and nobody does but me." Remarking that the mother who possesses "the real, hidden script" is "the character most closely aligned to the film's overall epistemic position," Smith sees the mother as speaking "on behalf of other misrepresented mothers as well as absent/silenced women generally in Hitchcock's films (most notably, Rebecca, Mrs. Bates, Carlotta and the real Madeleine Elster)."[17] Yet, as even this rather moving example suggests, although Smith gestures toward a possible feminist criticism of Hitchcock by naming some of his silenced women, she finds it difficult to sustain a feminist stand *against* Hitchcock. She appears far more comfortable saving Hitchcock from feminist criticism—hence the bizarre final chapter on *The Birds*, which sees all the violence against the protagonist Melanie Daniels as *positively redemptive*, at least as regards her particular character.

Smith argues in general that contrary to what many critics have maintained, the bird attacks are *not* irrational. What the birds signify, however, is not one single thing; rather their meaning "alters substantially depending upon which character perspective we consider them through."[18] In Melanie's case, her abandonment by her mother, mentioned briefly at Cathy's birthday party, where Mitch and Melanie share a private moment, and her consequent emotional isolation are what must be "worked through" in the course of the film, and the bird attacks actually serve to assist her in this. The final brutal attack in the attic confirms Melanie's knowledge that she was abandoned as a child but "as a result of her experience in the attic she now knows and understands this to be true in a much more visceral, emotional kind of way." She undergoes a "catharsis" in the attic, and the bandage then placed around her head by Mitch's mother Lydia suggests a "healing" by a now benign mother figure. "The subtle, tentative suggestion thus raised is that Melanie will now be able to *see* her way forward" (Smith's italics).[19] Never mind that the last view we have of her is of an *un*seeing, catatonic woman.

The manner in which the birds invade the attic "by breaking through the skylight window" suggests a "form of emotional breakthrough," according to Smith.[20] Now, granted we are dealing with a work of art, and Smith is speaking symbolically; but can we really take seriously this form of tough love, which has more in common with Satanic ritual than with what Smith calls a therapeutic "working through"?

The oddness of Smith's reading does not end here, however, nor do the chilling implications of her interpretation for sexually independent women. When, after discussing what the birds represent for Lydia and Mitch's ex-girlfriend Annie, Smith turns her attention to Mitch, she reverts to a more "standard" feminist interpretation of the film and Mitch's role in it, seeing the attacks as at least in part an intensification of the "aggressive, punitive behaviour displayed by him towards Melanie" earlier in the film. Smith says it is even possible to see the attacks as Mitch's "symbolic rape" of Melanie.[21] Now, I realize that in considering the signification of the birds, Smith wants to keep the strands separate—a different meaning for each character. But surely we expect all this to add up, come together somehow, and what it seems to add up to is this: Mitch's "symbolic rape" of Melanie is coincident with her "emotional breakthrough." I think I've encountered this attitude before, but never, or at least never so baldly, in a piece of criticism written by an avowed feminist.

Mitch, Smith points out, largely escapes the devastation wrought upon the other characters, but she confidently declares that the birds massing at the end are massing "for *him*," despite the fact that they blow their chance to get at him as he readies the family car to drive everyone away. Smith assures us that Mitch's "emotional crisis" awaits him at a point "beyond the narrative." In the meantime, until he has the good fortune of undergoing savage bird attacks in order to experience catharsis and be redeemed, he remains, sadly, the only character who is "emotionally unfree."[22]

In the end Smith confesses she doesn't know quite how to read Mitch, as his point of view is seldom rendered. Pointing out the rhyming of the nicknames of character and director—Mitch/Hitch—she assigns both to the space of unknowability. In the concluding sentence of her final chapter, Smith writes, "*The Birds* ultimately constructs not the woman but M/Hitch as its final, most irresolvable enigma, its underlying mystery that can't be known."[23] While Smith appears to believe she has struck a blow for womankind, since feminist theory has so often discussed the way woman is constructed as enigma and pecked and probed for her "meaning," she does not realize that putting a male in the role of a "mystery that can't be known," especially one who has been bowed down to as much as Hitchcock, is putting him in a godlike position. After many pages (the unfortunate chapter on *The Birds* excepted) in which she demonstrates her own critical mastery of the films, Smith takes the feminine tack of disclaiming her knowledge/power in relation to the Master. Hitchcock is once again "divinized," constructed as the unknown knower, *le sujet supposé savoir*.

### More Than You Wanted to Know about Žižek: (In Which the Identity of the "Second Mr. Lacan" is Revealed)

Although Slavoj Žižek has said that his work on Hitchcock and on popular culture more generally is not meant just to illustrate Lacanian thought, but to illuminate Hitchcock, the very terms in which he speaks about popular entertainment suggest that he takes one seriously and not the other: juxtaposing high and low culture, he avers, can serve as an excuse to indulge in "the idiotic enjoyment of popular culture."[24] Film analysis is something of a one-way street for Žižek. As a result, while he may advance Lacanian thought, in doing so, in trying to make Hitchcock "fit" Lacan, he frequently ends up simplifying what goes on in the films. Is it necessary to add that in every respect Žižek restores to us a Hitchcock untainted (one is tempted to say "unstained") and uncomplicated by feminist analysis?

While of course some of Žižek's criticism is fascinating, we can note at least three reductionist tendencies in Žižek's freewheeling "analyses" of Hitchcock: (1) he generalizes, sometimes with wild inaccuracy, about the various "stages" of Hitchcock's career; (2) he psychologizes the films' characters with bits and pieces of out of date, not to say long-discredited, pop psychology and sociology; and (3) he recycles nuggets of received wisdom about the various films, announcing them with an *éclat* that suggests he believes these ideas originate with him.[25]

An example of the first tendency is his assertion that there are "three main stages of Hitchcock's career" and that each "can be conceived precisely as three variations on the [Lacanian] theme of the impossibility of the sexual relationship." Referring to the Selznick period, Žižek notes that the stories are generally "narrated from the point of view of a woman divided between two men, the elderly figure of a villain … and the younger, somewhat insipid good guy."[26] His examples and omissions demonstrate how loyalty to Lacanian dogma prevents Žižek from noticing aspects of Hitchcock that are far more interesting and complicated than his summaries suggest. His characterizations of the conflicts in these films do not fit *Rebecca*, the central work from the Selznick period, and they greatly simplify the conflicts in *Shadow of a Doubt* (not a Selznick picture), which Žižek says is about young Charlie's being divided between her murderous uncle (played by a hardly elderly Joseph Cotten) and the policeman out to capture her uncle, who turns out to be the "merry widow murderer." Žižek neglects what is really interesting about Charlie's divided loyalties—that in an important sense she is caught between her Uncle Charlie, with whom she has a rather incestuous relationship, and her *mother* Emma who, young Charlie laments, "works just like a dog" and who, she insists, *ought* to have the fur stole Uncle Charlie bestows on Emma, no doubt after taking it from the shoulders of one of the widows he has killed.[27] The desire to do something for her mother motivates Charlie's decision to send a telegram to her uncle inviting him for a visit, a visit he has already, as if telepathically, decided to pay. Charlie in effect makes a "merry widow" out of her mother, who neglects her husband in favor of her brother. One might think that such perverse dynamics would be grist for the psychoanalytic mill, but so intent is Žižek on thinking about the couple (even if it's the "necessary failure" of the couple) and woman's relation to man that he falls back on less interesting conflicts than the ones that engaged Hitchcock.

And what could be the reason for Žižek's neglect of the powerful film *Rebecca*—the Selznick film par excellence? Again it's clear that Žižek prefers to think about women and men rather than women in relation to one another, and it is quite simply impossible to sideline female–female relations in *Rebecca*. It is interesting to me, given my argument about the centrality of *Rebecca* in Hitchcock's "oeuvre," a position that I contend put Hitchcock's identity and the notion of what constitutes a true "Hitchcock picture" into question, that Žižek appears determined to support Hitchcock's own characterization of the film as "not a Hitchcock picture." No doubt he would justify the omission on the grounds that *Rebecca* is, as he elsewhere says of films he chooses not to discuss because they don't fit his schema, one of the "'exceptions,' the results of various compromises."[28] That there can be a film made without compromise, without what Peter Wollen in his discussion of the auteur theory called "noise," is an astonishing notion, coming from a theorist who elsewhere mocks the belief in the possibility of "undistorted communication."[29] Furthermore, all one has to do is read the Truffaut interviews to see how almost *all* of Hitchcock's pictures are the results of various compromises (often having to do with his not being granted his choice of stars, for example). Žižek's tendency to fall back on a notion of Hitchcock as an auteur in complete control of his pictures (and, for that matter, of his unconscious!) would seem to go against his own project in taking up Hitchcock's oeuvre, which is to show ultimately how Hitchcock's films often undermine the very notion of personal identity, how they lead to a position beyond subjectivity and beyond what Žižek calls "subjectivization"—to a place where identity is emptied out.

In light of the fact that Žižek frequently refers to the idea that man depends for his existence on woman, or as he says, "man literally ex-sists: his entire being lies 'out there,' in woman," it might seem curious that Žižek would back away from Truffaut's insight that Hitchcock found his true subject and his true method in du Maurier's text.[30] But of course du Maurier is not Woman as "sublime object"; she is a "common woman," as Žižek says of Judy in relation to Madeleine. It must seem intolerable to have Hitchcock's mastery shown to be subjected in part to that of a common woman. Yet so it is: du Maurier in important ways anticipated *Vertigo*—a film which at its core is about man's fascination with woman's fascination with woman—in writing a novel about a woman who appears to be *everyone's* sublime object until her drowned body is discovered and her widower husband reveals her to have been, as Žižek says happens to *Vertigo's* Madeleine when she becomes Judy, "a disgusting lump of slime." Interestingly, in invoking the slime analogy, Žižek refers to one of Jacques Cousteau's television broadcasts in which the octopus is shown to be a magnificent creature at sea but "when removed from the water, it becomes a disgusting lump of slime."[31] Let us not forget that the sea is Rebecca's element.

According to Žižek *Vertigo* demonstrates how the power exerted by a "sublime object" like Madeleine (and surely the same applies to Rebecca) "always announces a lethal dimension." This accords with my argument about Madeleine, which draws on Cixous's notion that "woman for man is death," a point Žižek elaborates on at some length: the sublime object, he writes, "presents the paradox of an object that is able to subsist only in shadow, in an intermediary, half-born state, as something latent, implicit, evoked."[32] Žižek essentially agrees with Hitchcock, who himself pointed out the necrophilic aspects of *Vertigo*. Žižek writes, "The hero loves [Judy] as Madeleine, that is to say *insofar as she is dead*," and concludes, "Although shot almost exclusively from a masculine perspective *Vertigo* tells us more about the impasse of the woman's being a symptom of man than most 'women's films.'"[33] Of course, this gratuitous swipe at women's films serves to further distance the men, Hitchcock and Žižek, from the woman's film *Rebecca* and its title "character," the s(ub)lime object, and it ignores the way critics have shown how crucial the woman's point of view is in *Vertigo*, even if (or perhaps because) it is given to us only at brief moments. These moments are of utmost importance for they serve to remind us of how the "common woman" feels on realizing that to her beloved she represents "slime," or to invoke another word Žižek uses to characterize what Judy is to Scottie, "shit."

Žižek might retort that the woman's point of view, or female subjectivity, is beside the point, as his purpose is ultimately to find in Hitchcock evidence of what he, Žižek, calls "the subject beyond subjectivity." Yet to such an objection I would point out that Žižek himself is capable of departing from his main goals to speculate on characters' personalities, feelings, etc. Thus, for example, he actually draws rather extensively, and it would appear sincerely, on the pop guru of the 1980s, Christopher Lasch, of all people, in offering what he calls a "wider frame of reference enabling us to confer a kind of theoretical consistency on the ... forms of (the impossibility of) sexual relationship" demonstrated by Hitchcock's work."[34] He goes on to speak at some length about "the pathological narcissist" who is the product of "a fundamental disorder in family relationships" caused by the mother usurping the paternal function. Writing about the mother of "pathological narcissist" Roger Thornhill in *North by Northwest* and utterly missing the appeal of the mother in the film and the screwball-comic nature of the mother/son "couple," Žižek observes that at the beginning of the film Roger is shown with "his scornful, mocking mother, and it is not difficult to guess why he has been four times divorced"! The "possessive" mother "disturbs the 'normal' sexual relationship," Žižek remarks. Even more harshly, Žižek in writing hyperbolically of the mother in *The Birds* (who seems to me rather frail and fearful) speaks of the "'irrational' maternal superego, arbitrary, wicked, blocking 'normal' sexual relationship (only possible under the sign of the paternal metaphor)."[35]

But while the birds in *The Birds* may be read as symbolic of troubled intersubjective relations caused by the possessive mother and the irrational, arbitrary, wicked maternal superego, Žižek concludes with some justification that the intersubjective family drama he has been discussing is, when all is said and done, completely overshadowed by the traumatic bird attacks. The birds therefore "play a direct part in the story as something inexplicable, as a *lawless impossible real*"[36] which Žižek significantly winds up equating with something he calls, without explication, "the Bad Object of fascination and the maternal law."[37] The terms don't in fact seem all that different from the psychology and sociology he draws on earlier in the chapter.

If the Real is associated with the maternal law, itself equated with lawlessness, it is also in Žižek insistently linked to what he calls, the "Maternal Thing/Body," which he believes we confront in the final image of the son in *Psycho*. As with *The Birds*, Žižek in his analysis of *Psycho* seeks to go beyond subjectivity and intersubjectivity. The disembodied "Voice" of the mother finds "embodiment" in the son, and "we confront a kind of 'zombie,' an 'absolute Otherness' which precludes any identification." *Psycho*, says Žižek, thus forces us to "identify with the abyss beyond subjectivity."[38]

Žižek's notion of the Real—the abyss beyond subjectivity—as the "maternal Thing/Body," seems to resemble Kristeva's notion of the abject, discussed in Chapter 7, not least because it so intensely evokes horror. Indeed, Elsie B. Michie points out that Žižek *invariably* sees the maternal body as a locus of fears," not of fantasies (whereas Kristeva sees the mother as the site of both, although the fears seem dominant in her later work). In "Unveiling Maternal Desires: Hitchcock and American Domesticity," Michie, whose task is to look at the *mother's* desires (to be something else besides a wife and mother) that are revealed briefly in two films, *Shadow of a Doubt* and the remake of *The Man Who Knew Too Much*, quotes Žižek apropos of the song, "Que sera sera" sung by the mother in *The Man Who Knew Too Much* to her son who is being held captive in a foreign embassy. According to Žižek, the song, which begins with a boy or a girl asking his/her mother, "What will I be?" and receiving the reply, "What will be, will be," reveals "malevolent indifference." In speaking of the shots which "track" the mother's voice up the deserted stairs of the embassy, Žižek also writes:

> This incestuous song which links the subject to the Thing (the maternal body), i.e. by means of which the Thing catches him with its tentacles is, of course, none other than the notorious 'Che sara, sara' [*sic*] sung by Doris Day. … It is … a song through which *the mother reaches, 'catches,' her son*, that is to say a song which expressly establishes the incestuous umbilical link."[39]

In addition to welcoming our old friend the octopus, which makes its reappearance in the above quotation, I want to consider how Žižek gets away with recycling tattered stereotypes about mothers, stereotypes redolent of fairy tales and of fifties' "Momism," of which, despite being made in the 1950s, *The Man Who Knew Too Much* is *not* an example. Žižek explains that, appearances to the contrary, in discussing the mother in the film he is not really talking about women, or mothers, at all. His "procedure," he assures us, "is … strictly allegorical: the 'mother' *qua* diegetic personality is ultimately an agency which, within the narrative content of Hitchcock's film stands in for, holds the place of, a certain formal disturbance, a stain which blurs the field of vision."[40] Here we see that Žižek himself can be as slippery as certain sea creatures. In jettisoning a presumably older model of psychoanalytic interpretation, he takes refuge in pure formalism, ignoring the entire realm of representation, which is the central concern of feminism. For feminism, the question is this: why is it that in Hitchcock and in Žižek the "clinging," "possessive," "irrational," "malevolent," "wicked" "arbitrary" and life-sucking parent is invariably *represented* as a mother, as a person of the feminine gender?

I have one other question as well, this one in relation to Žižek's characterization of the mother's song, "Que sera sera": "*Malevolent indifference*"? Even as a little girl, I loved this song about the possibilities of an unknown and unknowable future in which I might "paint pictures," "sing songs," "have rainbows," a song which told me to go with the flow. Such openness on the part of the mother and the others—teacher, sweetheart—in the song is entirely antithetical to the snaring and clutching of Žižek's boogey woman, who would bind her son to her for life. Finally, we might well ask, what's a mother to do? Should she lie and say the child will be handsome and rich and have rainbows day after day? Should she pretend to be able to predict the future, to be *le sujet supposé savoir*, to be the woman who knows not indeed too much, but *everything*

## Whose Hole?

In the nineties there emerged a new approach to Hitchcock focusing on issues of homosexuality and homophobia. These critiques came from both gay men and lesbians, but each involves very different kinds of issues and approaches; hence, I shall treat them separately.

If feminist film theorists had frequently compared the cut (or, in the words of D.A. Miller, "a penetrable hole in the celluloid film body") to the vagina, a hole that signified castration for men and thus inspired fear in them, some gay critics now argued that the cut signifies not the vagina, but a different hole, the anus, *more* feared than the vagina. Indeed, in his famous essay, "Anal Rope," D.A. Miller contends that compared with the idea of recognizing the anus as a hole to be penetrated, the idea of the woman's hole, although it provokes fears of castration, may be stimulating an anxiety that is oxymoronically a comfort to men who identify as heterosexual. Castration anxiety, Miller contends, is a "normalizing anxiety," resolved along with the Oedipus complex in order for the male subject to accede to his place in the symbolic order.[41]

But Miller is not ready to cut woman's cut out of the analysis altogether. "Recall how regularly, in the child's fantasy that Freud calls the primal scene, sexual intercourse between the parents takes place from behind—or in other words, for all the child knows of anatomy, at the anus, where the mother's penis, somehow lost, perhaps severed, in this very aggression is supposed to have been." Miller plausibly suggests that the anus may raise for the little boy the frightening possibility of being "in the mother's place," of, that is, "being fucked." Since the possession of an anus means the boy cannot simply project the possibility "of being fucked" solely onto the woman's vagina, the straight man requires another "other" "to enter into a polarization that exorcises the 'woman' in man through assigning it to a class of man who may be considered no 'man' at all. Only between the woman and the homosexual together may the normal male subject imagine himself covered front and back."[42]

I am in full agreement that homophobia and misogyny are complexly intertwined, and although parts of Miller's discussion of *Rope* at times seem a little strained to me, I welcome his analysis as one that furthers our understanding of the interconnectedness of woman hating and homophobia. Still, I want to stress the point that Miller doesn't press. If we—women and gay men, that is—perform similar psychic tasks for the straight man, helping to ensure his normalization, it is nevertheless the possibility of *being in the woman's place* that scares the little boy straight. Let's face it, a lot of people are loath to be in the woman's place, including—as we know from the essentialism debates of the late eighties and early nineties—a not insignificant number of women themselves.

Acknowledging a debt to Miller, Lee Edelman, the great punster of academic discourse, has written several articles on Hitchcock's films that follow up on some of Miller's insights and focus in on issues related to male homosexuality. While Miller's focus had been on one of the few Hitchcock films in which two men—rather than a man and a woman—are at the center of the action, two men, moreover, whose story was supposed to be based on the real-life murder of a man by two "homosexuals," Edelman's work probes films that center on heterosexual couples like *Rear Window, Notorious,* and *Psycho* for evidence of anal obsession and anal desire, and finds it in such apparently unlikely places as the shower sequence in *Psycho* and the scene from *Notorious* in which, "deep in the bowels" of the mansion, Alicia and Devlin kiss, hoping to throw Sebastian off the scent of their espionage activity.[43]

In one essay, "*Rear Window*'s Glasshole," Edelman distances himself in the very first paragraph from feminist analysis and claims that while feminism has taught "us" some lessons ("all too well"), it is wedded to the binary of sexual difference and so colludes with a homophobic, phallocentric order. In equating the male gaze with power, feminism, he argues, works "complicitously with the seductions of dominant cinema to keep us from seeing a no less significant—and no less significantly male-associated—desire to *escape* the phallic regime ...," a desire Edelman links to anal pleasure. It may be true that many feminists have not focused on male desires to "escape the phallic regime" (although Kaja Silverman's work certainly has), but this does not mean, as I believe Edelman is implying, that feminists have not themselves desired to "escape" the regime. Ignoring everything that has come after Laura Mulvey's "Visual Pleasure and Narrative Cinema," Edelman cites her brief discussion of two Hitchcock films and admonishes feminism in general by saying that its focus on woman as the object of the voyeuristic male gaze "can ... conceal the intrinsic ambivalence analogous to that by which Homi Bhabha identifies colonial discourse—shaping a Symbolic order founded, however blindly, on the clear-cut distinctions that carve out the landscape of meaningful forms from the umbrage of the Imaginary's ambiguating overgrowth through the power, always already seen, of the castratory saw."[44]

Now, anyone who's read even a part of the vast feminist criticism that exists today knows that it is hardly a unified system of thought; that it has focused for a long time now on issues of gender and sexuality rather than "sexual difference." Moreover, I take umbrage at Edelman's claims to be the first to attend to the "umbrage of the Imaginary's ambiguating overgrowth," since I've spent more than a little time there myself, discussing, precisely, "ambivalence" in Hitchcock, the very topic Edelman suggests that feminists have not broached. What is noteworthy in the quoted passage is not only Edelman's dismissal of feminists' "psychoanalytically oriented theorization of narrative cinema" but the appropriation of the work of Homi Bhabha. Thus, while feminist film theory as Edelman understands it has nothing of relevance to offer a gay male reading of Hitchcock, is in fact said to be complicit with the forces of homophobia, other theories like those of Homi Bhabha, who has had precious little to say about the asshole, are capable of lending some prestige to the gay male project: hence Edelman's effort to colonize (or as he might put it, colon-ize) colonialist discourse.

Edelman is nothing if not himself perverse in the way he goes about seeking perverse desire in Hitchcock's texts, especially that which centers on the anus, partly because he sees it in the oddest of places—for example, the scene in which Lisa has stolen into Thorwald's apartment and wiggles her finger behind her back to show Jeff that she is wearing Thorwald's wife's wedding ring. The ring, as interpreted by most critics, signals Lisa's desire to be married. In contrast to this critical commonplace, however, Edelman draws on Lacan's belief that rings signify the anus—not the vagina, as Ernest Jones had maintained. (Once upon a time feminists and Marxists used to argue about which had primacy—women's oppression or working class oppression; now, it seems gay men pick quarrels with feminists over whose hole has primacy.) Moreover, Edelman observes, Lisa is pointing at her backside in those scenes. Nevertheless, he insists, it isn't *her* ass "on the line" (despite the fact that she here occupies the classically dangerous position of the Hitchcock heroine, caught between the forces of law and the criminal). Lisa's ass "substitutively doubles" for *Jeff's*, since it leads to Thorwald's looking across the courtyard at Jeff and ultimately entering his apartment to menace him.[45] Edelman goes on to link the anus to a paradoxical kind of vision. The lens, he writes, is a ring too. "The blinding image of this blood-red hole [from the flash bulbs going off as Jeff tries to slow Thorwald's advance] gives visible form to the formlessness of the anal cut or opening from out of which the Symbolic order of visual relations emerges as the law of form as such ..."[46]

Finally, it's not clear (but then as the previous sentence indicates, hindsight for Edelman is not 20-20) where this leaves women, who have been excluded from the Symbolic by theorists' insistence on the primacy of castration and now seem to be ejected from the Imaginary realm in which the male anus is said to dominate. Edelman does, very briefly, touch on the misogyny in the film when he says that Jeffries' compulsion to find the woman's body and Thorwald's act of dismembering it both have as their aim "to find the cut in the woman or find the woman cut in order to cast out, project, or excrete the cut that threatens to rupture the Symbolic's structure from within."

There's something ghastly in the casual punning way in which Edelman dismisses the central concern of the story—the murder and dismemberment of a woman, which critics have traditionally seen as reflecting Jeff's ambivalence toward Lisa and marriage. For Edelman, it all amounts to the same thing: Regardless of whether one aims to find the cut in the woman, or to find the woman cut, that is to say, murdered and chopped to bits, the effect is to bow to "the ideological imperative to find the body of woman as such in obedience to the Symbolic contract that demands an account of [men's] relation to it."[47] From the point of view of the woman, or at least this woman, it matters *a whole lot* whether one is seen as a symbolic castrata or is turned into a mutilated corpse, and under such circumstances it is not unreasonable to "demand an account" of the men who don't much care what kind of shape it is in when they *do* find the body.

If Edelman generally lacks interest in the wrongs done to women in Hitchcock films, he is equally uninterested in what is positive about the depictions of female characters within the terms of his own interpretive scheme. Yet, looked at from one point of view, Lisa is, as Susan McCabe has memorably put it, "the anal ideal."[48] She is a perfectionist—"too perfect," Jeff laments throughout the film, as she takes control of the apartment and arranges lovely little dinners and sleepovers. The little suitcase about which Lisa says, "I'll bet *yours* isn't this small" isn't only, as I contended in my book, a double entendre that bespeaks "a *genital* bravado," as Edelman paraphrases me, it's an emblem of Lisa's ability to organize things and retain them neatly packed in tight little suitcases and thus suggests the kind of traits associated with the anal-retentive character.[49] These character traits link her to Hitchcock himself, the man who is *openly* playful about his own anal compulsiveness. Like Lisa, he too famously wanted to get everything just right, down to the smallest detail (in fact, no doubt some of those who worked with him on the set thought he was "*too* perfect"), and of course he constantly solicited recognition of himself as the controlling figure behind the films. Here we are back to my thesis about Hitchcock's identification with and desire for female characters, a thesis that Edelman seems to want to shy away from at all costs, concerned as he seems to be with making sexuality into an entirely male–male affair.

Earlier, I alluded to Edelman's claim to be breaking away from Mulvey's thesis (as if he were not the latest in a very, very long line), by suggesting that he is interested (like Homi Bhabha) in pointing out ambivalences that challenge a Symbolic order dependent on binary distinctions of a genital kind. Edelman finds evidence of this ambivalence in, for example, the shots of the flashbulb going off when Thorwald approaches Jeff; Jeff's is "a desire that wants both to destroy and preserve—to dazzle Thorwald in order to stop him, to arrest his imminent threat, but also and at once to prolong that threat, to dilate and retain it, etc."[50] Again, I hope the reader will recall how central the concept of ambivalence was in my reading of Hitchcock's portrayal of women whom, I argued, the director seemed to want "both to destroy and preserve." What is more, while I did not link that ambivalence to anal desire, I did in fact locate it in the other pre-genital phase theorized by Freud, a different component instinct than the one that preoccupies Edelman—not, then, the anal but the oral instinct/phase which precedes it. I do not see Edelman's approach and mine as mutually exclusive; far from it. Taken together (especially when coupled with all the cross-gender identifications I noted in *Rear Window*—Jeff's with the invalid wife of Thorwald, and even Lisa with Thorwald) they suggest the extraordinarily complicated way desires and identities collide in a Hitchcock film, often with the most disastrous consequences.

Turning briefly to another essay by Edelman, an extraordinarily complicated and in many ways impressive analysis of *The Birds*, "Hitchcock's Future," Edelman here too is intent on diminishing, and finally eradicating entirely, the role of the woman. In this essay, rather than situating his investigations in the realm of the Imaginary, Edelman joins forces with Žižek in drawing heavily on the late Lacan, who was more interested in theorizing the Real, the place where meaning and subjectivity founder, than the Symbolic with which film critics have previously been preoccupied. Edelman coins the term "sinthome-osexuality," which he defines as that which threatens "meaning insofar as meaning is invested in reproduction's promise of coming ... into the presence that reconciles meaning with being."[51] "Sinthome-osexuality" is allied with the birds, for whose attacks there appears to be no adequate explanation and who thus represent a challenge to meaning itself. To support his argument that *The Birds* savage the reproductive imperative on which the meaning of life is generally held to depend and represent a grave (but to Edelman a heartening) threat to the family, Edelman focuses on the attacks on the children to the virtual exclusion of all the other attacks (invoking the figure of the pedophile, and noting that the birds are first seen in "San Francisco" as they "flit through the air"). While he admits that others in the film are victims of "avian violence," he insists that the threat of the birds achieves "its most vividly iconic representation" in the two crucial scenes where they single out young children to attack.[52] Surely this is a very debatable point. In all my years of teaching the film and discussing it with people, I have *never* known anyone who finds the most horrifying scenes to be the attacks on children. *Everyone*, male and female, emphasizes the prolonged scenes in which Melanie is threatened or outright attacked—once in the phone booth, where she largely escapes injury, and once in the attic, where she is very nearly killed and ends up, as a result, in a catatonic state. Critics may endlessly seek to answer the interpretive question, "Why do the birds attack?" but the man on the street's question is "Why does Melanie go up to the attic?" Here is one of the answers supplied by Edelman: Referring to the opening scene in which a young boy wolf-whistles at Melanie, Edelman positively crows over what the film is about to do to her, "Just as the boy's sweet tweet is cheapened by the echoing cheep of the birds, so the reassuring meaning of heterosexuality as the assurance of meaning itself confronts in the birds a resistance, call it *sinthome*-osexuality, that fully intends to wipe the satisfied smile off Melanie's face."[53]

Rather than spending any time whatsoever focusing on the brutal scenes in which Melanie gets the smile wiped off her face, Edelman shockingly ignores her torment at the climax of the movie and replaces Melanie, the film's victim with whom most viewers identify, with a victim from real life, Matthew

Shepherd, the young gay man from Laramie, Wyoming, beaten, tied to a fence, and left to die. Edelman invokes Shepherd early in the essay and then again at the end, when, after describing how the film's "family" drives "through danger," the audience presumably rooting for its survival, he writes, "Somewhere, someone else will be savagely beaten and left to die …"[54]

Yes, and that someone could be a battered wife, just as much as it could be a gay man. I feel an affinity with some of what Edelman has to say in this article. Feminist analyses of the family have seen it as a locus for women's oppression, and there is plenty of reason to think that, for all their differences, feminists (straight and lesbian) and gay men have a common stake in loosening the hold of the ideology of the family. But why is Edelman so intent on erasing the representation of a woman's suffering to redirect our sympathies to the suffering of a gay man? Edelman creates a new and deadly binary, pitting one set of victims against another, and in the process colludes with the powers that have made women into scapegoats representing the evils of the patriarchal institution of the family.

## Matricide: Take Two

While theorists of gay male sexuality who have written about Hitchcock have looked at my work only glancingly, if at all, I have been directly criticized by several lesbians, either for neglecting the lesbian subtexts of a couple of films or for inadequately theorizing lesbianism—in fact, "bisexuality was a much more central term than lesbianism in *The Women Who Knew Too Much*. Some of these criticisms seem to me well founded, although as is usual in scholarly fields, they prove well founded largely in hindsight. That is to say that the conceptual tools for theorizing lesbianism in a way acceptable to lesbians today were not yet available. Some important lesbian film critics at that time were themselves not yet working on lesbian issues but were writing primarily within the framework of sexual difference (between men and women), a framework they would later denounce.

Since the criticism I will be analyzing reflects the work of Teresa de Lauretis, who has most fully elaborated theories informing this criticism in her monumental study of lesbian desire, *The Practice of Love*, I will move back and forth between these criticisms and de Lauretis's study. The three other works to which I will be referring include "The Queer Voice in *Marnie*," by Lucretia Knapp, "'I'm not the sort of person men marry': Monsters, Queers, and Hitchcock's *Rebecca*," by Rhona J. Berenstein, and a discussion of *Rebecca* and Berenstein's article by Patricia White in *Uninvited*, her path-breaking book on lesbians and film.[55]

All of these works by lesbians take issue with me and other feminists who have stressed the role of the mother and the importance of the preoedipal period in the lives of women. In my introduction I wrote that women's bisexual nature was "rooted in preoedipality," referring in particular to the fact that the mother serves as first love object for both the boy *and* the girl. In "Queer Marnie," Lucretia Knapp writes of the "limitations of film theory, such as Mary Ann Doane's and Tania Modleski's valorization of the bisexual space and its precursor, the preoedipal," and remarks that these terms are not *solely suffi-cient* in theorizing lesbian or gay positions in life or in the theater" (my ital-ics).[56] Let me be clear. It is a fact not lost on me that the majority of women are not lesbians. So when I say that women's bisexuality is "rooted" in the pre-oedipal, I am not arguing that either lesbianism or bisexuality are explicable solely in these terms. (After all, "rooted" plants need certain conditions of cli-mate and soil to stay alive; this would in part mean, in the case of bisexuality or lesbianism, a climate in which heterosexuality is not compulsory.) The closeness of daughters' preoedipal bonds with mothers *predispose* women to the kind of passionate intensities characteristic of many female/female rela-tionships, which in *some* cases, though by no means the majority, could lead to same-sex relations. (As I read Patricia White's book, these intensities are what lead her to call certain films "lesbian films," even though such films obviously had to operate through what D.A. Miller calls "connotation.")

Nevertheless, it is understandable that some lesbians would balk at formu-lations like mine. Lesbian sexuality may not be entirely explicable in terms of the preoedipal, but too many of us were content with invoking this stage of mother/daughter relations, rather than moving beyond it in speaking of female same-sex desire. The arrested development of our theories led to the impression that in our view lesbian sexuality was itself a case of arrested development.

Yet in compensating for what is no doubt rightly seen as mainstream femi-nist theory's overemphasis on mother/daughter relations, particularly very early ones, there has been a felt need on the part of some lesbian critics to see the mother as completely irrelevant to the development of lesbian desire. Berenstein and White's central disagreement with my reading of *Rebecca* has to do with the fact that I speak of Rebecca as a kind of mother figure with whom the heroine identifies so closely that she can't assert her own individuality and be recognized as an object of desire by her husband Maxim de Winter. In focusing on identifications, they say, particularly mother/daughter ones, I not only neglect to see the film's hints of Rebecca's lesbianism, but I fail to con-sider the way in which Rebecca herself is an object of *desire* for the heroine as well as for Mrs. Danvers. For this desire to be considered lesbian, Rebecca's "status as a maternal figure must," says Berenstein, "be separated from her role as an object of female sexual desires."[57]

Berenstein's criticism appears to draw on the work of Teresa de Lauretis while stopping short of the extreme to which de Lauretis takes this line of thinking. De Lauretis doesn't in fact see the mother/daughter relation as irrel-evant to lesbian desire. She assigns the mother a crucially *negative* role in the development of female same-sex desire. Speaking of two texts through which she works out her theory, Radclyffe Hall's *The Well of Loneliness* and Cherrie Moraga's *Giving up the Ghost*, de Lauretis writes: "Both fantasies [in the two texts under discussion] speak a failure of narcissism: I cannot love myself, says the subject of fantasy, because the (M)Other does not love me (the Victorian mother was repulsed by her daughter's body, the Chicana mother preferred her son). I want another to love me and to love me sexually."[58] Although de Lauretis arrives at this conclusion solely through the reading of two texts, she generalizes from it in her chapter titled "Perverse Desire," where she most explicitly advances her psychoanalytic account of lesbian desire: "Failing the mother's narcissistic validation of the subject's body-image, which constitutes the imaginary matrix or first outline of the ego, the subject is threatened with a loss of body-ego, a lack of being."[59] It is this awareness of lack that constitutes for the lesbian the castration complex, and requires another woman's body to enter the picture and make good on the lack.

As often as I read this passage I cannot believe I am interpreting it correctly. Does de Lauretis really mean that if a mother like Stephen's (in *The Well of Loneliness*) or Marisa's (in *Giving up the Ghost*) were to have loved their daughters' bodies, the daughters would have been heterosexual? Or does the term Mother (as suggested by the parenthetical and capitalized "M") expand to include all (female?) elements of a society inhospitable to lesbians and not necessarily (just) the biological mother? In short, does lesbianism require the mother's homophobia? In the end it is ironic, in light of the way mothers have been "blamed" for the homosexuality of their sons, that de Lauretis seems to be in effect holding them responsible for the homosexuality of their daughters insofar as the former are cold and withholding.

In the very way de Lauretis describes the mother's relation to her lesbian daughter, I am reminded of the image of Mrs. Danvers, who I argued was a kind of "mother" figure in a film with several such figures. We recall that Mrs. Danvers (whom I call the "emissary" to Rebecca, another mother figure) devotes herself to making the heroine feel her inferiority to Mrs. Danvers' beloved Rebecca, with her black satin and pearls, her "breeding, beauty, and brains." When she tricks the heroine into wearing to the costume ball the same outfit Rebecca had worn for a previous ball and Maxim becomes distraught, Mrs. Danvers taunts, "Even in that dress you couldn't compare." (Mrs. Danvers fails to narcissistically "validate the subject's body image.") She then very nearly succeeds in coaxing her to commit suicide. ("The subject is threatened with a lack of being.") This is the turning point in the movie; it precedes the moment when Rebecca's body is discovered, the truth comes out, Maxim declares his hatred for his ex-wife, and the heroine becomes complicit in her husband's wife-hating crimes and attitudes. If Berenstein and White are correct in maintaining that the heroine vacillates between two object choices throughout much of the film, this is the moment when she definitively embraces the male object choice. Indeed, it is not so strange to imagine that a "mother" like

Mrs. Danvers would succeed in driving her "daughter" into the arms of a strong, protective father figure who *will* validate "the subject's body image."

One of the main quarrels de Lauretis and Berenstein have with feminist film theory's discussion of lesbian desire has been with its tendency to see female identification as bound up with desire (desire first and foremost for the mother). Both vehemently insist on the necessity of keeping desire and identification separate in part so as to rescue lesbian specificity from the lesbian continuum, according to which "women-identified" heterosexual women are granted honorary status as lesbians without actually *being* lesbians or engaging in lesbian activity. It must be said, however, that on this point de Lauretis and Berenstein are now in a distinct minority. Today *most* lesbian psychoanalytic theorists as well as clinicians, following the work of Judith Butler in both *Gender Trouble* and *Bodies that Matter* emphatically reject the strict separation of desire and identification in the etiology of lesbian subjectivity. Adria E. Schwartz writes, "The construction of identification and desire as two mutually exclusive relations supports a normative heterosexuality."[60] Certainly Freud, who put men on the side of "having" and women on the side of "being," was supporting a "normative heterosexuality" in doing so. Indeed, returning to *Rebecca,* it is unclear to me how anyone can maintain that identification and desire are separate with respect to the film's heroine. For, granting Berenstein's contention that the second Mrs. De Winter is attracted to the "lesbian" Rebecca, it is clear that the former begins by doing everything possible to imitate Rebecca so that Maxim will desire her, and then, like everyone else in Rebecca's world, is herself seduced for a time by the very image she tries to emulate.

Schwartz also writes, "The theory [that desire and identification are mutually exclusive] presumes a unitary subject who makes a unified, discrete, and coherent gendered identification through incorporation or internalization." In our society, it is of course the male who is most capable of assuming what he often desperately needs to see as a "unified, discrete, and coherent gendered identification."[61] This is perhaps the place, then, to emphasize that a great part of my book was devoted to showing how desire and identification become entangled, not primarily in the girl's psychosexual development, but in the *male's.* That seemed to me at the time a radical insight, since, as I have said, it appears to be so frightening for men to find themselves in the woman's place. Hitchcock's being forced to film *Rebecca* in a way that did not allow him to take as much distance from du Maurier's novel as he had wanted to do ended in an identification with the female (text) that stayed with him always. Given how often feminist film theory deplored women's supposed tendency to over-identify with texts, I thought it would be fun, as well as productive, to use the theory to apply, for once, to the *male* spectator—and indeed to show how feminine identifications on the part of the (male) spectator seemed frequently to be solicited by Hitchcock, thereby threatening man's sense of stable gender identity and troubling Hitchcock's texts themselves.

When all is said and done, I have to acknowledge that I was in error to have noted Mrs. Danvers' association with lesbianism and not Rebecca's. White writes, "[Modleski's] vivid evocation of Rebecca's sexual daring is disappointingly revealed to refer to marital infidelity, although, as Berenstein points out, Max's reference to the 'unspeakable' nature of Rebecca's confession to him draws out the connotation of homosexuality."[62] I did overlook what, once pointed out, seems obvious—that Rebecca, insofar as the film hints at her lesbian activity, is in a long line of what Terry Castle has called "apparitional lesbians" haunting literature and film. While I do not wish to downplay the significance of this blind spot in a book committed to fostering the return of the repressed woman, I do not believe the acknowledgement of such a blind spot negates all I have had to say about the film. On the contrary, the positing of Rebecca's "lesbianism" strengthens my case that the title "character" is deeply threatening to the patriarchal order. I also want to point out, however, that the film clearly indicates a relationship of a sexual nature between Rebecca and her cousin Jack Favell; moreover, Rebecca goes to the doctor *thinking she is pregnant*, only to learn she has a malignant tumor. For Berenstein and White, the need to repudiate the thesis that female bisexuality is one of the underpinnings of lesbianism leads them to efface the bisexual woman altogether.

Let us turn to *Marnie*, a film in which the objects of same-sex desire are at least alive, to pursue a bit further the question of woman's sexual desire for the mother. In *Marnie*, Lucretia Knapp detects "a queer voice" that she herself links partly to the mother. In the film, Mark's sister-in-law, Lil, sees Marnie as a rival for Mark's affections and so does some research about Marnie's past. Giving Mark a clue about this past, Lil pointedly remarks, "I always thought a girl's best friend was her mother." But I would argue that Marnie and her mother are, to mischievously use the words of Norman Bates, "*more* than friends"—at least in the daughter's psyche. I'm not talking (solely) about pre-oedipal "desire" here. I am talking about a sexual and fetishistic attachment to the mother that has the hallmarks of the perverse desire de Lauretis celebrates. Like the other critics, Knapp claims not to want any truck with the preoedipal theories of critics she confidently labels heterosexual. Yet, oddly, she continually makes claims about the "women's space" in the film, and on occasion makes it seem a lot more blissful than I see it: "The space where Marnie's mother lives is a community of women, where little girls inhabit the street, skipping, jumping, and singing rhyme. Marnie's mom tells her that she's thinking of sharing a household with a neighbor girl, Jessie, and her mother. Like a thief within patriarchy, Marnie moves between this women's community and the world of men, stealing from patriarchy and then returning to the mother."[63] Although Knapp admits elsewhere that the female community is, in the film's presentation of it, "a dark cloud that hangs over the heterosexual narrative," Knapp's words here evoke a kind of fantasy that is very much at odds with what goes on in this space and with how it is configured: tenements and dead-end streets, young girls "singing rhyme" about disease, resentment expressed by Marnie at the very idea of sharing a household with the detested Jessie. Knapp further writes, "The maternal bond is a threat because it opens up the possibility for a desire that is not informed by, or in harmony with, the masculine."[64] Well, that's what many of us were saying once upon a time. One of the values of Knapp's essay for me is that it illustrates how difficult it is even for some lesbian critics not to be seduced by a fantasy of the preoedipal even as they denounce its importance in the work of other critics.

Knapp makes much of fetishes in the film, hoping to draw Marnie away from the preoedipal even as she, Knapp, idealizes it. For example, she sees the key to the safe in Rutland's offices (placed inside the masculine fetish of the purse) as a lesbian fetish, because it provokes a couple of knowing smiles between the secretary and Marnie. (This is, to say the least, a tepid evocation of lesbian desire. More persuasive are Knapp's remarks about the highly charged gazes of Lil as she relates to Marnie and searches for clues about her past.) But there is one fetish that no one to my knowledge has remarked upon, oddly enough since it is one of the most classic fetishes of all time—the fur piece. On the first visit to her mother, Bernice, Marnie brings her this fur and wraps it around her mother's neck. A few minutes later, the fur set aside, Marnie watches with longing as Bernice combs Jessie's hair, captured in a signature shot of Hitchcock tracking into the hair at the back of the head, evoking desire and longing on the part of the one who looks (*Vertigo* provides the most famous instances of this shot). Jessie leaves the house, and Marnie immediately places the fur around her mother's neck. Shortly thereafter the two go into the kitchen (to make "Jessie's pie") and they quarrel. Stung by her mother's insinuation that there is something suspicious about Marnie's relationship with her boss, the fictitious Mr. Pemberton, Marnie raises her voice and asks if her mother thinks she's having an affair with him. Becoming increasingly shrill, she demands, "Is that how you think I've gotten the money to *set you up*?" Bernice slaps Marnie hard across the face, and the pecans for Jessie's pie are knocked over and go flying. These words and the physical chastisement attendant on them suggest to me that what we are witnessing is a fully fetishistic, sadomasochistic incestuous desire for the mother, whose daughter in a moment of rage goes so far as to call her a whore—*her* whore (the whore, in effect, of a whore).

The preoedipal fantasy of the film comes to the fore, and comes in *as* frankly a fantasy, when Marnie watches Jessie's hair being combed while Bernice admits she never had the time to fuss with Marnie's hair (first her injury, then her work prevented her, she says). The fur is just one of many gifts Marnie brings hoping to cover over the narcissistic wounds inflicted on her by a poverty-stricken and desperate mother with a horrible secret she must keep from her daughter. One might have thought this sexualized, sadomasochistic and fetishistic relationship *to the mother* that goes well beyond the preoedipal would have captured the attention of more lesbian critics; that it hasn't, I suggest, has to do with the fact that is hard to talk about the mother in terms that are not idealized, and hard to think of the mother in genuinely sexual terms at all, much less of a sexual daughter/mother relationship that has little to do with feelings of oceanic bliss. It's just plain politically incorrect to "set up" your Mom.

Were I to write *The Women Who Knew Too Much* today in light of the voluminous amount of work in queer theory that has appeared since its publication, I would still maintain that the preoedipal is one source of women's bisexuality or lesbianism (and insofar as that is the case, woman is threatening to man) but I would focus more on sexualities as well as identifications. This would in part involve examining the less permissible and more highly sexualized feelings the "daughter" (be it the second, not that second, and also Mrs. De Winter or Marnie or the female spectator) may experience in relation to the "mother." In particular, I would speak not only of the preoedipal but the pre-genital (which Laplanche and Pontalis say it is important not to conflate).[65] According to Freud, the pregenital "phases"—the oral and the anal—involve sado-masochistic feelings toward the primary caregiver. Helene Deutsch in her work with homosexual women, conducted over 70 years ago, discovered the importance of sado-masochistic elements of mother/daughter relations (such as those we see enacted in the scene between Marnie and her mother) that get played out in adult lesbian relations. Deutsch's findings have been important to more than one contemporary theorist thinking about questions of lesbian desire.[66] Teresa de Lauretis herself gives pride of place to Deutsch's case studies (two of them) in formulating her own theories, crediting her with moving beyond the preoedipal conceived as involving blissful fusion and merger between mother and daughter.

But while Deutsch speaks of lesbian relations as a "return" to the mother, de Lauretis will have none of it. Needless to say, Deutsch was not speaking literally. In fact, what struck her as extremely positive about lesbian relations was the fluidity with which roles could shift so that one woman was now the daughter, now the mother, with respect to her lover. Granted, it is extremely limited to think of any relationship as a simple playing out of mother–child, or even mother–father–child relations, yet it would seem to make sense that early formative feelings and fantasies do to a greater or lesser extent persist throughout life and inform adult sexual fantasies, fantasy being the essence, according to de Lauretis following Laplanche and Pontalis, of *all* sexual desire.

Even the male child does not cut himself off from the mother to the extent that de Lauretis and others claim is necessary for the lesbian. The male, we recall, does have to renounce his desire for the mother and identify with the father, *but* he gets to choose a substitute for the lost object, the mother, when he reaches adulthood. There is, then, for the male, a possibility of a kind of "return to the mother." As Laplanche and Pontalis put it, "The choice of love object ... after puberty bears the stamp both of the object-cathexes and identifications which are inherent in the Oedipus complex."[67] The situation for the lesbian, according to de Lauretis, is different: she must cut the tie cleanly. She writes, "My divergence from Deutsch on this point bears restating: as a result of her successful analysis, the patient does not 'return to the mother' empowered by phallic and Oedipal drives, but effectively resolves the complex, with its 'pendulum swing of the libido' and exits the Oedipal stage."[68]

It is understandable that de Lauretis is wary of the way heterosexual women have used the mother/daughter relation as a metaphor for female sexual desire, without their feeling the need to account for lesbian difference within the category of "woman." De Lauretis in particular is reacting against heterosexual feminists' appropriation of Julia Kristeva, who sees lesbian relations as nothing more than an offshoot of mother/daughter relations, what she calls the "homosexual maternal." For Kristeva, lesbian relations are *nothing but* a playing out of early mother/child symbiosis. Such relations are fine for Kristeva when they are "a sidelight of phallic eroticism, its parenthesis and its rest," but "when it aspires to set itself up as absolute of a mutual relationship the nonrelationship that it is bursts into view." The potential consequences are dire: "lost identity, lethal dissolution of psychosis, anguish on account of lost boundaries, suicidal call of the deep."[69] This is truly nasty stuff (although, in light of the fact that *Rebecca* has been seen as a lesbian text—and even allowing for the fact that those who celebrate it as such acknowledge its homophobia—it is uncanny how much Kristeva's words seem to encapsulate the dilemma of the film's heroine—lost identity, lost boundaries, and the suicidal call of the deep: recall Mrs. Danvers' whispering to the heroine to leap to her death from the window overlooking the sea where Rebecca's body lies).

Given de Lauretis's emphatic rejection of Kristeva's representation of lesbian desire, it is more than a little unsettling that both Kristeva and de Lauretis come, in the end, to very similar conclusions regarding the necessary banishment of the mother. "Matricide is our vital necessity," wrote Julia Kristeva some time ago, and when some of us feminists came across this passage, it raised the hair on the back of our necks.[70] *The Women Who Knew Too Much* was in part dedicated to keeping the mother from being killed, symbolically speaking, or, when all else failed, from remaining dead.

Yet here I am, so many years later, fighting the same battle on so many fronts. As regards lesbianism, I am prepared to admit that such is the infinite variety of human relationships, mother–daughter ones included, that the fantasies of some lesbians are matricidal (such fantasies, it might be supposed, tie the daughter all the more securely to the mother) and that the fantasies of others are incestuous (and probably for most there is something of each, layer upon layer, in fact, of love and hate, envy and greed, the wish to preserve and the wish to destroy). One of my lesbian friends, an artist, told me she became aware of her lesbianism at the precise moment that she realized she was in love with her mother, of whom she remains enamored to this day. From the start, the mother was always fully supportive of her daughter's lesbianism. Here then was a woman who, in loving her daughter and her daughter's bodily image, did not threaten her with a loss of being, but helped her come into being as a woman loving women. Is it really controversial to maintain that the daughter's relations with her female lovers were the stronger for it?

## The Future of Hitchcock Criticism: Is It Ours to See?

In my book, I wrote the following lines:

> According to Jameson ... consciousness on the part of the oppressed classes, expressed 'initially, in the unarticulated form of rage, helplessness, victimization, oppression by a common enemy', generates a 'mirror image of class solidarity among the ruling groups.... This suggests ... that the *truth* of ruling-class consciousness ... is to be found in working-class consciousness.' Similarly, in Hitchcock, the 'truth' of patriarchal consciousness lies in feminist consciousness and depends precisely on the depiction of victimized women found so often in his films.

In a penetrating discussion of feminist responses to *Vertigo*, Susan White quotes these lines, and in her analysis of them does something akin to what so many other critics, I have argued on these pages, do to feminist criticism—misrepresents it and holds it to a different and more rigorous standard than other kinds of criticism are held to. She writes, "Modleski changes the status of Jameson's 'political unconscious' [although note that Jameson is here speaking of ruling class *consciousness*] when she says that women consciously know the truth of patriarchy." She continues, "This is obviously an essentialist position."[71] Put like that, it certainly is. Yet it is White who is changing the status of *my* position by substituting the word "woman" for "feminist." I most definitely do not think that all women consciously know the truth of patriarchy. Blind spots in my work there may well be, but I am not *completely* blind. Rather, my position has been that a feminist consciousness comes about in part through bringing a political analysis to bear on the "unarticulated form[s] of rage, helplessness [and] victimization" that women may experience but do not always have a way to understand. I take it that Jameson is making exactly the same point with respect to the working class.

White also says that I believe there is "a single truth" of the "patriarchal unconscious." I had hoped my arguments in the book were supple enough to demonstrate that, in fact, I think "the truth" is multiple and complicated (although I never meant to suggest I grasped the whole of it). "The truth"—a word that can and was intended to signify plurality, not simply something singular—changes with the times, and along with it, so does the status of feminist consciousness. "Feminist consciousness," like "working class consciousness," is not the same for all people: just as the working class is divided by race, gender, and sexuality, so too are women divided by race, class, and sexuality.

My book, it is true, relies heavily on psychoanalysis and was avowedly dedicated to understanding (some of) the appeal of Hitchcock to both men and women in our time. As years have gone by, gay men and lesbians have also sought to consider the appeal of Hitchcock to gay and lesbian viewers. The work of Edelman or Berenstein and Patricia White seems, to me at least, also to be speaking largely about the relevance of Hitchcock's films to today's viewers. (None of these critics, in any case, spends any significant amount of time situating Hitchcock in his historical moment.) I welcome analyses that complicate even further the complex workings of desire and identification I showed to be at work in Hitchcock's texts, but I am concerned when such analyses scapegoat women or feminist theory or when they reproduce some of the very misogynist and "matrophobic" attitudes found in Hitchcock's work. The decision to write a new chapter was motivated by the desire to call attention to the way some newer Hitchcock criticism was simplifying, ignoring, or setting back the gains made not just in feminist work on Hitchcock, but feminist film theory in general. In the process I have also tried to indicate how feminist analysis, and, say, gay male analyses (like Edelman's) don't need to be pitted against one another but can indeed be complementary.

Robert J. Corber's book *In the Name of National Security: Hitchcock Homophobia and the Politics of Gender in Postwar America*, is one of the few works that have attempted to show this complementarity. It exhibits a refreshing concern to demonstrate the workings of the interlocking categories of sexuality, including gay male sexuality, and gender. His ideas about how the male spectator's identification with male characters both entails desire and works as a defense against that desire seem very compatible with my own.[72] In addition to drawing on psychoanalysis (intermittently), *In the Name of National Security* represents a significant attempt to situate the later Hitchcock in his historical moment. The book contains genuinely exciting insights: I think particularly of its mapping of the idea of surveillance—the spying on one's neighbors in the McCarthy era—onto the category of voyeurism, particularly as it has been elaborated in psychoanalytic theory. Indeed, it seems to me that much of the best work being done these days on Hitchcock is work that historicizes the films. The anthology *Hitchcock's America*, edited by Jonathan Freedman and Richard Millington, contains some of the strongest writing I've seen on the director's American period—and the editors' essays in particular, along with Elsie B. Michie's "Unveiling Maternal Desires" and Amy Lawrence's "American Shame: *Rope*, James Stewart, and the Postwar Crisis in American Masculinity," are especially thought provoking. There is a great deal more criticism of interest in recent Hitchcock studies from which I have profited but have not been able to accommodate in these pages. I suspect the frenzy of Hitchcock criticism won't be abating any time soon. I must admit that I for one look to the future of this criticism with anything but malevolent indifference.

10.  Thorwald in *Rear Window*.

**In Hitchcock films, women's purses and jewelry take on a vulgar Freudian significance.**

11.  Lisa in *Rear Window*.

**The woman has the last look in a film about the power of the gaze.**

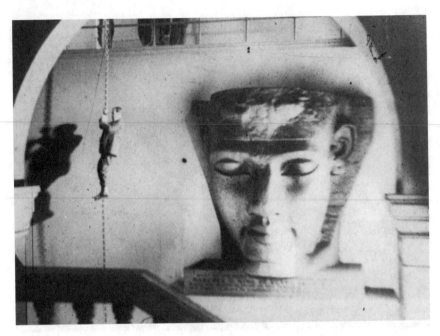

**12.** Tracy in *Blackmail*.

**13.** Scottie in *Vertigo*.

"Being hung, or suspended, from some contraption happens to be among the favorite masochistic practices. Presumably, it gives a functional objectivity to the sensation of suspense" (Theodor Reik, *Masochism and Modern Man*).

**14.** Madeleine and the portrait of Carlotta Valdez in *Vertigo*.

"It is no exaggeration to say that Masoch [from whom the word masochism is derived] was the first novelist to make use of suspense as an essential ingredient of romantic fiction. This is partly because the masochistic rites of torture and suffering imply actual physical suspension (the hero is hung up, crucified, or suspended), but also because the woman torturer freezes into postures that identify her with a statue, a painting or a photograph" (Gilles Deleuze, *Masochism: An Interpretation of Coldness and Cruelty*).

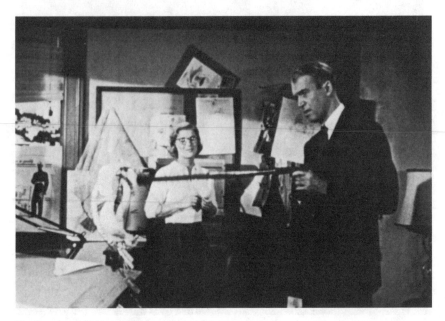

**15.** Scottie and Midge in *Vertigo*.

**Femininity by design.**

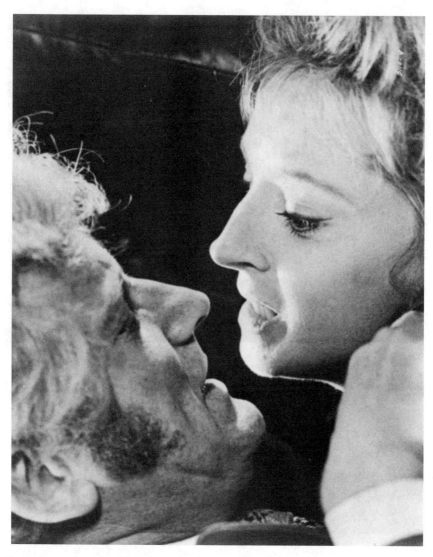

**16.** Rusk and Brenda in *Frenzy.*

**The murderous "lusts of men."**

17. Blaney and Babs in *Frenzy.*

**The murderous "lusts of men."**

18.   The father, the scout, and Charlotte in *Stage Fright*.

**A parable of patriarchial cinema.**

**19.** Eve and Charlotte in *Stage Fright*.

An alternative to patriarchal cinema (a preview of coming attractions): Woman holds the mirror up to woman.

# Notes

## Introduction

1. Laura Mulvey, "Visual Pleasure and Narrative Cinema," *Screen* 16, no. 3 (1975): 6–18.
2. Tania Modleski, "Never to be Thirty–Six Years Old: *Rebecca* as Female Oedipal Drama," *Wide Angle* 5, no. 1 (1982): 34–41.
3. The most explicit statement of this can be found in an interview with Bellour conducted by Janet Bergstrom, "Alternation, Segmentation, Hypnosis: Interview with Raymond Bellour," *Camera Obscura*, nos. 3–4 (1979): 93.
4. Teresa de Lauretis, *Alice Doesn't: Feminism, Semiotics, Cinema* (Bloomington: Indiana University Press, 1984), p. 153.
5. In an unpublished paper delivered at the conference "New Narrative Cinema," Simon Fraser University, September 1983.
6. Susan Lurie, "The Construction of the Castrated Woman in Psychoanalysis and Cinema," *Discourse*, no. 4 (Winter 1981–82): 52–74.
7. Robin Wood, "Fear of Spying," *American Film* (November 1982): 28–35.
8. Fredric Jameson, *The Political Unconscious: Narrative as a Socially Symbolic Act* (Ithaca: Cornell University Press, 1981), pp. 289–90.
9. For one account of this process see Mary Ann Doane, "Misrecognition and Identity," *Ciné-Tracts* 3, no. 3 (Fall 1980), pp. 25–32.
10. In *From Reverence to Rape: The Treatment of Women in the Movies* (New York: Penguin, 1974), Molly Haskell notes the "complex interplay of misogyny and sympathy in Hitchcock" (p. 32).
11. Michelle Citron, Julia Lesage, Judith Mayne, B. Ruby Rich, and Anna Maria Taylor, "Women and Film: A Discussion of Feminist Aesthetics," *New German Critique* 13 (Winter 1978): 87. Hereafter cited in the text.
12. Freud discussed differences between female and male sexual development in "Female Sexuality," *The Standard Edition of the Complete Psychological Works of Sigmund Freud*, trans. James Strachey (London: Hogarth, 1974), Vol. 21, and "Femininity," *New Introductory Lectures on Psychoanalysis*, trans. James Strachey (New York: Norton, 1965), pp. 99–119.
13. Gertrud Koch, "Why Women Go to Men's Films," *Feminist Aesthetics*, Ed. Gisela Ecker (Boston: Beacon, 1985), p. 110.
14. E. Ann Kaplan, *Women and Film: Both Sides of the Camera* (New York and London: Methuen, 1983), p. 6.
15. E. Ann Kaplan, "The Case of the Missing Mother: Maternal Issues in Vidor's *Stella Dallas*," *Heresies* 16 (1983): 81–85.
16. Linda Williams, "Something Else Besides a Mother: *Stella Dallas* and the Maternal Melodrama," *Cinema Journal* 24, no. 1 (Fall 1984): 2–27.
17. Mary Ann Doane, "Film and the Masquerade: Theorising the Female Spectator," *Screen* 23, nos. 3–4 (September–October 1982): 79.
18. Hélène Cixous, "Castration or Decapitation?" trans. Annette Kuhn, *Signs* 7, no. 1 (Autumn 1981): 48.
19. Citron et al., "Women and Film," p. 87. Quoted in Williams, "Something Else," pp. 19–20.
20. Doane, "Film and the Masquerade," p. 80.
21. The term "passionate detachment" is Mulvey's, but it has been picked up by Annette Kuhn, who uses it as the title for the opening chapter of her book *Women's Pictures: Feminism and Cinema* (London: Routledge & Kegan Paul, 1982), pp. 3–18.
22. Teresa de Lauretis, "Aesthetic and Feminist Theory: Rethinking Women's Cinema," *New German Critique*, no. 34 (Winter 1985): 163. Some of the reviews of the Kuhn and Kaplan books strongly criticized their tendency to focus on patriarchal cinema instead of

concentrating on the female vision of women filmmakers. See, in particular, Sarah Halprin, "Writing in the Margins: Review of E. Ann Kaplan's *Women and Film*," *Jump Cut*, no. 29 (1984): 31–33.

23. Gaylyn Studlar, "Masochism and the Perverse Pleasures of the Cinema," *Movies and Methods*, Vol. 2, Ed. Bill Nichols (Berkeley and Los Angeles: University of California Press, 1985), p. 616. D.N. Rodowick challenges Mulvey's reliance on binary oppositions by pointing to Freud's essay "'A Child is Being Beaten.'" See Rodowick, "The Difficulty of Difference," *Wide Angle* 5, no. 1 (1982): 4–15. This little essay of Freud's on a childhood masochistic fantasy has proved inspirational to several critics in thinking about spectatorship and identification. See, for example, Mary Ann Doane, "The 'Woman's Film': Possession and Address," in *Re–vision: Essays in Feminist Film Criticism*, Eds. Mary Ann Doane, Patricia Mellencamp, and Linda Williams, The American Film Institute Monograph Series. Vol. 3 (Frederick MD: University Publications of America. 1984), pp. 67–80; and Miriam Hansen, "Pleasure, Ambivalence, Identification: Valentino and Female Spectatorship," *Cinema Journal* 25, no. 4 (Summer 1986): 6–32. See also Gaylyn Studlar's response to Hansen's essay, *Cinema Journal* 26, no. 2 (Winter 1987): 51–53. The Freud essay, " 'A Child is Being Beaten': A Contribution to the Study of the Origin of Sexual Perversions," can be found in the *Standard Edition*, Vol. 17.

24. Quoted in Rodowick, "The Difficulty of Difference," p. 15n. See Freud's *Three Essays on the History of Sexuality*, trans. James Strachey (New York: Basic Books, 1962), pp. 7–14. Also relevant is Freud's paper "Hysterical Phantasies and Their Relation to Bi–sexuality" in the *Standard Edition*, Vol. 19.

25. Janet Bergstrom, "Sexuality at a Loss: The Films of F.W. Murnau," *Poetics Today* 6, nos. 1–2 (1985): 193n. For an excellent critique of this essay, see Patrice Petro, *Joyless Streets: Women and Melodramatic Representation in Weimar Germany* (Princeton, NJ: Princeton University Press, 1989), 155–57.

26. Bergstrom, "Sexuality at a Loss," p. 200.

27. Janet Bergstrom, "Enunciation and Sexual Difference," *Camera Obscura*, nos. 3–4 (1979): 58.

28. See Sigmund Freud, "Some Psychical Consequences of the Anatomical Distinction Between the Sexes," *Standard Edition*, Vol. 19.

29. See Claire Johnston's "Towards a Feminist Film Practice: Some Theses," in *Movies and Methods*, Vol. 2, p. 321.

30. Studlar, "Masochism and the Perverse Pleasures," p. 605.

31. Christian Metz, *The Imaginary Signifier*, trans. Celia Britton, Anwyl Williams, Ben Brewster, and Alfred Guzzetti (Bloomington: Indiana University Press, 1982), p. 49.

32. Kaja Silverman, "Masochism and Subjectivity," *Framework* 12 (1980): 4. Hereafter cited in the text.

33. In other works, Silverman takes this dialectic more fully into account. See, for example, her relevant analysis of *Psycho*, which she considers in the light of theories of suture. In *The Subject of Semiotics* (New York: Oxford University Press, 1983), pp. 203–13. For his discussion of the dreamwork, see Sigmund Freud, *The Interpretation of Dreams*, trans. James Strachey (New York: Avon, 1965), pp. 311–546. It should be noted that in his book on masochism, Gilles Deleuze insists that the process by which apparently masochistic urges of the tormentor are displaced onto the victim, thereby allowing an identification with the victim, is entirely compatible with sadism. Deleuze speaks of the "pseudo–masochism in sadism" and the "pseudo-sadism of masochism." See his *Masochism: An Interpretation of Coldness and Cruelty*, trans. Jean MacNeil (New York: George Braziller, 1971), p. 109. Deleuze maintains that the two perversions ought to be kept entirely separate, and, indeed, such separation is preferable to the kind of confusion that reigns in the current theorizing of the problem. However, my own study does not follow Deleuze's line, but rather accords more closely with the Sartrean model of masochism and sadism as the two poles between which the subject oscillates in his attitude toward the other. In an excellent, unpublished paper, "Masochism and Feminist Theory," Sonia Rein points out some of the more problematic aspects of film theory's adoption of the masochistic aesthetic and shows how masochism as it is theorized by Deleuze (upon whom Studlar heavily relies), is no more liberating for feminism than the sadistic model proposed by Mulvey.

34. Alice Jardine, *Gynesis: Configurations of Woman and Modernity* (Ithaca: Cornell University Press, 1985), p. 48.

35. Jardine, *Gynesis,* p. 98.
36. Edward Said, *The World, the Text, and the Critic* (Cambridge: Harvard University Press, 1983), p. 53.

## *Blackmail*

1. See Linda Williams, "When the Woman Looks," *Re–vision: Essays in Feminist Film Criticism,* Eds. Mary Ann Doane, Patricia Mellencamp, and Linda Williams, The American Film Institute Monograph Series. Vol. 3 (Frederick, MD): University Publications of America. 1984). p. 96.
2. This, as we shall see, is part of Mary Ann Doane's argument in "Film and the Masquerade: Theorising the Female Spectator," *Screen* 23, nos. 3–4 (September–October 1982): 80. Doane is drawing on Laura Mulvey's discussion "Afterthoughts on 'Visual Pleasure and Narrative Cinema,' Inspired by *Duel in the Sun*," *Framework* 15/16/17 (Summer 1981):13.
3. Ronald Dworkin, "Law as Interpretation," in *The Politics of Interpretation,* Ed. W.J.T. Mitchell (Chicago: University of Chicago Press, 1983), pp. 249–70. Catharine MacKinnon, "Feminism, Marxism, Method, and the State: Toward Feminist Jurisprudence," *Signs* 8, no. 4 (Summer 1983): 639.
4. MacKinnon, "Feminism, Marxism, Method," p. 652.
5. Adrienne Rich, "When We Dead Awaken: Writing as Re-vision," in *On Lies, Secrets, and Silence: Selected Prose 1966–1978* (New York: Norton, 1979), p. 35. "Re-vision—the act of looking back, of seeing with fresh eyes, of entering an old text from a new critical direction—is for women more than a chapter in cultural history: it is an act of survival."
6. Hitchcock shot this film twice—once as a silent film and then again as a sound film. For an interesting discussion of the slight differences in the two texts, see Charles Barr, "*Blackmail:* Silent and Sound," *Sight and Sound* 52, no. 5 (1983): 189–93.
7. Sigmund Freud, *Jokes and Their Relation to the Unconscious,* trans. James Strachey (New York: Norton, 1960), p. 99.
8. Hélène Cixous, "Castration or Decapitation?" trans. Annette Kuhn, *Signs* 7, no. 1 (Autumn 1981): 42–43. See also Judith Mayne's discussion of Demeter's laughter as an "emblem of what the rethinking of spectacle might entail" for feminist film theory. "The Limits of Spectacle," *Wide Angle* 6, no. 3 (1984): 15.
9. Maurice Yacowar, *Hitchcock's British Films* (Hamden, CT: Archon, 1977), p. 110.
10. Yacowar, *Hitchcock's British Films,* p. 111.
11. Donald Spoto, *The Dark Side of Genius: The Life of Alfred Hitchcock* (New York: Ballantine, 1983), p. 133.
12. Yacowar, *Hitchcock's British Films,* p. 103. Beverle Houston and Marsha Kinder also pursue this line in their analysis of the film. See their *Close-Up* (New York: Harcourt Brace Jovanovich, 1972), pp. 52–58.
13. Yacowar, *Hitchcock's British Films,* p. 108.
14. Deborah Linderman, "The Screen in Hitchcock's *Blackmail*," *Wide Angle* 4, no. 1 (1980): 26.
15. Linderman, "The Screen," p. 25.
16. Lindsay Anderson, "Alfred Hitchcock," in *Focus on Hitchcock,* Ed. Albert J. LaValley (Englewood Cliffs, NJ: Prentice-Hall, 1972), p. 50.
17. Donald Spoto, *The Art of Alfred Hitchcock* (New York: Doubleday, 1976), p. 19.
18. John Russell Taylor, *Hitch* (London: Faber and Faber, 1978), p. 100.
19. Francois Truffaut, *Hitchcock* (New York: Simon and Schuster, 1983), p. 63; and Alfred Hitchcock, "Direction," in *Focus on Hitchcock,* p. 33.
20. Eric Rohmer and Claude Chabrol, *Hitchcock: The First Forty-Four Films* (New York: Ungar, 1979), p. 20.
21. Raymond Durgnat, *The Strange Case of Alfred Hitchcock, Or the Plain Man's Hitchcock* (Cambridge: MIT Press, 1974), p. 88. While Durgnat's analysis purports to explore the moral ambiguity of the film, and while he even concludes that Alice experiences too much guilt relative to the other characters, nevertheless such remarks as the one I have quoted indicate his confusion about the issue of rape that he treats in such a high-handed manner. And like Hitchcock, he too appears to use the words "rape" and "seduction" interchangeably.
22. See, for example, Elizabeth Weis, *The Silent Scream: Alfred Hitchcock's Sound Track* (East Brunswick, NJ: Fairleigh Dickinson University Press, 1982), pp. 28–59. Weis's discussion of

the film is heavily influenced by male critics and is even more emphatic than many of them in its insistence that the woman is subconsciously inviting her own rape.

23. Taylor, *Hitch,* p. 100.

24. See Kaja Silverman's analysis of *Histoire d'O* for an extensive demonstration of how a text works to construct the sexualized woman. *"Histoire d'O:* The Construction of a Female Subject," *Pleasure and Danger: Exploring Female Sexuality,* Ed. Carole S. Vance (London: Routledge & Kegan Paul, 1984), pp. 320–49.

25. I am referring, of course, to Judith Fetterley's book *The Resisting Reader: A Feminist Approach to American Fiction* (Bloomington: Indiana University Press, 1978). Daniel Cottom forcefully makes the point about interpretation that I am stressing: "No way of reading is wrong in itself; it can only be declared wrong under specific political conditions, which therefore must be treated as the subject of sociohistorical differences within any literary [or film] theory that would not blindly identify itself with an imaginary law." "The Enchantment of Interpretation," *Critical Inquiry* 11, no. 4 (June 1985): 580. Interestingly, Cottom focuses his essay on the interpretation of jokes. He cites the following example: "Why do women have vaginas? So men will talk to them," and points out that this joke may be "brutally sexist, cynically feminist, or something else entirely," depending on the context in which it is told (p. 576). A joke in Yvonne Rainer's film *The Man Who Envied Women,* illustrates this point. The joke, told by one woman to another as they sit in a restaurant, is as follows: "a man is a human being with a pair of testes attached, whereas a woman is a vagina with a human being attached." In the context of Rainer's film, what might in other situations be locker-room humor becomes "cynically feminist," as are many of the other jokes in the film.

26. Rohmer and Chabrol, *Hitchcock: The First Forty-Four Films,* p. 23.

27. See also Spoto, *The Art of Alfred Hitchcock,* p. 20: "This White girl is certainly for purity. She even kills for it!"

28. Given this merger of the voices of Alice and the landlady, it is interesting to consider that it is the landlady—another woman—who is unwittingly responsible for Alice's ultimate escape from patriarchal "justice."

29. Doane, "Film and the Masquerade," p. 85. Hereafter cited in the text.

30. In any case, Samuel Weber has pointed out that the distinction between obscene jokes and aggressive jokes cannot be strictly maintained. *The Legend of Freud* (Minneapolis: University of Minnesota Press, 1982), p. 103.

31. Freud wrote, "Throughout history people have knocked their heads against the riddle of the nature of femininity. ... Nor will *you* have escaped worrying over this problem—those of you who are men; to those of you who are women this will not apply—you are yourselves the problem." Quoted in Shoshana Felman, "Rereading Femininity," *Yale French Studies,* no. 62 (1981): 19.

32. Spoto's biography, *The Dark Side of Genius,* dwells on this obsession in fascinated and obsessive detail.

33. For a discussion of interpretive triangles in literary theory, see Mary Jacobus, "Is There a Woman in This Text?" *New Literary History* 14, no 1 (Autumn 1982): 117–42; and for a discussion of triangles in literature, see Eve Kosofsky Sedgwick, *Between Men: English Literature and Male Homosocial Desire* (New York: Columbia University Press, 1985). An interesting analysis of Samuel Richardson's *Clarissa* in terms of the issues of rape and the silencing of women can be found in Terry Castle, *Clarissa's Ciphers: Meaning and Disruption in Richardson's* Clarissa (Ithaca: Cornell University Press, 1982).

34. Hitchcock, "Direction," pp. 32–33.

35. Quoted in Spoto, *The Dark Side of Genius,* p. 133.

36. Alexander Welsh considers this possibility in his analysis of the film in *George Eliot and Blackmail* (Cambridge: Harvard University Press, 1985).

## *Murder!*

1. For an interesting discussion of the "psychic consequences" of the "Great Masculine Renunciation" in male dress that occurred in the eighteenth century, see Kaja Silverman, "Fragments of a Fashionable Discourse," *Studies in Entertainment: Critical Approaches to Mass Culture,* Ed. Tania Modleski (Bloomington, Indiana University Press, 1986), pp. 139–52.

2. Roland Barthes, *S/Z,* trans. Richard Miller (New York: Hill and Wang, 1974), pp. 70–71.

3. For another discussion of theatrical motifs in *Murder!*, see William Rothman's lengthy discussion of the film in *Hitchcock: The Murderous Gaze* (Cambridge: Harvard University Press, 1982), pp. 53–106.

4. Georges Didi-Huberman, *Invention de l'hysterie: Charcot et iconographie photographique de la Salpêtrière* (Paris: Macula, 1982).

5. These quotations are discussed by Andreas Huyssen in light of the development of modernism and its repudiation of femininity. See "Mass Culture as Woman: Modernism's Other," in my *Studies in Entertainment*, pp. 188–207. For an interesting discussion of femininity and theater, see Lucy Fischer's chapter contrasting Ingmar Bergman's *Persona* with Mai Zetterling's *The Girls*, in *Shot/Countershot: Film Tradition and Women's Cinema* (Princeton, NJ, 1989), pp. 63–88.

6. Luce Irigaray, *Speculum of the Other Woman*, trans. Gillian C. Gill (Ithaca: Cornell University Press, 1985), p. 245.

7. Kaja Silverman, "Lost Objects and Mistaken Subjects: Film Theory's Structuring Lack," *Wide Angle* 7, nos. 1–2 (1985): 23.

8. This, for example, is Francois Truffaut's understanding. See *Hitchcock* (New York: Simon and Schuster, 1983), p. 75.

9. O.B. Hardison, quoted in Maurice Yacowar. *Hitchcock's British Films* (Hamden. CT: Archon, 1977). p. 135. Yacowar hereafter cited in the text.

10. As was the case with his discussion *of Blackmail*, Yacowar's analysis is very perceptive at the descriptive level, but he gives his interpretation the most ideologically conservative slant possible.

11. See Sigmund Freud, "Psychoanalytic Notes Upon an Autobiographical Account of a Case of Paranoia (Dementia Paranoides)," in *Three Case Histories*, Ed. Philip Rieff (New York: Collier, 1963), pp. 103–86. For a discussion of paranoia in relation to the structuring of shots in the classical cinema, see Jacqueline Rose, "Paranoia and the Film System," *Screen* 17, no. 4 (Winter 1976–77): 85–104. Rose focuses her remarks on Hitchcock's film *The Birds*.

12. Laura Mulvey, "Afterthoughts on 'Visual Pleasure and Narrative Cinema,' Inspired by *Duel in the Sun*," *Framework* 15/16/17 (Summer 1981): 12.

13. Janet Bergstrom, "Alternation, Segmentation, Hypnosis: Interview with Raymond Bellour," *Camera Obscura*, nos. 3–4 (1979): 93.

14. Richard Klein, quoted in Eve Kosofsky Sedgwick, *Between Men: English Literature and Male Homosocial Desire* (New York: Columbia University Press, 1985), p. 23.

15. Eve Kosofsky Sedgwick, *Between Men*. p. 24.

16. Didi-Huberman, *Invention de l'hystérie*, p. 240.

17. Didi-Huberman, *Invention de l'hystérie*, p. 270.

18. Stephen Heath, "Lessons from Brecht," *Screen* 15, no. 2 (Summer 1974): 103–28.

19. Paul Willemen, "Distanciation and Douglas Sirk," *Screen* 12, no. 2 (Summer 1971): 63–67.

20. The thesis that female spectators tend to overidentify with film characters is most elaborately developed by Mary Ann Doane, "Film and the Masquerade: Theorising the Female Spectator," *Screen* 23, nos, 3–4 (September–October 1982): 80. See as well her *The Desire to Desire: The Woman's Film of the 1940's* (Bloomington: Indiana University Press, 1987).

21. Willemen, "Distanciation and Douglas Sirk," p. 66.

22. Irigaray, *Speculum of the Other Woman*, p. 270.

## *Rebecca*

1. Robin Wood, *Hitchcock's Films* (South Brunswick and New York: A.S. Barnes and Tantivy, 1966), p. 44.

2. Francois Truffaut, *Hitchcock* (New York: Simon and Schuster, 1983), p. 127.

3. See Donald Spoto. *The Dark Side of Genius: The Life of Alfred Hitchcock* (New York: Ballantine. 1983). p. 220.

4. Rudy Behlmer, Ed., *Memo from: David O. Selznick* (New York: Avon, 1972), pp. 309–10.

5. Mary Ann Doane, *The Desire to Desire: The Woman's Film of the 1940's* (Bloomington: Indiana University Press, 1987).

6. Janet Bergstrom, "Alternation, Segmentation, Hypnosis: Interview with Raymond Bellour," *Camera Obscura*, nos. 3–4 (1979): 93.

7. Raymond Durgnat, *The Strange Case of Alfred Hitchcock, or the Plain Man's Hitchcock* (Cambridge: MIT Press, 1974), p. 168.

8. Geoffrey Nowell-Smith uses the term "family romance" in connection with Hollywood melodrama. By this term he means the Freudian "imaginary scenario played out by children in relation to their paternity." He is taken to task by Griselda Pollack for his "dangerously misleading," improper use of the term, which has been used by Stephen Heath to describe "a filmic notion of narrativisation and memory which concerns process, rather than content or setting." See "Dossier on Melodrama," *Screen* 18, no. 2 (Summer 1977): 105–19. Nowell–Smith's article is entitled "Minnelli and Melodrama"; Pollack's is "Report on the Weekend School." I use the term here in its improper sense.

9. Truffaut, *Hitchcock*, pp. 129–30.

10. See, for example, Sigmund Freud, *Beyond the Pleasure Principle*, trans. James Strachey (New York: Norton, 1961), p. 10.

11. Eugénie Lemoine-Luccioni, in *Partage des femmes* (Paris: Seuil, 1976), p. 85. For discussions of Lemoine-Luccioni's ideas in relation to feminist film theory, see Stephen Heath, "Difference," *Screen* 19, no. 3 (Autumn 1978): 92; and Claire Pajakowska, "Imagistic Representation and the Status of the Image in Pornography," *CineTracts* 3, no. 3 (Fall 1980): 20.

12. Bergstrom, "Alternation, Segmentation, Hypnosis: Interview with Raymond Bellour," p. 93.

13. Raymond Bellour, "Hitchcock, the Enunciator," *Camera Obscura*, no. 1 (Fall 1977): 66–91.

14. See Daniel Dayan, "The Tutor Code of Classical Cinema," in *Movies and Methods*, Vol. 1, Ed. Bill Nichols (Berkeley and Los Angeles: University of California Press, 1976), pp. 438–51.

15. Sigmund Freud, "Femininity," *New Introductory Lectures on Psychoanalysis*, trans. James Strachey (New York: Norton, 1965), pp. 105–7.

16. Laura Mulvey, "Visual Pleasure and Narrative Cinema," *Screen* 16, no. 3 (1975).

17. Kaja Silverman, *The Subject of Semiotics* (New York: Oxford University Press, 1983), p. 225.

18. Silverman, *The Subject of Semiotics*, p. 204.

19. Pascal Bonitzer, "Partial Vision: Film and the Labyrinth," trans. Fabrice Ziolkowski, *Wide Angle* 4, no. 4 (1981): 58.

20. For another discussion of this shot, see Mary Ann Doane, *"Caught* and *Rebecca:* The Inscription of Femininity as Absence," *Enclitic* 5–6, nos. 1–2 (Fall 1981–Spring 1982): 84. Not surprisingly, given the different emphases in our work, which I discussed in the first chapter, our conclusions are very different. Doane is concerned to show "the impossibility of female spectatorship" (p. 89), whereas I want to suggest not only its possibility, but also the film's problematization of *male* spectatorship and of masculine identity in general.

21. For a relevant analysis of the struggle between these two orders in another film, see Pam Cook, "Duplicity in *Mildred Pierce*," in *Women in Film Noir*, Ed. E. Ann Kaplan (London: British Film Institute, 1978), p. 50.

22. Luce Irigaray, "Ce sexe qui n'en est pas un," in *New French Feminisms*, Eds. Elaine Marks and Isabelle de Courtivron (Amherst: University of Massachusetts Press, 1980), p. 102.

23. Irigaray, "Ce sexe qui n'en est pas un," p. 104.

24. See, for examples, Charles Higham, who condemns the film's "falsity and women's magazine values" in "Hitchcock's World," *Film Quarterly* 16, no. 2 (Winter 1962): 10; and Lindsay Anderson, who, after speaking *of Jamaica Inn*, writes, "It was curious and unhappily prophetic that Hitchcock's first film in Hollywood should also be an adaptation from a Daphne du Maurier bestseller, *Rebecca*—a less boring book, but equally Boots Library in its level of appeal" ("Alfred Hitchcock," *Focus on Hitchcock*, Ed. Albert J. LaValley, [Englewood Cliffs, NJ: Prentice-Hall, 1972], p. 54). The most profound repugnance toward the film is expressed by Mark Crispin Miller in a grotesquely elitist and misogynistic article entitled "Hitchcock's Suspicions and *Suspicion*," *Modern Language Notes* 98, no. 5 (December 1983): 1181. For Miller, *Suspicion* is a great work of art, a consummate example of "adversary cinema," insofar as it manages to subvert and ridicule the "woman's film" and its implied audience. Miller sees *Suspicion* as Hitchcock's revenge on Selznick/du Maurier, and he argues that in myriad ways the film manages to make Lina—and, by extension, the audience that shares her fears— look foolish in their Gothic imaginings. Picking up on Johnny's nickname for Lina—"Monkeyface"—Miller concludes his article by pointing to the (all male) theorists and artists who have "attempted variously (and so far without success) to induce the viewer to break out of his long simian trance and discern his human face." Presumably when women begin to look less like apes they will begin to look more like men.

25. Jean Laplanche and J.-B. Pontalis, *The Language of Psycho-Analysis*, trans. Donald Nicholson Smith (London: Hogarth, 1973), p. 205.

26. Truffaut, *Hitchcock*, p. 129.

## Notorious

1. See the volume of essays, *The Female Gothic*, Ed. Juliana E. Fleenor (London: Eden, 1983). See also my chapter on the female gothic in *Loving with a Vengeance: Mass-Produced Fantasies for Women* (New York and London: Methuen, 1984), pp. 59–84; and Diane Waldman, "At last I can tell it to someone!: Feminine Point of View and Subjectivity in the Gothic Romance Films of the 1940's," *Cinema Journal* 23, no. 2 (1983): 29–40.
2. Stephen Heath remarks that the name is "as crushing as the image." "Narrative Space," *Questions of Cinema* (Bloomington: Indiana University Press, 1981), p. 19.
3. For a phenomenological description of *Notorious*, see William Rothman, "Alfred Hitchcock's *Notorious*," *Georgia Review* 39, no. 4 (1975): 884–927; for a structuralist one, see Richard Abel, "*Notorious*: Perversion par Excellence," in *A Hitchcock Reader*, Eds. Marshall Deutelbaum and Leland Poague (Ames: Iowa State University Press, 1986), pp. 162–69.
4. See for example, the essays on noir in *Women in Film Noir*, Ed. E. Ann Kaplan (London: British Film Institute, 1978). On the de-eroticization of the female gaze in the woman's film, see Mary Ann Doane, "The 'Woman's Film': Possession and Address," in *Revision: Essays in Feminist Film Criticism*, Eds. Doane, Patricia Mellencamp, and Linda Williams. The American Film Institute Monograph Series. Vol. 3 (Frederick. MD: University Publications of America. 1984).
5. Donald Spoto, *The Art of Alfred Hitchcock*, (New York: Doubleday, 1976), p. 162.
6. Jean-Paul Sartre, *Being and Nothingness*, trans. Hazel Barnes (New York: Washington Square, 1966), p. 708. In a controversial article on Hitchcock's *Vertigo* entitled, "The Critic as Consumer: Film Study in the University, *Vertigo*, and the Film Canon," *Film Quarterly*, 39, no. 3 (Spring 1986): 32–41 Virginia Wright Wexman discusses the way the film effects a collapse of the "political" and the personal similar to the one I have been discussing here. Her argument is that psychoanalytic feminist film theory, by focusing primarily on questions of sexual difference, repeats the gestures of Hollywood texts in displacing "explicitly political" and economic issues "into the sphere of sexuality." To counter this tendency, Wexman's strategy is to show how what she calls "political anxieties" having to do with such problems as the cold war are projected onto the woman, who becomes the locus of male fear and paranoia. But Wexman's analysis seems to me misguided, in that her discussion of popular films' tendency to reduce the political to the personal presupposes an older hierarchy of values that feminists have been concerned to call into question—a hierarchy in which the political (consisting of world historical events) is opposed to and privileged over the personal, conceived of as the realm of sexuality. A more feminist approach would, I believe, need to ask how it is that woman becomes the figure for so much displacement. For example, how is it that in *Notorious*, one woman is made to atone for the sins of the Nazi father, while the other woman, the mother, becomes the incarnation of Nazi evil? By turning to psychoanalysis to understand male sexual development (and men's relations with their mothers), feminists have begun to be able to understand how such outrageous scapegoating attitudes toward women can take psychic hold in the male subject. Psychoanalysis has been for feminism a way of continuing to politicize the personal realm (even the unconscious)—*not* of personalizing politics.
7. Roland Barthes, *The Pleasure of the Text*, trans. Richard Miller (New York: Hill and Wang, 1975), p. 10.
8. Janet Bergstrom, "Alternation, Segmentation, Hypnosis: Interview with Raymond Bellour," *Camera Obscura*, nos. 3–4 (1979): 92–93.
9. Teresa de Lauretis, *Alice Doesn't: Feminism, Semiotics, Cinema* (Bloomington: Indiana University Press, 1984), p. 120.
10. Dana Polan, *Power and Paranoia: History, Narrative, and the American Cinema, 1940–1950* (New York: Columbia University Press, 1986). See also his specific comments on *Notorious*, arguing for its generic roots in the female Gothic, p. 280. See also Judith Mayne's excellent and very relevant discussion of female audiences in the 1940s in her essay "The Female Audience and the Feminist Critic," *Women and Literature* 4 (1988): 22–40.
11. At one point, though, the film shows *Sebastian* to be victim—when it takes a high-angle shot of him as he moves slowly across the floor after his discovery of Alicia's betrayal.
12. Michael Renov, "From Identification to Ideology: The Male System of Hitchcock's *Notorious*," *Wide Angle* 4, no. 1 (1980): 32.

13. The whole question of how we come to identify with certain characters needs to be addressed by film theory in a far more complex manner than has generally been done. For one effort in this direction, see Nick Browne's analysis of a segment from John Ford's *Stagecoach*, "The Spectator in the Text: The Rhetoric of *Stagecoach*," *Movies and Methods*, Vol. 2, Ed. Bill Nichols (Berkeley and Los Angeles: University of California Press, 1985), pp. 458–75.

14. Doane, "The 'Woman's Film,'" p. 77.

15. Theodor Reik, *Masochism and Modern Man*, trans. Margaret H. Biegel and Gertrud M. Kurth (New York: Farrar, Straus, 1941), p. 241. Hereafter cited in the text.

16. Spoto, *The Art of Alfred Hitchcock*, p. 173. He is referring to Alicia's manner at the end of the film.

17. Leo Bersani, *The Freudian Body: Psychoanalysis and Art* (New York: Columbia University Press, 1986), pp. 58–59.

## Rear Window

1. Laura Mulvey, "Visual Pleasure and Narrative Cinema," *Screen* 16, no. 3 (1975): 17.

2. Mulvey, "Visual Pleasure," p. 16.

3. Jean Douchet, "Hitch et son Public," *Cahiers du Cinema*, no. 113 (November 1960): 10. For the most recent discussion of the film in relation to questions of spectatorship, see R. Barton Palmer, "The Metafictional Hitchcock: The Experience of Viewing and the Viewing of Experience in *Rear Window* and *Psycho*," *Cinema Journal* 26, no. 2 (Winter 1986): 4–29.

4. Robin Wood, "Fear of Spying," *American Film* (November 1982): 31–32.

5. Linda Williams. "When the Woman Looks." in *Revision: Essays in Feminist Film Criticism*, Eds. Mary Ann Doane. Patricia Mellencamp. and Linda Williams. The American Film Institute Monograph Series. Vol. 3 (Frederick. MD: University Publications of America. 1984).

6. Robert Stam and Roberta Pearson do, however, devote one brief paragraph to this issue in their article "Hitchcock's *Rear Window*: Reflexivity and the Critique of Voyeurism," *Enclitic* 7, no. 1 (Spring 1983): 143.

7. Stam and Pearson, "Hitchcock's *Rear Window*: Reflexivity," p. 140.

8. A constant theme in the writings of Stephen Heath is the way cinema works to "remember" the (male) spectator: e.g., "the historical reality it encounters [is] a permanent crisis of identity that must be permanently resolved by remembering the history of the individual subject." "Film Performance," *Questions of Cinema* (Bloomington: Indiana University Press, 1981), p. 125.

9. Ruth Perlmutter, "*Rear Window*: A Construction Story," *Journal of Film and Video* 37 (Spring 1985): 59.

10. Susan Lurie, "Pornography and the Dread of Women: The Male Sexual Dilemma," *Take Back the Night: Women on Pornography*, Ed. Laura Lederer (New York: William Morrow, 1980), p. 166.

11. François Truffaut, *Hitchcock* (New York: Simon and Schuster, 1983), p. 166.

12. This point is developed at great length in Raymond Bellour, "*The Birds*: Analysis of a Sequence," Mimeograph, The British Film Institute Advisory Service, n.d.

13. That he is so reluctant to do so provides an interesting confirmation of Christian Metz' thesis that in narrative cinema, it is the story, rather than any particular character, that "exhibits itself." "History/discourse: a note on two voyeurisms," *Theories of Authorship*, Ed. John Caughie (London: Routledge & Kegan Paul, 1981), p. 231.

14. Virginia Woolf, *A Room of One's Own* (New York: Harbinger, 1957), p. 77.

15. Kaja Silverman, "Lost Objects and Mistaken Subjects: Film Theory's Structuring Lack," *Wide Angle* 7, nos. 1–2 (1985): 24. In many respects, Silverman's position is close to Lurie's. However, Lurie, in common with many "American" feminists (as opposed to French or French-influenced feminists), seems to share to some extent the little boy's fantasy, which he comes to deny, of woman's "wholeness," whereas for Silverman all subjects are inevitably divided, but in patriarchal culture men are able to project division onto women, thus maintaining the illusion of their own completeness.

16. On this point see Perlmutter, "*Rear Window*: A Construction Story," p. 58.

17. Metz speaks of "that *other* mirror, the cinema screen, in this respect a veritable psychical substitute, a prosthesis for our primally dislocated limbs." Quoted in Stam and Pearson, "Hitchcock's *Rear Window*: Reflexivity," p. 138.

18. Susan Stewart, *On Longing: Narratives of the Miniature, the Gigantic, the Souvenir, the Collection* (Baltimore: Johns Hopkins University Press, 1984), p. 63. It is important to recognize, as John Belton has pointed out, that Jeff does not merely watch, but actively manipulates his neighbors, "writing a blackmail letter ('What have you done with her?'), which keeps the suspected killer from leaving town and later luring him out of his apartment with a phone call so that it can be searched." *Cinema Stylists* (Metuchen, N.J.: Scarecrow, 1983), p. 15. Stewart hereafter cited in the text.

19. In his meditation on the miniature in *The Poetics of Space,* Gaston Bachelard makes a similar point. However, unlike Stewart, Bachelard celebrates the tendency of the miniature to place us in a position of transcendence. See *The Poetics of Space,* trans. Maria Jolas (Boston: Beacon, 1964), pp. 148–82.

20. Jean Laplanche and J.-B. Pontalis, *The Language of Psychoanalysis,* Trans. Donald Nicholson Smith (London: Hogarth, 1973), p. 251.

21. Jacques Lacan, *Ecrits: A Selection,* trans. Alan Sheridan (New York: Norton, 1977), pp. 1–7.

22. I again refer the reader to the opening pages of Mary Ann Doane's *The Desire to Desire: The Woman's Film of the 1940's* (Bloomington: Indiana University Press, 1987).

23. Truffaut, *Hitchcock,* p. 223. Hereafter cited in the text.

24. The phrase is taken from James B. McLaughlin's excellent discussion of Hitchcock's *Shadow of a Doubt,* "All in the Family: Alfred Hitchcock's *Shadow of a Doubt,*" *Wide Angle* 4, no. 1 (1980): 18.

25. Theodor Reik, *Masochism and Modern Man,* trans. Margaret H. Biegel and Gertrud M. Kurth (New York: Farrar, Straus, 1941), pp. 59–71. On the primacy of masochism in human development, see Jean Laplanche, *Life and Death in Psychoanalysis,* trans. Jeffrey Mehlman (Baltimore: Johns Hopkins University Press, 1976), p. 89.

26. Robert Scholes, "Narration and Narrativity in Film," in *Film Theory and Criticism,* Eds. Gerald Mast and Marshall Cohen (New York: Oxford University Press, 1985), p. 393. Hereafter cited in the text.

27. Peter Brooks speaks of the same activity in similar terms, terms recalling the way in which "femininity" is perceived and constructed under patriarchy: "The assumption of another's story, the entry into narratives not one's own, runs the risk of an alienation from self that in Balzac's work repeatedly evokes the threat of madness and aphasia." See his *Reading for the Plot: Design and Intention in Narrative* (New York: Vintage, 1985), p. 219.

28. Teresa de Lauretis borrows this term, "narrative image," from Stephen Heath: "In cinema … woman properly represents the fulfillment of the narrative promise (made, as we know, to the little boy), and that representation works to support the male status of the mythical subject. The female position, produced as the end result of narrativization, is the figure of narrative closure, the narrative image in which the film, as Heath says, 'comes together.'" *Alice Doesn't: Feminism, Semiotics, Cinema* (Bloomington: Indiana University Press, 1984), p. 140.

29. Sigmund Freud, "On Narcissism: An Introduction," *The Standard Edition of the Complete Psychological Works of Sigmund Freud,* Vol. 14, trans. James Strachey (London: Hogarth, 1974), pp. 88–89.

30. Jean-Louis Baudry, "Ideological Effects of the Basic Cinematographic Apparatus," trans. Alan Williams, *Apparatus: Cinematographic Apparatus: Selected Writings,* Ed. Theresa Hak Kyung Cha (New York: Tanam, 1980), p. 29.

31. Jean-Louis Baudry, "Author and Analyzable Subject," in *Apparatus,* p. 68.

32. Baudry, "Ideological Effects," p. 32. In light of the "headless woman" motif in Hitchcock, consider the following remark by Joan Copjec, "We know that the dreamer dreams of himself when he dreams of a person whose head he cannot see." "The Anxiety of the Influencing Machine," *October* 23 (Winter 1982): 44.

## *Vertigo*

1. Robin Wood, "Fear of Spying," *American Film* (November 1982): 35. This discussion of *Vertigo,* which attempts to "save Hitchcock for feminism," is not, in my opinion, nearly as provocative nor, ironically, ultimately as useful for feminism as his earlier discussion of the film in his book, a discussion Wood now sees as "shot through with a subtle and insidious sexism."

2. Laura Mulvey, "Visual Pleasure and Narrative Cinema," *Screen* 16, no. 3 (1975): 16.

3. Richard Abel, *"Stage Fright:* The Knowing Performance," *Film Criticism* 9, no. 2 (1984–85): 50n.

4. Wood, "Fear of Spying," p. 35.

5. The term is Roland Barthes'. See *S/Z,* trans. Richard Miller (New York: Hill and Wang, 1974), p. 8.

6. See Kaja Silverman's "Fragments of a Fashionable Discourse," in *Studies in Entertainment: Critical Approaches to Mass Culture,* Ed. Tania Modleski (Bloomington: Indiana University Press, 1986).

7. In the scene we have been discussing, for example, he tries to overcome his vertigo by climbing onto a footstool, and counters Midge's skepticism by querying, "What do you *want* me to start with? The Golden Gate Bridge?"

8. Hélène Cixous, "Castration or Decapitation?" trans. Annette Kuhn. *Signs,* 7. no. 1 (Autumn 1981): 48.

9. See Raymond Bellour, "Hitchcock the Enunciator," *Camera Obscura,* no. 1 (Fall 1977): 66–91.

10. Donald Spoto, *The Art of Alfred Hitchcock,* (New York: Doubleday, 1976) p. 309.

11. Sarah Kofman, *The Enigma of Woman,* trans. Catherine Porter (Ithaca: Cornell University Press, 1985), p. 56.

12. See Sigmund Freud, "The 'Uncanny,'" in *On Creativity and the Unconscious: Papers on the Psychology of Art, Literature, Love, Religion,* Ed. Benjamin Nelson (New York: Harper Torch-books, 1958), p. 148. Besides explicitly connecting the uncanny to the figure of the double, Freud also links it to repetition compulsion—a connection that is clearly pertinent to *Vertigo,* with its continual repetitions at the level of character and plot, and with its circular constructions at the level of form. For one explanation of the connection between the uncanny and repetition, see J. Hillis Miller, *Fiction and Repetition: Seven English Novels* (Cambridge: Harvard University Press, 1982), pp. 236–37n.

13. On the distinction between the "real" father and the "dead" father, see Juliet Mitchell, *Psychoanalysis and Feminism* (New York: Vintage, 1974), p. 395.

14. Kofman, *The Enigma of Woman,* p. 207.

15. Shoshana Felman, "Women and Madness: The Critical Phallacy," *Diacritics,* no. 5 (Winter 1975): 9. Hereafter cited in the text.

16. "If the woman looks, the spectacle provokes, castration is in the air, the Medusa's head is not far off; thus, she must not look, is absorbed herself on the side of the seen, seeing herself, Lacan's femininity." Stephen Heath, "Difference," *Screen* 19, no. 3 (Autumn 1978): 92.

17. Sigmund Freud, "Mourning and Melancholia," *The Standard Edition of the Complete Psychological Works of Sigmund Freud,* Vol. 14, trans, James Strachey (London: Hogarth, 1974), p. 246. It is noteworthy that in *Speculum of the Other Woman,* trans. Gillian C. Gill (Ithaca: Cornell University Press, 1985), Luce Irigaray shows how Freud's account of femininity coincides point for point with his account of melancholia. In this way, we could say that Scottie, both by virtue of his identification with the woman and the fact that he has succumbed to melancholia, is doubly emasculated, "feminized." Freud hereafter cited in the text.

18. In "The Ego and the Id," Freud notes that in fact it is a very *common* situation for the ego to regress to identification with the object. See *The Ego and the Id,* trans. Joan Rivière (New York: Norton, 1960), pp. 13–24.

19. Many instances could be cited. In *Notorious,* as we saw, we get a point-of-view shot of Alicia driving while drunk, and she mistakes her hair for "fog." Later in the film, other point-of-view shots show the blurring of her vision when she is nearly poisoned to death. Marnie is afflicted with fits whenever she sees the color red, and, again, as spectators we experience her disorientation through point-of-view shots. In *Psycho,* Janet Leigh's sightless eye after she has been stabbed to death in the shower is emphasized through the use of a still photograph, and at the end of the film Mother's eye sockets are visually underscored by showing the reflection of a swinging lightbulb in them.

20. Francois Truffaut, *Hitchcock* (New York: Simon and Schuster, 1983), p. 248.

21. Truffaut, *Hitchcock,* p. 244.

22. Sigmund Freud, "Femininity," *New Introductory Lectures on Psychoanalysis,* trans. James Strachey (New York: Norton, 1965), quoted in Kofman, *The Enigma of Woman,* p. 104. See also Lucy Fischer's discussion of bisexuality in "Two-Faced Woman: The 'Double' in Women's Melodrama of the 1940's." For Fischer, the bisexuality expressed in the figure of

the female double is entirely negative from a feminist viewpoint, and her analysis, unlike Kofman's, condemns the Freudian imposition of a "false bifurcation" on the female body, which thus, according to Fischer, becomes the "battleground of hostile masculine and feminine forces." *Cinema Journal* 23, no. 1 (Fall 1983): 39.

23. Teresa de Lauretis, *Alice Doesn't: Feminism, Semiotics, Cinema* (Bloomington: Indiana University Press, 1984), p. 153.
24. De Lauretis, *Alice Doesn't*, p. 143.
25. Kofman, *The Enigma of Woman*, p. 223.
26. I am not necessarily speaking of a represented biological mother and daughter. It could be a daughter and mother-in-law, as it is in *Notorious* and *The Birds;* in both these films, the resemblance between the mother-in-law and the daughter is striking, suggesting the truth of Susan Lurie's argument that, in a film like *The Birds*, the project is to kill off the mother *in* the daughter. See her "The Construction of the Castrated Woman in Psychoanalysis and Cinema," *Discourse*, no. 4 (Winter 1981–82): 52–74.
27. Truffaut, *Hitchcock*, p. 243.

# Frenzy

1. Donald Spoto, *The Dark Side of Genius: The Life of Alfred Hitchcock* (New York: Ballantine, 1983), p. 545. See also the discussion of the reviews *of Frenzy in* Jeanne Thomas Allen, "The Representation of Violence to Women: Hitchcock's *Frenzy,*" *Film Quarterly* 38, no. 3 (Spring 1985): 31. Allen quotes Vincent Canby, "I suspect that films like *Frenzy* may be sicker and more pernicious than your cheapie, hum-drum porno flick, because they are slicker, more artistically compelling versions of sadomasochistic fantasies and because they leave me (sic.) feeling more angry and more impotent simultaneously."
2. Virginia Wright Wexman, "The Critic as Consumer: Film Study in the University, *Vertigo,* and the Film Canon," *Film Quarterly* 39, no. 3 (Spring 1986): 32–73.
3. Robin Wood, "Fear of Spying," p. 31. *American Film* (November 1982): 31.
4. Raymond Durgnat, alone among critics that I am aware of, has noticed that food and pollution function together in an important way in the film. However, he never gets around to saying *how* they function, and is content simply to point out the existence of these elements. See *The Strange Case of Alfred Hitchcock, or the Plain Man's Hitchcock* (Cambridge: MIT Press, 1974), pp. 394–401.
5. Claude Lévi-Strauss, *The Savage Mind* (Chicago: University of Chicago Press, 1966), p. 105.
6. Lévi-Strauss, *The Savage Mind*, p. 106.
7. Claude Lévi-Strauss, *The Raw and the Cooked: Introduction to a Science of Mythology*, Vol. 1, trans. John and Doreen Weightman (Chicago: University of Chicago Press, 1969).
8. See, for example, Freud's remarks on cannibalism in *Totem and Taboo*. "By incorporating parts of a person's body, through the act of eating, one at the same time acquires the qualities possessed by him." *The Standard Edition of the Complete Psychological Works of Sigmund Freud,* Vol. 13, trans. James Strachey (London: Hogarth, 1974), p. 82.
9. Julia Kristeva, *Powers of Horror: An Essay on Abjection,* trans. Leon S. Roudiez (New York: Columbia University Press, 1982), p. 64. Kristeva herself has something to say about Hitchcock and horror in her essay entitled "Ellipsis on Dread and the Specular Seduction," trans. Dolores Burdick, *Wide Angle* 3, no. 3 (1979): 42–47. But her prejudice against anything that has mass appeal is such that she simply cannot see the extent to which Hitchcock's cinema, being an exercise in sustained abjection, is of relevance to her theories. For an extremely interesting discussion of Hitchcock's British film *The Lady Vanishes* in the light of Kristeva's work, see Patrice Petro, "Rematerializing the Vanishing 'Lady': Feminism, Hitchcock, and Interpretation," *A Hitchcock Reader*, Eds. Marshall Deutelbaum and Leland Poague (Ames: Iowa State University Press, 1986), pp. 122–33. Kristeva hereafter cited in the text.
10. For an excellent discussion of these motifs in *Psycho,* see James Naremore, *Filmguide to Psycho* (Bloomington: Indiana University Press, 1973). This analysis is, I believe, the best ever written about the film.
11. Kaja Silverman, "Lost Objects and Mistaken Subjects: Film Theory's Structuring Lack," *Wide Angle* 7, nos. 1–2 (1985): 24. See also Christian Metz on the relation of the technology of photography to orality. *The Imaginary Signifier,* trans. Celia Britton, Anwyl Williams, Ben Brewster, and Alfred Guzzetti (Bloomington: Indiana University Press, 1982), p. 50.

12. Sigmund Freud, "Mourning and Melancholia," *Standard Edition*, Vol. 14, p. 250. See also *Three Essays on the Theory of Sexuality*, trans. James Strachey (New York: Basic Books, 1962), p. 64.
13. See the entries on cannibalism and incorporation in Jean Laplanche and J.-B. Pontalis, *The Language of Psychoanalysis*, trans. Donald Nicholson Smith (London: Hogarth, 1973).
14. Mary Douglas, *Purity and Danger: An Analysis of the Concepts of Pollution and Taboo* (New York: Praeger, 1966), p. 142.
15. Spoto, *The Dark Side of Genius*, p. 545.
16. As an example, see V. F. Perkins, *Film as Film: Understanding and Judging Movies* (New York: Penguin, 1972), pp. 107–15.
17. I could not disagree more strongly with Jeanne Thomas Allen, who analyzes the rape sequence in detail to demonstrate Hitchcock's thoroughgoing misogyny. Allen sees "a suggestion of submissive cooperation" here, in particular in Brenda's request to remove her own clothing rather than have it ripped off by Rusk. "The gesture allows for an element of ambiguity and projection for the male viewer" (p. 34). Later Allen is even more forceful in her condemnation of the scene, claiming that there is *no* ambiguity whatsoever: "It is the objectification of a particularly pathological but culturally logical male subjectivity in patriarchy, and the film spectator, male or female, is unambiguously forced to share it" (p. 35). See "The Representation of Violence to Women: Hitchcock's *Frenzy*," *Film Quarterly* 28, No 3 (Spring 1985).

## Afterword 1

1. Quoted in Sarah Kofman, *The Enigma of Woman*, trans. Catherine Porter (Ithaca; Cornell University Press, 1985), p. 51.
2. Kofman, *The Enigma of Woman*, p. 67.
3. In "When the Woman Looks." Linda Williams discusses the "distorting mirror" of patriarchy. See *Re–vision: Essays in Feminist Film Criticism*, Eds. Mary Ann Doane. Patricia Mellencamp. and Linda Williams. The American Film Institute Monograph Series. Vol. 3 (Frederick. MD: University Puhlications of America. 1984).
4. Jean–Paul Sartre, *Being and Nothingness*, trans. Hazel Barnes (New York: Washington Square, 1966), p. 10.
5. Thus Kristin Thompson calls the film a "duplicitous text." See "The Duplicitous Text: An Analysis *of Stage Fright*," *Film Reader* 2 (1977): 52–64.
6. William Rothman, *Hitchcock: The Murderous Gaze*, (Cambridge: Harvard University Press, 1982), p. 106.
7. Rothman, *Hitchcock: The Murderous Gaze*, p. 107.
8. In an early and highly influential essay on women and cinema, Claire Johnston pointed out the way woman *as* woman was absent in patriarchal cinema. See "Women's Cinema as Countercinema" in *Movies and Methods*, Vol. 1, Ed. Bill Nichols (Berkeley and Los Angeles: University of California Press, 1976), pp. 208–17.
9. Fredric Jameson, "Reading Hitchcock," *October* 23 (Winter 1982): 15.
10. Quoted in Jameson, "Reading Hitchcock," p. 15.

## Afterword 2

1. But it is not without assistance that I arise. I am deeply grateful to Devon Hodges and Susan McCabe for their support and for their astute criticisms of this chapter.
2. Slavoj Žižek, "Alfred Hitchcock, or, The Form and Its Historical Mediation," in *Everything You Always Wanted to Know about Lacan (But Were Afraid to Ask Hitchcock)*, Ed. Slavoj Žižek (London: Verso, 1992) p. 10.
3. The author of at least one avowedly feminist study of Hitchcock that looks at the centrality of the father/daughter relation in Hitchcock's life and his films directly allies herself with Rothman in arguing that Hitchcock's films in the 1950s show "a greater trust in the audience to respond *correctly* to his films, to recognize him as "master" (in Rothman's terms), as 'father' in my terms—and by recognizing him, to be assigned a position of relative equality to him" (my italics). The reader may recall that for Rothman too, bowing before the godlike creator of the films would somehow put the viewer in a relation of equality with the master/

father. See Paula Marantz Cohen, *Alfred Hitchcock: The Legacy of Victorianism* (Lexington, Kentucky: The University Press of Kentucky, 1995), p. 85.

4. Robert E. Kapsis, *Hitchcock: The Making of a Reputation* (Chicago and London: The University of Chicago Press, 1992), p. 137.
5. Quoted in Kapsis, p. 134. See Rebecca Bailin, "Feminist Readership, Violence, and *Marnie*," *Film Reader* 5 (1982): 24–35.
6. Quoted in Kapsis, pp. 134–35.
7. Kapsis, p. 138.
8. Kapsis, p. 138.
9. Kapsis, p. 137.
10. Michelle Piso, "Mark's Marnie," in *A Hitchcock Reader*, Ed. Marshall Deutelbaum and Leland Poague (Ames, Iowa: Iowa State Press, 1986), p. 296.
11. Piso, p. 296.
12. Piso, p. 297.
13. Piso, p. 295.
14. Piso, p. 291.
15. Piso, p. 293. So much for Kapsis's claim that Piso seems unaware of the "ambiguous" presentation of the rape. Indeed, *pace* Kapsis, Piso exhibits keen awareness that *Marnie's* "narrative levels are inconsistent," that the film conveys "conflicting ideologies," p. 303.
16. Kapsis, p. 146.
17. Susan Smith, *Hitchcock: Suspense, Humour and Tone* (London: British Film Institute, 2000), p. 137.
18. Smith, p. 135.
19. Smith, p. 140.
20. Smith, p. 139.
21. Smith, p. 145.
22. Smith, p. 148.
23. Smith, p. 149.
24. Žižek, "Everything You Always Wanted to Know," p. viii.
25. As an example of the latter, see his discussion of *Rear Window* in which he notes that what goes on across the courtyard in the film are "*fantasy figurations of what could happen to him and Grace Kelly*" (his italics). *Looking Awry: An Introduction to Jacques Lacan through Popular Culture* (Cambridge and London: MIT Press, 1991), p. 92.
26. Žižek, *Looking Awry*, p. 101.
27. "Leave my mother alone, or I'll kill you myself," says young Charlie to her uncle at one point. It is out of fear for what the knowledge about Charlie's identity as a murderer will do to her mother that Charlie must bear the burden of this knowledge herself. As for the policeman/possible future husband he is, as Paula Marantz Cohen points out with a bit of understatement, "hardly a weighty presence in the film" (p. 72).
28. Žižek, *Looking Awry*, p. 98.
29. Peter Wollen, *Signs and Meaning in the Cinema* (Bloomington, Indiana: University of Indiana Press, 1972), p. 104. Slavoj Žižek, "From Desire to Drive: Why Lacan is not Lacaniano," *Atlantica de las Artes* 14 (1996), p. 7.
30. Slavoj Žižek, *Enjoy Your Symptom! Jacques Lacan in Hollywood and Out* (New York and London: Routledge, 1992), p. 155
31. Žižek, *Looking Awry*, p. 84.
32. Žižek, *Looking Awry*, pp. 83–84.
33. Žižek, *Looking Awry*, p. 85.
34. Žižek, *Looking Awry*, p. 102.
35. Žižek, *Looking Awry*, p. 99.
36. Žižek, *Looking Awry*, p. 105.
37. Žižek, *Looking Awry*, p. 106.
38. Žižek, "In His Bold Gaze My Ruin is Written," *Everything You Wanted to Know*, p. 234. Tom Cohen has pointed to a weakness in certain of Žižek's formulations, like this one that posits the viewer's "identification" with the "abyss beyond identification." The rhetoric suggests Žižek's inability to go the distance. "While Žižek closes the model of identification and subjectivization, he does so by moving to the perverse endpoint and inversion (emptying) of the same discursive terms—not quite 'beyond' it." See his *Anti-Mimesis from Plato to Hitchcock* (Cambridge: Cambridge University Press, 1994), p. 232.

39. Quoted in Michie, p. 42.
40. Žižek, *Enjoy Your Symptom!*, p. 119.
41. D.A. Miller, "Anal Rope," *Representations* 32 (Fall 1990), p. 127.
42. Miller, p. 128.
43. Lee Edelman, "Piss Elegant: Freud, Hitchcock, and the Micturating Penis," *GLQ* 2 nos. 1–2 (1995), p. 155. See Kaja Silverman, *Male Subjectivity at the Margins* (New York: Routledge, 1992).
44. Lee Edelman, "*Rear Window*'s Glasshole," *Out Takes: Essays on Queer Theory and Film*, Ed. Ellis Hanson (Durham, North Carolina: Duke University Press, 1999), p. 72.
45. Edelman, "*Rear Window*'s Glasshole," p. 84
46. Edelman, "*Rear Window*'s Glasshole," p. 89.
47. Edelman, "*Rear Window*'s Glasshole," p. 91.
48. In conversation.
49. Edelman, "*Rear Window*'s Glasshole," p. 81.
50. Edelman, "*Rear Window*'s Glasshole," p. 87.
51. Lee Edelman, "Hitchcock's Future," in *Alfred Hitchcock: Centenary Essays*, Eds. Richard Allen and S. Ishii-Gonzales (London: British Film Institute, 1999), p. 240.
52. Edelman, "Hitchcock's Future," p. 243.
53. Edelman, "Hitchcock's Future, p. 245.
54. Edelman, "Hitchcock's Future," p. 254.
55. De Lauretis's book was published after the articles, but many of her ideas circulated before its publication in essay form.
56. Lucretia Knapp, "Queer *Marnie*," *Cinema Journal* 32 (Summer 1993), p. 8.
57. Rhona J. Berenstein, "I'm Not the Sort of Person Men Marry: Monsters, Queers, and Hitchcock's *Rebecca*," *CineAction* 29 (Fall 1992), p. 90. Speaking of my casting both Rebecca and Mrs. Danvers as mother figures for the heroine, Patricia White remarks that neither woman seems "remotely maternal." I don't know about that. I've known plenty of cold and withholding mothers. Is White here indulging in a little nostalgia for the preoedipal dyad? See *Uninvited: Classical Hollywood Cinema and Lesbian Representability* (Bloomington, Indiana: Indiana University Press, 1999), p. 66.
58. Teresa de Lauretis, *The Practice of Love: Lesbian Sexuality and Perverse Desire* (Bloomington, Indiana: Indiana University Press, 1994), p. 249.
59. De Lauretis, p. 262.
60. Adria E. Schwartz, *Sexual Subjects: Lesbians, Gender, and Psychoanalysis* (New York: Routledge, 1998), p. 20.
61. Schwartz, p. 20.
62. White, p. 66.
63. Knapp, p. 17.
64. Knapp, p. 18.
65. "'Preoedipal' refers to the interpersonal situation (absence of the Oedipal triangle), while 'pregenital' concerns the type of sexual activity in question." J. Laplanche and J.-B. Pontalis, *The Language of Psychoanalysis*, trans. Donald Nicholson-Smith (New York: W.W. Norton, 1973), p. 328.
66. See, for example, Noreen O'Connor and Joanna Ryan, *Wild Desires and Mistaken Identities: Lesbianism and Psychoanalysis* (New York: Columbia University Press, 1993), esp. pp. 62–72.
67. Laplanche and Pontalis, p. 285.
68. De Lauretis, p. 290.
69. Quoted in de Lauretis, p. 179.
70. Julia Kristeva, *Black Sun*, trans Leon S. Roudiez (New York: Columbia University Press, 1989), p. 27.
71. Susan White, "*Vertigo* and the Problem of Knowledge in Feminist Film Theory," in *Centenary Essays*, p. 283. For more discussion of my "essentializing way," see White's "Allegory and Referentiality: *Vertigo* and Feminist Criticism," *MLN*, 106 (December 1991), pp. 910–32.
72. In other respects, the book is somewhat disappointing, especially when it relies, as it often does, on a kind of reflection theory of art in relation to its historical moment. Take, for example, Corber's analysis of the 1950s version of *The Man Who Knew Too Much*. Corber draws heavily on Dr. Spock to show that Hitchcock's film is complicit with the forces that pushed women back into the home and defined the mother's role as a full-time job. He

argues that *although we identify primarily with Jo*, the Doris Day character, the film some-how also judges her to be a bad mother—for example, when she reads a magazine on the bus while her son Hank gets up and inadvertently pulls the veil off the head of a Muslim woman (my italics). Hank, Corber concludes from the boy's wandering part way down the aisle of the bus, "has not been adequately socialized and is failing to develop 'normally'"! Jo has "been too busy with her career to bond 'properly' with him." What Corber neglects to note is that *Jo has given up her career for marriage and motherhood*. Although she would like to return to singing, it is simply incorrect to say she has been "busy with her career." Nor, I think, does the film in any way show her to be delinquent in reading a magazine while her child sits between her and his father and gets a little restive. (Had she been keeping an eagle eye on this rather big boy, Dr. Spock would have had plenty to say about *that*.) Even Corber, earlier in the very same paragraph, remarks that, "Hank seems relatively well adjusted." Nevertheless, he insists in the next clause, the boy "does not promise to contribute to the reproduction of the national security state." (As exaggerated as this claim may seem, it is nothing compared with Žižek's that Hank when he grows up will be Norman Bates. Has film criticism gone mad? Well, I suppose we all go a little mad sometimes.) Later Corber quotes some passages from Dr. Spock and then moves immediately to apply them to the film, exactly as if they were part of the film text itself: "This formulation [that is, Dr. Spock's] of the Oedipus complex, which was typical during the 1950s, *suggests that Hitchcock was critical* of Jo's desire to function as a point of identification for Hank because it conflicted with the Oedipal structure of the middle-class nuclear family" (my italics). Robert J. Corber, *In the Name of National Security: Hitchcock, Homophobia, and the Political Construction of Gender in Postwar America* (Durham, North Carolina: Duke University Press, 1993), pp. 145–48.

Corber's analysis of *The Man Who Knew Too Much*, I think, illustrates perfectly the dangers inherent in trying to see films as reflections of their times—it is easy to end up downplaying those elements of the text that might go against the normalizing thought of their period and thus to find oneself unintentionally complicit with the forces of normalization. While Corber admits to the fact that our sympathies lie with Jo in this film and even to the fact that Hank appears to be developmentally on course, he ends up arguing against his own best insights to make the film into the mouthpiece of the dominant ideology.

# Works Cited

Abel, Richard. *"Notorious:* Perversion par Excellence." *A Hitchcock Reader.* Eds. Marshall Deutel-baum and Leland Poague. Ames: Iowa State University Press. 1986.

———. *"Stage Fright:* The Knowing Performance." *Film Criticism* 9, no. 2 (1984–85): 41–50.

Allen, Jeanne Thomas. "The Representation of Violence To Women: Hitchcock's *Frenzy." Film Quarterly* 38, no. 3 (Spring 1985): 30–38.

Anderson, Lindsay. "Alfred Hitchcock." *Focus on Hitchcock.* Ed. Albert J. LaValley. Englewood Cliffs, NJ: Prentice-Hall, 1972.

Bachelard, Gaston. *The Poetics of Space.* Trans. Maria Jolas. Boston: Beacon, 1964.

Barr, Charles. *"Blackmail:* Silent and Sound." *Sight and Sound* 52, no. 5 (1983): 189–93.

Barthes, Roland. *The Pleasure of the Text.* Trans. Richard Miller. New York: Hill and Wang, 1975.

———. *S/Z.* Trans. Richard Miller. New York: Hill and Wang, 1974.

Baudry, Jean Louis. "Author and Analyzable Subject." Trans. Alan Williams. *Apparatus: Cinemato-graphic Apparatus: Selected Writings.* Ed. Theresa Hak Kyung Cha. New York: Tanam, 1980.

———. "Ideological Effects of the Basic Cinematographic Apparatus." Trans. Alan Williams. *Apparatus: Cinematographic Apparatus: Selected Writings.* Ed. Theresa Hak Kyung Cha. New York: Tanam, 1980.

Behlmer, Rudy, Ed. *Memo From: David O. Selznick.* New York: Avon, 1972.

Bellour, Raymond. *"The Birds:* Analysis of a Sequence." Mimeograph. The British Film Institute Advisory Service, n.d.

———. "Hitchcock, the Enunciator." *Camera Obscura,* no. 1 (Fall 1977): 66–91.

Belton, John. *Cinema Stylists.* Metuchen, NJ: Scarecrow, 1983.

Berenstein, Rhona J. "I'm Not the Sort of Person Men Marry: Monsters, Queers, and Hitchcock's *Rebecca," CineAction* 29 (Fall 1992): 82–96.

Bergstrom, Janet. "Alternation, Segmentation, Hypnosis: Interview with Raymond Bellour." *Camera Obscura,* nos. 3–4 (1979): 71–104.

———. "Enunciation and Sexual Difference." *Camera Obscura,* nos. 3–4 (1979): 33–70.

———. "Sexuality at a Loss: The Films of F.W. Murnau." *Poetics Today* 6, nos. 1–2 (1985): 185–203.

Bersani, Leo. *The Freudian Body: Psychoanalysis and Art.* New York: Columbia University Press, 1986.

Bonitzer, Pascal. "Partial Vision: Film and the Labyrinth." Trans. Fabrice Ziolkowski. *Wide Angle* 4, no. 4 (1981): 56–64.

Brooks, Peter. *Reading for the Plot: Design and Intention in Narrative.* New York: Vintage, 1985.

Browne, Nick. "The Spectator in the Text: The Rhetoric of *Stagecoach." Movies and Methods,* Vol. 2. Ed. Bill Nichols. Berkeley and Los Angeles: University of California Press, 1985.

Castle, Terry. *Clarissa's Ciphers: Meaning and Disruption in Richardson's* Clarissa. Ithaca: Cornell University Press, 1982.

Citron, Michelle, Julia Lesage, B. Ruby Rich, and Anna Maria Taylor. "Women and Film: A Dis-cussion of Feminine Aesthetics." *New German Critique,* no. 13 (Winter 1978): 83–108.

Cixous, Hélène. "Castration or Decapitation?" Trans. Annette Kuhn. *Signs* 7, no. 1 (Autumn 1981): 41–55.

Cohen, Paula Marantz. *Alfred Hitchcock: The Legacy of Victorianism.* Lexington, KY: The Univer-sity Press of Kentucky, 1995.

Cohen, Tom. *Anti-Mimesis from Plato to Hitchcock.* Cambridge: Cambridge University Press, 1994.

Cook, Pam. "Duplicity in *Mildred Pierce." Women in Film Noir.* Ed. E. Ann Kaplan. London: Brit-ish Film Institute, 1978.

Copjec, Joan. "The Anxiety of the Influencing Machine." *October,* no. 23 (Winter 1982): 43–60.

Corber, Robert J. *In the Name of National Security: Hitchcock, Homophobia, and the Political Construction of Gender in Postwar American.* Durham, NC: Duke University Press, 1993. pp. 145–48.

Cottom, Daniel. "The Enchantment of Interpretation." *Critical Inquiry* 11, no. 4 (June 1985): 573–94.

Dayan, Daniel. "The Tutor Code of Classical Cinema." *Movies and Methods*, Vol. 1. Ed. Bill Nichols. Berkeley and Los Angeles: University of California Press, 1976.

de Lauretis, Teresa. "Aesthetic and Feminist Theory: Rethinking Women's Cinema." *New German Critique*, no. 34 (Winter 1985): 154–75.

———. *Alice Doesn't: Feminism, Semiotics, Cinema.* Bloomington: Indiana University Press, 1984.

———. *The Practice of Love: Lesbian Sexuality and Perverse Desire.* Bloomington: Indiana University Press, 1994.

Deleuze, Gilles. *Masochism: An Interpretation of Coldness and Cruelty.* Trans. Jean McNeil. New York: George Braziller, 1971.

Didi-Huberman, Georges. *Invention de l'hystérie: Charcot et l'iconographie photographique de la Salpêtrière.* Paris: Macula, 1982.

Doane, Mary Ann. *"Caught* and *Rebecca;* The Inscription of Femininity as Absence." *Enclitic* 5–6, nos. 1–2 (Fall 1981–Spring 1982): 175–89.

———. *The Desire to Desire: The Woman's Film of the 1940's.* Bloomington: Indiana University Press, 1987.

———. "Film and the Masquerade: Theorising the Female Spectator." *Screen* 23, nos. 3–4 (September-October 1982): 74–87.

———. "Misrecognition and Identity." *Cine-Tracts* 3, no. 3 (Fall 1980): 25–32.

———. "The 'Woman's Film': Possession and Address." *Revision: Essays in Feminist Film Criticism.* Eds. Mary Ann Doane, Patricia Mellencamp, and Linda Williams. The American Film Institute Monograph Series, Vol. 3. Frederick, MD: University Publications of America, 1984.

Douchet, Jean. "Hitch et son Public." *Cahiers du Cinéma*, no. 113 (November 1960): 7–15.

Douglas, Mary. *Purity and Danger: An Analysis of the Concepts of Pollution and Taboo.* New York: Praeger, 1966.

Durgnat, Raymond. *The Strange Case of Alfred Hitchcock, or the Plain Man's Hitchcock.* Cambridge: MIT Press, 1974.

Dworkin, Ronald. "Law as Interpretation." *The Politics of Interpretation.* Ed. W.J.T. Mitchell. Chicago: University of Chicago Press, 1983.

Edelman, Lee. "Hitchcock's Future," in *Alfred Hitchcock: Centenary Essays.* Eds. Richard Allan and S. Ishii-Gonzales. London: British Film Institute, 1999.

———. "Piss Elegant: Freud, Hitchcock, and the Micturating Penis." *GLQ* 2, vol. 2, no. 1–2 (1995): 149–77.

———. *"Rear Window's* Glasshole," *Out Takes: Essays on Queer Theory and Film.* Ed. Ellis Hanson. Durham, NC: Duke University Press, 1999.

Felman, Shoshana. "Rereading Femininity." *Yale French Studies*, no. 62 (1981): 19–44.

———. "Women and Madness: The Critical Phallacy." *Diacritics*, no. 5 (Winter 1975): 2–10.

Fetterley, Judith. *The Resisting Reader: A Feminist Approach to American Fiction.* Bloomington: Indiana University Press, 1978.

Fischer, Lucy. *Shot/Countershot: Film Traditions and Women's Cinema.* Princeton, NJ: Princeton University Press, 1989.

———. "Two-Faced Woman: The 'Double' in Women's Melodrama of the 1940's." *Cinema Journal* 23, no. 1 (Fall 1983): 24–43.

Fleenor, Juliann E., Ed. *The Female Gothic.* London: Eden, 1983.

Freud, Sigmund. "'A Child is Being Beaten': A Contribution to the Study of the Origin of Sexual Perversions." *The Standard Edition of the Complete Psychological Works of Sigmund Freud,* Vol. 17. Trans. James Strachey. London: Hogarth, 1974.

———. *Beyond the Pleasure Principle.* Trans. James Strachey. New York: Norton, 1961.

———. *The Ego and the Id.* Trans. Joan Riviere. New York: Norton, 1960.

———. "Female Sexuality." *Standard Edition*, Vol. 21.

———. "Femininity." *New Introductory Lectures on Psychoanalysis.* Trans. James Strachey. New York: Norton, 1965.

———. "Hysterical Phantasies and Their Relation to Bisexuality." *Standard Edition*, Vol. 19.

―――. *Jokes and Their Relation to the Unconscious*. Trans. James Strachey. New York: Norton, 1960.

―――. "Mourning and Melancholia." *Standard Edition,* Vol. 14.

―――. "On Narcissism: An Introduction." *Standard Edition,* Vol. 14.

―――. "Psychoanalytic Notes upon an Autobiographical Account of Paranoia (Dementia Paranoides)." *Three Case Histories*. Ed. Philip Rieff. New York: Collier, 1963.

―――. "Some Psychical Consequences of the Anatomical Distinction between the Sexes." *Standard Edition,* Vol. 19.

―――. *Three Essays on the History of Sexuality*. Trans. James Strachey. New York: Basic Books, 1962.

―――. "The 'Uncanny.'" *On Creativity and the Unconscious: Papers on the Psychology of Art, Literature, Love, Religion*. Ed. Benjamin Nelson. New York: Harper Torchbooks, 1958.

―――. *Totem and Taboo, Standard Edition,* Vol. 13.

Halprin, Sarah. "Writing in the Margins: Review of E. Ann Kaplan's *Women and Film.*" *Jump Cut,* no. 29 (1984): 31–33.

Hansen, Miriam. "Pleasure, Ambivalence, Identification: Valentino and Female Spectatorship." *Cinema Journal* 25, no. 4 (Summer 1986): 6–32.

Haskell, Molly. *From Reverence to Rape: The Treatment of Women in the Movies*. New York: Penguin, 1974.

Heath, Stephen. "Difference." *Screen* 19, no. 3 (Autumn 1978): 59–112.

―――. "Lessons from Brecht." *Screen* 15, no. 2 (Summer 1974): 103–28.

―――. *Questions of Cinema*. Bloomington: Indiana University Press, 1981.

Higham, Charles. "Hitchcock's World." *Film Quarterly* 16, no. 2 (Winter 1962): 3–16.

Hitchcock, Alfred. "Direction." *Focus on Hitchcock*. Ed. Albert J. LaValley. Englewood Cliffs, NJ: Prentice-Hall, 1972.

Houston, Beverle and Marsha Kinder. *Close-Up*. New York: Harcourt Brace Jovanovich, 1972.

Huyssen, Andreas. "Mass Culture as Woman: Modernism's Other." *Studies in Entertainment: Critical Approaches to Mass Culture*. Ed. Tania Modleski. Bloomington: Indiana University Press, 1986.

Irigaray, Luce. "Ce Sexe qui n'en est pas un." *New French Feminisms*. Eds. Elaine Marks and sabelle de Courtivron. Amherst: University of Massachusetts Press, 1980.

―――. *Speculum of the Other Woman*. Trans. Gillian C. Gill. Ithaca: Cornell University Press, 1985.

Jacobus, Mary. "Is There a Woman in This Text?" *New Literary History* 14, no. 1 (Autumn 1982): 117–42.

Jameson, Frederic. *The Political Unconscious: Narrative as a Socially Symbolic Act*. Ithaca: Cornell University Press, 1981.

―――. "Reading Hitchcock." *October,* no. 23 (Winter 1982): 15–42.

Jardine, Alice. *Gynesis: Configurations of Woman and Modernity*. Ithaca: Cornell University Press, 1985.

Johnston, Claire. "Towards a Feminist Film Practice: Some Theses." *Movies and Methods,* Vol. 2. Ed. Bill Nichols. Berkeley and Los Angeles: University of California Press, 1985.

―――. "Women's Cinema as *Countercinema,*" *Movies and Methods,* Vol. 1. Ed. Bill Nichols. Berkeley and Los Angeles: University of California Press, 1976.

Kaplan, E. Ann. "The Case of the Missing Mother: Maternal Issues in Vidor's *Stella Dallas.*" *Heresies,* no. 16 (1983): 81–85.

―――. *Women and Film: Both Sides of the Camera*. New York and London: Methuen, 1983.

―――, Ed. *Women in Film Noir*. London: British Film Institute, 1978.

Kapsis, Robert E. *Hitchcock: The Making of a Reputation*. Chicago: The University of Chicago Press, 1992.

Knapp, Lucretia. "Queer *Marnie,*" *Cinema Journal* 32, no 4 (Summer 1993): 6–23.

Koch, Gertrud. "Why Women Go to Men's Films." *Feminist Aesthetics*. Ed. Gisela Ecker. Boston: Beacon, 1985.

Kofman, Sarah. *The Enigma of Woman*. Trans. Catherine Porter. Ithaca: Cornell University Press, 1985.

Kristeva, Julia. *Black Sun*. Trans. Leon S. Roudiez. New York: Columbia University Press, 1989.

―――. "Ellipsis on Dread and the Specular Seduction." Trans. Dolores Burdick. *Wide Angle* 3, no. 3 (1979): 42–47.

————. *Powers of Horror: An Essay on Abjection.* Trans. Leon S. Roudiez. New York: Columbia University Press, 1982.

Kuhn, Annette. *Women's Pictures: Feminism and Cinema.* London: Routledge & Kegan Paul, 1982.

Lacan, Jacques. *Ecrits: A Selection.* Trans. Alan Sheridan. New York: Norton. 1977.

Laplanche, Jean. *Life and Death in Psychoanalysis.* Trans. Jeffrey Mehlman. Baltimore, MD: The Johns Hopkins University Press, 1976.

Laplanche, Jean and J.B. Pontalis. *The Language of Psycho-Analysis.* Trans. Donald Nicholson Smith. London: Hogarth, 1973.

Lemoine-Luccioni, Eugénie. *Partage des femmes.* Paris: Seuil, 1976.

Lévi-Strauss, Claude. *The Raw and the Cooked: Introduction to a Science of Mythology,* Vol. 1. Trans. John and Doreen Weightman. Chicago: University of Chicago Press, 1969.

————. *The Savage Mind.* Chicago: University of Chicago Press, 1966.

Linderman, Deborah. "The Screen in Hitchcock's *Blackmail.*" *Wide Angle* 4, no. 1 (1980): 20–29.

Lurie, Susan. "The Construction of the Castrated Woman in Psychoanalysis and Cinema." *Discourse,* no. 4 (Winter 1981–82): 52–74.

————. "Pornography and the Dread of Women: The Male Sexual Dilemma." *Take Back the Night: Women on Pornography.* Ed. Laura Lederer. New York: William Morrow, 1980.

MacKinnon, Catharine. "Feminism, Marxism, Method and the State: Toward Feminist Jurisprudence." *Signs* 8, no. 4 (Summer 1983): 635–58.

Mayne Judith. "The Female Audience and the Feminist Critic." *Women and Literature,* forthcoming.

————. "The Limits of Spectacle." *Wide Angle* 6, no. 3 (1984): 5–14.

McLaughlin, James B. "All in the Family: Alfred Hitchcock's *Shadow of a Doubt.*" *Wide Angle* 4, no. 1 (1980): 12–19.

Metz, Christian. "History/discourse: a note on two voyeurisms." *Theories of Authorship.* Ed. John Caughie. London: Routledge & Kegan Paul, 1981.

————. *The Imaginary Signifier.* Trans. Celia Britton, Anwyl Williams, Ben Brewster, and Alfred Guzzetti. Bloomington: Indiana University Press, 1982.

Miller, D.A. "Anal Rope," in *Representations* 32 (Fall 1990): 114–133.

Miller, J. Hillis. *Fiction and Repetition: Seven English Novels.* Cambridge: Harvard University Press, 1982.

Miller, Mark Crispin. "Hitchcock's Suspicions and *Suspicion.*" *Modern Language Notes* 98, no. 5 (December 1983): 1143–86.

Mitchell, Juliet. *Psychoanalysis and Feminism.* New York: Vintage, 1974.

Modleski, Tania. *Loving with a Vengeance: Mass-Produced Fantasies for Women.* New York and London: Methuen, 1984.

————. "Never to be Thirty-six years old: *Rebecca* as Female Oedipal Drama," *Wide Angle* 5, no. 1 (1982): 34–41.

Mulvey, Laura. "Afterthoughts on 'Visual Pleasure and Narrative Cinema,' Inspired by *Duel in the Sun.*" *Framework* 15/16/17 (Summer 1981): 12–15.

————. "Visual Pleasure and Narrative Cinema." *Screen* 16, no. 3 (1975): 6–18.

Naremore, James. *Filmguide to Psycho.* Bloomington: Indiana University Press, 1973.

Nowell-Smith, Geoffrey. "Minnelli and Melodrama." *Screen* 18, no. 2 (Summer 1977): 113–19.

O'Connor, Noreen and Joanna Ryan. *Wild Desires and Mistaken Identities: Lesbianism and Psychoanalysis.* New York: Columbia University Press, 1993.

Pajakowska, Claire. "Imagistic Representation and the Status of the Image in Pornography." *Cine-Tracts* 3, no. 3 (Fall 1980): 13–24.

Palmer, R. Barton. "The Metafictional Hitchcock: The Experience of Viewing and the Viewing of Experience in *Rear Window* and *Psycho.*" *Cinema Journal* 26, no. 2 (Winter 1986): 4–29.

Perlmutter, Ruth. "*Rear Window:* A Construction Story." *Journal of Film and Video,* no. 37 (Spring 1985): 53–65.

Perkins, V.F. *Film as Film: Understanding and Judging Movies.* New York: Penguin, 1972.

Petro, Patrice. *Joyless Streets: Women and Melodramatic Representation in Weimar Germany.* Princeton, NJ: Princeton University Press, 1989.

————. "Rematerializing the Vanishing 'Lady': Feminism, Hitchcock, and Interpretation." *A Hitchcock Reader.* Ed. Marshall Deutelbaum and Leland Poague. Ames: Iowa State University Press, 1986.

Piso, Michelle. "Mark's Marnie," *A Hitchcock Reader.* Ed. Marshall Deutelbaum and Leland Poague. Ames: Iowa State University Press, 1986.

Polan, Dana. *Power and Paranoia: History, Narrative, and the American Cinema, 1940–1950.* New York: Columbia University Press, 1986.

Pollack, Griselda. "Report on the Weekend School." *Screen* 18, no. 2 (Summer 1977): 105–13.

Reik, Theodor. *Masochism and Modern Man.* Trans. Margaret H. Biegel and Gertrud M. Kurth. New York: Farrar, Straus, 1941.

Rein, Sonia. "Masochism and Feminist Theory." Unpublished manuscript.

Renov, Michael. "From Identification to Ideology: The Male System of Hitchcock's *Notorious.*" *Wide Angle* 4, no. 1 (1980): 30–37.

Rich, Adrienne. "When We Dead Awaken: Writing as Re-vision." *On Lies, Secrets, and Silence: Selected Prose, 1966–78.* New York: Norton, 1979.

Rodowick, David. "The Difficulty of Difference." *Wide Angle* 5, no. 1 (1982): 4–15.

Rohmer, Eric and Claude Chabrol. *Hitchcock: The First Forty-Four Films.* New York: Ungar, 1979.

Rose, Jacqueline. "Paranoia and the Film System." *Screen* 17, no. 4 (Winter 1976–77): 85–104.

Rothman, William, "Alfred Hitchcock's *Notorious.*" *Georgia Review* 39, no. 4 (1975): 884–927.

———. *Hitchcock: The Murderous Gaze.* Cambridge: Harvard University Press, 1982.

Said, Edward. *The World, the Text, and the Critic.* Cambridge: Harvard University Press, 1983.

Sartre, Jean-Paul. *Being and Nothingness.* Trans. Hazel Barnes. New York: Washington Square, 1966.

Scholes, Robert. "Narration and Narrativity in *Film.*" *Film Theory and Criticism.* Ed. Gerald Mast and Marshall Cohen. New York: Oxford University Press, 1985.

Schwartz, Adria E. *Sexual Subjects: Lesbians, Gender, and Psychoanalysis.* London and New York: Routledge, 1998.

Sedgwick, Eve Kosofsky. *Between Men: English Literature and Male Homosocial Desire.* New York: Columbia University Press, 1985.

Silverman, Kaja. "Fragments of a Fashionable Discourse." *Studies in Entertainment: Critical Approaches to Mass Culture.* Ed. Tania Modleski. Bloomington: University Press, 1986.

———. "*Histoire d'O:* The Construction of a Female Subject." *Pleasure and Danger. Exploring Female Sexuality.* Ed. Carole S. Vance. New York; Routledge and Regan Paul, 1984.

———. "Lost Objects and Mistaken Subjects: Film Theory's Structuring Lack." *Wide Angle* 7, nos. 1–2 (1985): 14–29.

———. "Masochism and Subjectivity." *Framework* no. 12 (1980): 2–9.

———. *The Subject of Semiotics.* New York: Oxford University Press, 1983.

Smith, Susan. *Hitchcock: Suspense, Humour and Tone.* London: British Film Institute, 2000.

Spoto, Donald. *The Art of Alfred Hitchcock.* New York: Doubleday, 1976.

———. *The Dark Side of Genius: The Life of Alfred Hitchcock.* New York: Ballantine, 1983.

Stam, Robert and Roberta Pearson. "Hitchcock's *Rear Window:* Reflexivity and the Critique of Voyeurism." *Enclitic* 7, no. 1 (Spring 1983): 136–45.

Stewart, Susan. *On Longing: Narratives of the Miniature, the Gigantic, the Souvenir, the Collection.* Baltimore, MD: Johns Hopkins University Press, 1984.

Studlar, Gaylyn. "Masochism and the Perverse Pleasures of the Cinema." *Movies and Methods,* Vol. 2. Ed. Bill Nichols. Berkeley and Los Angeles: University of California Press, 1985.

———. Response to Miriam Hansen, "Pleasure, Ambivalence, Identification, Valentino, and Female Spectatorship," *Cinema Journal* 26, no. 2 (Winter 1987): 51–53.

Taylor, John Russell. *Hitch.* London: Faber and Faber, 1978.

Thompson, Kristin. "The Duplicitous Text: An Analysis of *Stage Fright.*" *Film Reader,* no. 2 (1977): 42–64.

Truffaut, François. *Hitchcock.* New York: Simon and Schuster, 1983.

Waldman, Diane. "At Last I Can Tell It to Someone! Feminine Point of View and Subjectivity in the Gothic Romance Films of the 1940's." *Cinema Journal* 23, no. 2 (1983): 29–40.

Weber, Samuel. *The Legend of Freud.* Minneapolis: University of Minnesota Press, 1982.

Weis, Elizabeth. *The Silent Scream: Alfred Hitchcock's Sound Track.* East Brunswick, NJ: Fairleigh Dickinson University Press, 1982.

Welsh, Alexander. *George Eliot and Blackmail.* Cambridge: Harvard University Press, 1985.

Wexman, Virginia Wright. "The Critic as Consumer: Film Study in the University, *Vertigo* and the Film Canon." *Film Quarterly* 39, no 2. (Spring 1986): 32–41.

White, Susan. "Allegory and Referentiality: Vertigo and Feminist Criticism," *MLN,* 106, (December 1991): pp. 910–32.

———. "*Vertigo* and the Problem of Knowledge in Feminist Film Theory," *Alfred Hitchcock: Centenary Essays.* Ed. Richard Allan and S. Ishii-Gonzales. London: British Film Institute, 1999. p. 240.

Willeman, Paul. "Distantiation and Douglas Sirk." *Screen* 12, no. 2 (Summer 1971): 63–67.

Williams, Linda. "Something Else Besides a Mother: *Stella Dallas* and the Maternal Melodrama." *Cinema Journal* 24, no. 1 (Fall 1984): 2–27.

———. "When the Woman Looks." *Re-vision: Essays in Feminist Film Criticism.* Eds. Mary Ann Doane, Patricia Mellencamp, and Linda Williams. The American Film Institute Monograph Series, Vol. 3. Frederick, MD: University Publications of America, 1984.

Wollen, Peter. *Signs and Meaning in the Cinema.* Bloomington: University of Indiana Press, 1972.

Wood, Robin. "Fear of Spying." *American Film* (November 1982): 28–35.

———. *Hitchcock's Films.* South Brunswick and New York: A.S. Barnes and Tantivy, 1966.

Woolf, Virginia. *A Room of One's Own.* New York: Harbinger, 1957.

Yacowar, Maurice. *Hitchcock's British Films.* Hamden, CT: Archon, 1977.

Žižek, Slavoj. *Enjoy Your Symptom! Jacques Lacan in Hollywood and Out.* New York and London: Routledge, 1992.

———. "From Desire to Drive: Why Lacan is not Lacaniano," *Atlantica de Las Artes* 14, 1996.

———. *Looking Awry: An Introduction to Jacques Lacan through Popular Culture.* Cambridge and London: MIT Press, 1991.

———, Ed. *Everything You Always Wanted to Know about Lacan (But Were Afraid to Ask Hitchcock).* London and New York: Verso, 1992.

# Index